Premises and Problems

FERNAND BRAUDEL CENTER
STUDIES IN HISTORICAL SOCIAL SCIENCE

Series Editor: Richard E. Lee

The Fernand Braudel Center Studies in Historical Social Science publishes works that address theoretical and empirical questions produced by scholars in or through the Fernand Braudel Center or who share its approach and concerns. It specifically promotes works that contribute to the development of the world-systems perspective engaging a holistic and relational vision of the world—the modern world-system—implicit in historical social science, which at once takes into consideration structures (long-term regularities) and change (history). With the intellectual boundaries within the sciences/ social sciences/humanities structure collapsing in the work scholars actually do, this series offers a venue for a wide range of research that confronts the dilemmas of producing relevant accounts of historical processes in the context of the rapidly changing structures of both the social and academic world. The series includes monographs, colloquia, and collections of essays organized around specific themes.

RECENT VOLUMES IN THIS SERIES:

Questioning Nineteenth-Century Assumptions about Knowledge: Determinism
Richard E. Lee, editor

Questioning Nineteenth-Century Assumptions about Knowledge: Reductionism
Richard E. Lee, editor

Questioning Nineteenth-Century Assumptions about Knowledge: Dualism
Richard E. Lee, editor

The Longue Durée and World-Systems Analysis
Richard E. Lee, editor

New Frontiers of Slavery
Dale Tomich, editor

Slavery in the Circuit of Sugar: Martinique and the World-Economy, 1848–1860
Dale Tomich

The Politics of the Second Slavery
Dale Tomich, editor

The Trade in the Living
Luiz Felipe de Alencastro

Race and Rurality in the Global Economy
Michaeline A. Crichlow, Patricia Northover, and Juan Guisti-Cordero, editors

Power, Political Economy, and Historical Landscapes of the Modern World: Interdisciplinary Perspectives
Christopher R. DeCorse, editor

Atlantic Transformations: Empire, Politics, and Slavery during the Nineteenth Century
Dale Tomich, editor

Premises and Problems: Essays on World Literature and Cinema
Louiza Franco Moreira

Premises and Problems

Essays on World Literature and Cinema

Edited and with an Introduction by

Luiza Franco Moreira

FERNAND BRAUDEL CENTER
STUDIES IN HISTORICAL SOCIAL SCIENCE

Published by State University of New York Press, Albany

© 2021 State University of New York

All rights reserved

Printed in the United States of America

No part of this book may be used or reproduced in any manner whatsoever without written permission. No part of this book may be stored in a retrieval system or transmitted in any form or by any means including electronic, electrostatic, magnetic tape, mechanical, photocopying, recording, or otherwise without the prior permission in writing of the publisher.

For information, contact State University of New York Press, Albany, NY
www.sunypress.edu

Library of Congress Cataloging-in-Publication Data

Names: Moreira, Luiza Franco, editor.
Title: Premises and problems : essays on world literature and cinema / Luiza Franco Moreira.
Description: Albany : State University of New York, 2021. | Series: SUNY series, Fernand Braudel center studies in historical social science | Includes bibliographical references and index.
Identifiers: LCCN 2020048816 (print) | LCCN 2020048817 (ebook) | ISBN 9781438482477 (hardcover : alk. paper) | ISBN 9781438482460 (pbk. : alk. paper) | ISBN 9781438482484 (ebook)
Subjects: LCSH: Literature—History and criticism. | Motion pictures—History.
Classification: LCC PN86 P74 2021 (print) | LCC PN86 (ebook) | DDC 801/.9509—dc23
LC record available at https://lccn.loc.gov/2020048816
LC ebook record available at https://lccn.loc.gov/2020048817

10 9 8 7 6 5 4 3 2 1

CONTENTS

List of Illustrations   vii

Introduction   1
Luiza Franco Moreira

1   In Search of Universal Laws: Averroes' Interpretation of Aristotle's *Poetics*   9
Tarek Shamma

2   Lost in Transliteration: Morisco Travel Writing and the *Coplas del hijante de Puey Monçón*   29
Benjamin Liu

3   Modern Hebrew Literature as "World Literature": The Political Theology of Dov Sadan   45
Hannan Hever

4   Islam in the Theory and Practice of World Literature: Translating *Adab* in the Middle Eastern Novel   83
Karim Mattar

5   Selective Invisibility: Elizabeth Bishop, Carlos Drummond de Andrade, and World Literature   111
Luiza Franco Moreira

6   Latin America and the World: Borges, Bolaño, and the Inconceivable Universal   145
Patrick Dove

7 Analysis of the Socio-Culture in the Study of the Modern
  World-System 167
  Richard E. Lee

8 Ethics of Skepticism: A Case Study in Contemporary World Cinema 183
  Jeroen Gerrits

9 Polycentrism, Periphery, and the Place of Brazilian Cinema in
  World Cinema 209
  Cecília Mello

Contributors 235

Index 239

ILLUSTRATIONS

Figures 8.1   The scene leading up to the accident in *The Headless Woman*.   190

Figures 8.2, 8.3   The immediate aftermath of the accident in *The Headless Woman*.   191

Figures 8.4, 8.5   The scene leading to the accident in *Three Monkeys*.   192

Figures 8.6   The immediate aftermath of the accident in *Three Monkeys*.   193

Figure 8.7 and close up   Virtual point of view.   195

Figures 8.8–8.10   Virtual point of view in *Three Monkeys*.   200

Introduction

Luiza Franco Moreira

A persistent problem for discussions of world literature in the United States lies at the starting point of this collection. World literature is generally understood as a systematic category, as Walter Cohen has stressed (Cohen 2017, 2). Like several other scholars in the field, Cohen stresses the role of prestigious literary languages in effectively shaping the system. In his view, a sequence of major languages has served varying functions historically in establishing a structure for world literature. In an analogous way, Pascale Casanova, in a pioneering work, has focused on the prestige of the French language and on Paris as a center of literary institutions to develop an argument about the modern world literary system. Alexander Beecroft, for his part, has stressed the role of literary languages in organizing complex systems of literary circulation.[1] However illuminating or accurate these accounts are, they inevitably move the focus away from the literary languages that do not hold a sufficiently high level of prestige.[2] As Beecroft has pointed out, the system inevitably reduces noise. The problem that motivates this collection is that of holding in mind at once the structure of world literature and the diversity of literary languages that systematic arguments cannot help but disregard.

A parenthetical remark by Franco Moretti in the influential essay "Conjectures on World Literature" suggests a productive way to work through this difficulty: a study of world literature, Moretti stresses, is inevitably "a study of the struggle for symbolic hegemony across the world" (Moretti 2013, 56). In the light of this observation, Casanova, Beecroft, and Cohen appear to converge in calling attention to the power of hegemonic languages to shape the system of world literature. Moretti's remark is all the more interesting for advancing a dynamic understanding of hegemony. In his view, hegemony is asserted in the process of a broad, worldwide, continuing struggle. The approach sketched in his essay opens the way for considering literary languages that are less than hegemonic, not simply in order to explore their role in the uneven and unequal field of world literature but also, more interestingly, in order to examine the overall system from their perspective.

The essays collected here focus on specific historical moments that afford dynamic and not quite central perspectives on hegemony and, more generally, into the conflicts between diverse literary and linguistic traditions. Rather than reproduce the point of view of the current hegemonic literatures, this collection is concerned with grasping the ways that hegemony is established and the costs of losing it; what hegemony masks and the ways that it is masked. Very often, as a result, these essays discuss literatures that fall beyond the small circle of prestigious modern European languages. Such comparatively unfamiliar traditions are helpful in directing our attention to the areas of obscurity that make it a considerable challenge to trace relationships between literatures that hold different levels of prestige, or that render key features of the system indistinct.

However, it seems necessary to stress the ways in which the approach of this collection diverges from Moretti's. The collection is informed by a concern with historical, linguistic, and textual specificity that stands in contrast to this critic's project of a sociological formalism. Moretti's approach is articulated in part through a dialogue with Roberto Schwarz, and especially this critic's understanding of literary forms as abstracts of social relations.[3] All too often, sociologically inspired literary analysis proceeds by deriving general hypotheses to be tested later, usually though not always, through reading. One of the difficulties embedded in this method is that the initial hypothesis may establish the direction of discussion so fully that readings will serve mainly to confirm an initial insight: Sociological formalism runs the risk of asking only questions that contain their own answers. Moretti's call for distant reading heightens the abstraction implicit in this approach, by proposing a shift of focus away from the complexities of specific texts and toward models, artificial constructs, or general structures (Moretti, 2005).

This collection grows out of a colloquium organized by the Fernand Braudel Center and Binghamton's Department of Comparative Literature in April 2016. This volume, and the colloquium that preceded it, signal a convergence of interests between the Center and the Department, or between the scholarship in historical social science that, since the 1970s, has developed around the Center and the work of Immanuel Wallerstein, and the current pedagogical practice and scholarly concerns of the faculty of comparative literature at Binghamton. However, even as social scientists, on the one hand, and literary scholars, on the other, share an interest it world literature, their approaches do not necessarily coincide. It will be helpful to discuss the nature and limits of such a convergence. It seems important to begin by noting that Richard E. Lee's contribution, "Analysis of the Socio-Culture in the Study of the Modern World-System," articulates a sociological approach to discussions of culture from the perspective of the world system that is consistent with Wallerstein's theses.

The vocabulary of world-systems analysis was brought into the field of comparative literature most directly by Franco Moretti, in the essay discussed above, "Conjectures on World Literature." Moretti's main objective in this text is to propose an account of the history of the novel that reverses the more usual narratives, which have centered invariably on European cases. Rather than focus on the rise of the novel in "Spain, France, and especially England," Moretti argues that the modern novel "arises just about everywhere" after 1750, as a compromise between West European formal patterns and "local material." Wallerstein's understanding of the modern world as a single capitalist world system, "bound together in a relationship of growing inequality," allows Moretti to distinguish between the core countries, where formal patterns are established, and the periphery, where take shape varying, often unstable compromises between, on the one hand, local realities and narrative traditions and, on the other, prestigious foreign forms (Moretti 2013, 46–57). In contrast to Moretti, again, the essays collected here do not refer directly to the account of the political economy of the modern world that has been developed more prominently by Wallerstein; neither do they rely on the conceptual distinction between core and periphery (or center and periphery, to mention two terms that are often used in literary discussions). Instead, this collection seeks to shed an oblique light on world literature by approaching the system from the perspective of literary languages that have not attained hegemonic power, no longer hold it, perhaps have never come to engage in the struggle for hegemony, or have fallen short of hegemonic power.[4]

The chapters that focus on Islamic Spain, Al-Andalus, are useful in illustrating how productive an oblique approach to hegemony can be for historical discussions of world literature. In chapter 1, "In Search of Universal Laws: Averroes' Interpretation of Aristotle's *Poetics*," Tarek Shamma discusses the translation of the *Poetics* into Classical Arabic by Abu Bishr Matta bin Yunus (completed AD 932) and the later commentaries by Ibn Rushd, or Averroes. Shamma's dual focus on a translation *into Classical Arabic* and the contemporaneous philosophical context of Averroes' commentary allows him to set aside familiar concerns with mistranslation and misunderstanding in order to call attention, instead, to the "creative transformation" of the *Poetics* by Islamic scholars and, more broadly, to the ways that foreign texts may "speak to other cultures across the limitations of time, place, and literary tradition."

In chapter 2, "Lost in Transliteration: Morisco Travel Writing and the *Coplas del hijante de Puey Monçón*," Benjamin Liu is concerned with a later period. Liu brings into sharp focus the ever-possible harmful effects of the limitations in tradition, time, and place that Shamma has alluded to. Liu discusses the verse narrative of a pilgrimage to Mecca that dates from the sixteenth century, a time when Iberian Muslims faced the systematic repression that culminated in their expulsion early in the seventeenth century. Liu considers the distinctive writing practice of *aljamiado*, which uses at once the Spanish language and Arabic script. This *aljamiado* travel narrative, he argues, embodies a tension between translation and transliteration, or between rendering familiar the distant lands visited by the pilgrim and rendering unfamiliar his everyday Spanish language. This poem, which strives to keep alive "a covert cultural memory," was nevertheless lost for centuries and had become nearly unreadable when it was recovered in the 1880s. By the time the text was recovered, Liu stresses, the community it addressed had long been dispersed to lands far from the Peninsula. If we look at this pair of chapters in the light of discussions of hegemony, Shamma's argument derives innovative insights by taking the perspective of the hegemony of Classical Arabic—which is so often obscured in narratives of the transmission of Greek philosophy—while Liu focuses on a period when Iberian Muslims had lost their hegemonic position.

The subsequent chapters of the collection are concerned predominantly with literature and film from the twentieth century on. The contributions by Hannan Hever and Karim Mattar question persistent, if generally silent, assumptions about modern world literature. Each of the two critics moves away from a focus on the literature of the nation-state, Hever by considering Hebrew literature broadly, in relation to Jewish nationality and religion, and Mattar by exploring Orhan Pamuk's engagement with Islam. Beyond that, and especially when taken together, the two chapters make a compelling case for rethinking our current understanding of modern literature as secular.

In chapter 3, "Modern Hebrew Literature as 'World Literature': The Political Theology of Dov Sadan," Hever takes the perspective of Jewish thought, and particularly of Dov Sadan (1902–1989) and the distinguished philosopher Nachman Krochmal (1785–1840), to reflect on the relationship between modern Hebrew literature and world literature. For Hever, there are clear limitations to the ways that Hebrew literature may be integrated into world literature because the theological dimension of Hebrew, a sacred language, cannot be translated. Rather than discuss a transition of Hebrew literature from sacred to secular, he maintains, it is necessary to keep in mind that Jewish nationality and the Jewish religion are conflated and fully present in Hebrew literature. Hebrew is never simply the language of a given, historical nation-state, Israel. Although it may certainly function as one among the many national literatures of the contemporary world, such an approach to Hebrew literature closes off its distinctive theological-political reach. Hever's essay addresses a topic of significant interest to comparatists: by discussing Auerbach's *Mimesis* in the context of reflections on translation by Jewish scholars, Hever calls attention to aspects of this seminal work that might otherwise escape consideration.

In chapter 4, "Islam in the Theory and Practice of World Literature: Translating *Adab* in the Middle Eastern Novel," Karim Mattar takes issue with the predominant reading of Pamuk's *The Black Book* as a secular, postmodern work. Mattar seeks to read through the modern overwriting of precolonial Arabic-Islamic literary practices in order to bring to light Pamuk's complex engagement with, at once, secularism and Islam. Together, Hever's and Mattar's chapters call attention to the irreducible religious and cultural diversity that cuts across world literature at the present time, yet remains masked by the image of a hegemonic secular modernity.

Two chapters of this collection approach world literature from the perspective of Latin America, Patrick Dove's and my own. My own contribution, "Selective Invisibility: Elizabeth Bishop, Carlos Drummond de Andrade, and World Literature," chapter 5, explores the difficulty of apprehending the complex yet fruitful literary relationship that Elizabeth Bishop's poetry establishes to the work of Brazilian poet Carlos Drummond de Andrade (1902–1987). The hegemonic power of English, I argue, renders Bishop's sustained engagement with Drummond nearly invisible. I suggest that we need to triangulate between languages in order to grasp literary relationships that remain masked when we consider hegemonic languages alone—much as binocular vision achieves depth perception through triangulation. In chapter 6, "Latin America and the World: Borges, Bolaño, and the Inconceivable Universal," Dove is concerned with a critical reevaluation of the terms, *world* and *literature*. He proceeds through readings of Borges and Roberto Bolaño, Latin American writers who have undeniably attained world literary status, approaching them in the light of a discussion of referentiality inspired by Derrida and Heidegger.

Richard E. Lee's "Analysis of the Socio-Culture in the Study of the Modern World-System," chapter 7, extends the field of discussions of world literature toward the social sciences and, specifically, toward world-systems analysis. Lee begins by outlining an understanding of capitalist modernity as a system defined by two large scale structures—a world-scale economic division of labor, which goes hand in hand with the interstate geopolitical system—and proceeds by proposing that the third arena of the system, culture, be approached through the lens of large-scale, enduring structures of knowledge. Lee concludes by offering three examples of the work that this perspective enables in approaching the contemporary university, in the understanding of the classification system of the Library of Congress, and in exploring the development of Western musical forms.

Finally, a pair of chapters discusses contemporary world cinema, moving the focus away from hegemonic film and the hegemonic traditions of reflection on cinema. In chapter 8, "Ethics of Skepticism: A Case Study in Contemporary World Cinema," Jeroen Gerrits discusses a subgenre of global art cinema, that of collision films, in particular Lucrecia Martel's *Headless Woman* and Nuri Bilge Ceylan's *Three Monkeys*. Gerrits proposes the concept of cinematic skepticism, drawing on Stanley Cavell's discussion of epistemological skepticism. Both Martel and Ceylan, he argues, introduce a virtual point of view and rely on this cinematic technique to suggest at once that "our forms of knowing have their limitations" and that "our (recovery from our broken) relation to the world is not grounded in knowledge." In chapter 9, "Polycentrism, Periphery, and the Place of Brazilian Cinema in World Cinema," Cecília Mello stages a dialogue between discussions of "world cinema" in English language scholarship and Brazilian academic debates about audiovisual media. Mello calls attention to the contribution of Brazilian scholars to articulating some of the recurrent terms in discussions of world cinema, notably the conceptual contrast between center and periphery. However, Mello notes, a paradoxical result of the persistent understanding of Brazilian cinema as peripheral and underdeveloped is that it is often discussed as if it were isolated from the rest of the world, and in particular from Asia and Africa. Even as a polycentric view of world cinema proves illuminating for contemporary cinematic production, if this approach is transplanted to the Brazilian context, it gives rise to a series of new questions: why, for instance, is the term *world cinema* so prevalent in English language scholarship, but not so frequent or comprehensible elsewhere?

∽

This collection, and the April 2016 colloquium that preceded it, would not have been possible without the support of the Fernand Braudel Center and its director, Richard E. Lee. Thanks are due to Amy Keough and Kelly Pueschel, administrative assistant and publications officer at the Center, and to Kathy Stanley, the secretary of Comparative Literature. Their tireless support made the event and this collection possible. The faculty and graduate students of Comparative Literature are the inspiration for this project, and have supported it at every step of the process. Our graduate students teach the yearlong sequence of introductory courses on world literature offered by the department; they always make it a success. Over the years, many students attended my seminar on the challenges of conceptualizing world literature. Their collegial and attentive engagement in our discussions helped clarify the arguments that inform the collection. An international and diverse group, our students have pushed me to broaden my own horizons on world literature. A special thanks is due Nadia K. Schumann, who patiently helped me copyedit these essays; many thanks are due also to Laura Tomich, Lior Libman, and Shmuel Sermoneta-Gertel for their support at various stages of the preparation of this manuscript. I am grateful, finally, to the speakers who took part in the 2016 colloquium and to the authors of the chapters collected here for their support of this project.

Notes

1. In contrast, David Damrosch's influential account of world literature focuses on the reader's activity rather than on the structure of the system.

2. See, in this respect, Gayatri Spivak's and Emily Apter's reservations about the category of world literature.

3. See Schwarz 1997, 51: "Neste sentido, formas são o abstrato de relações sociais determinadas." In Gledson's translation, "In this sense, forms are the abstract of specific social relationships" (Schwarz 1992, 53).

4. Pascale Casanova's arguments stand in contrast to Moretti's as well, but for a different reason. Casanova examines the modern world literary system directly from the perspective

of a sociology of literature. Rather than rely on a sociological argument for the hypothesis that enables literary discussion, Casanova is concerned with proposing an account of the world literary system by examining the institutions and mediations that shape it.

Works Cited

Apter, Emily. 2013. *Against World Literature: On the Politics of Untranslatability*. London: Verso.

Beecroft, Alexander. 2015. *An Ecology of World Literature: From Antiquity to the Present Day*. London: Verso.

Casanova, Pascale. 2004. *The World Republic of Letters*. Cambridge, MA: Harvard University Press.

Cohen, Walter. 2017. *A History of European Literature: The West and the World from Antiquity to the Present*. Oxford, UK: Oxford University Press.

Damrosch, David. 2003. *What Is World Literature?* Princeton, NJ: Princeton University Press.

Moretti, Franco. 2013. "Conjectures on World Literature." *Distant Reading*. London: Verso.

———. 2005. *Graphs, Maps, Trees: Abstract Models for Literary History*. London: Verso.

Schwarz, Roberto. 1997. "A importação do romance e suas contradições em Alencar." ["The Importing of the Novel to Brazil and Its Contradictions in the Work of Alencar."] *Ao vencedor as batatas*. São Paulo, Brazil: Duas Cidades. *Misplaced Ideas*. Introduction and translation by John Gledson. London: Verso.

Spivak, Gayatri. 2003. *Death of a Discipline*. New York: Columbia University Press.

Chapter 1

In Search of Universal Laws

Averroes' Interpretation of Aristotle's *Poetics*

Tarek Shamma

The first Arabic translation of Aristotle's *Poetics* has long been the subject of debate and speculation. Completed in AD 932 by Abu Bishr Matta bin Yunus, its "distortions" of the source text, and the subsequent "misunderstandings" of Aristotle's literary theories by philosophers and literary critics, have attracted the attention of contemporary and modern scholars. Some have criticized what they saw as the inaccuracies and misinterpretations to which the book was subjected. A modern Arabist referred to the transmission of Aristotle's *Poetics* in the Classical age of Islam as "the history of an error" (Gabrieli, qtd. in Gelder 1989, 96). Another lamented the missed opportunity, speculating that an accurate understanding of the book "could have changed the face of Arabic literature" (Badawi 1953, 56). In fact, these attitudes, which focus on what was lost rather than possibly gained, continue to this day. A modern Arab scholar called Matta's version "a crime against translation" ('Abdallah 2014, 357).

Even when allowance is given to the practically unbridgeable gap in literary traditions, it is in the spirit of not being too harsh on the Arabic translators and readers of Aristotle: "it is somewhat unfair to deride Abu Bishr for equating a Greek comedy with an Arabic invective poem if he only gave an approximation" (Gelder 1989, 97). Similarly, Dimitri Gutas, while recognizing the immense limitations facing the Arabic reception of the book, still views the translation and its interpretation by Averroes within the one-dimensional framework of comprehension and miscomprehension: "His understanding . . . was circumscribed *objectively* by the semantic and ideational range of the Arabic translation in front of him and of whatever commentaries were available to him" (1990, 93). Again, Uwe Vagelpohl describes the trajectory of Aristotle's *Poetics* and *Rhetoric* in Classical Arabic as a process defined squarely by the elementary values of preservation and loss: "the simple relation between comedy and tragedy on the one hand and their understanding by Aristotle's audience on the other was supplemented at every step of the reception; equally, additional strands were woven into the thread connecting Aristotle's *Poetics* and *Rhetoric* and its readers at various times while other strands frayed and ultimately snapped" (2015, 91).

This paper attempts to move the discussion away from this uncontextualized, either/or concern with mistranslation and misunderstanding. My argument is that, far from being a missed opportunity, Matta's translation, which adapted Aristotle's literary terms to Arabic ones, sometimes giving them completely different meanings, was instrumental in forming aesthetic views by philosophers such as Ibn Sina (Avicenna) and Ibn Rushd (Averroes). It was a case of creative adaptation that defies the simple designations of accuracy and faithfulness. While not denying that Aristotle's book was misunderstood (which was practically inevitable under the circumstances), what should be remembered is that the Arabic translators, and later philosophers and literary critics, were not interested in Aristotle's literary views as such, and much less in Greek literature itself, but in the relevance of the *Poetics* to their own philosophical and literary concerns. I believe this is the question we need to answer about the *Poetics*: what it meant to contemporaries (or what Gadamer calls their "horizon of interpretation")—beyond debating to what extent the translation, and later interpretations, deviated from the original or remained faithful to it. What were philosophers like al-Farabi, Avicenna, and Averroes looking for in a work which dealt with a literary tradition that they themselves realized was alien to them, and which, judging by their commentaries, they were not even very much interested in as such? This chapter tries to answer some of these questions, first, through an analysis of Matta's translation, within its linguistic and social context. The second part of the paper examines the reception of the translation in the works of later scholars and philosophers, with special focus on Averroes, whose commentary on the *Poetics* is undoubtedly the most thorough and creative engagement with the book in Classical Arabic. This paper will explore the manifestations of "tragedy" and "comedy," as adapted through the translation, in approaches to the *Poetics* in

Classical Arabic. My aim is to investigate how the translated terms were acculturated for contemporary intellectual pursuits in a new cultural context, above and beyond their original environment, which cannot be seen as the only, or even the primary, criterion in evaluating the translation.

Between Logic and Literature: Matta's Translation

It shouldn't be surprising that the early reception of the *Poetics* in Classical Arabic was mediated through philosophy. Considering Aristotle's reputation as the "First Teacher," the greatest of Greek and probably all philosophers, and notwithstanding the purely literary nature of the book, its influence was confined initially to philosophers, including some of the most eminent practitioners in Arabic, from al-Kindi, through Avicenna and Averroes. It was only in later stages that that its literary side was recognized, allowing some, mostly theorized, but never conclusively established, influence on rhetorical and aesthetic theories (e.g., Al-Musawi 2001, 32; Meisami 1998, 473). Apart from a conjectured early translation by the philosopher al-Kindi (see below), the first known translations of the book were made by Abu Bishr Matta bin Yunus (d. 940) and Yahia bin 'Adi (974–893), both philosophers and translators from Greek and Syriac. Of these, the only surviving translation is the one by Matta bin Yunus, described as "the leading logician of his time" (Ibn al-Nadim 1971, 309, 324).

Known as a logician and translator of philosophy, Matta did not seem to have been interested in literature or linguistics. Hence, his translation has to be seen in the context of the great interest among Islamic philosophers in making all Aristotle's works available in Arabic. Facilitating this integration into philosophy was the fact that it had become an established practice by that time to classify *The Poetics* among the *Organon*, the collection of Aristotle's six books on logic. As early as the sixth century, Aristotle's exegists in the School of Alexandria included the *Poetics* and the *Rhetoric* in the Organon, in addition to the original *Categories, On Interpretation, Prior Analytics, Posterior Analytics, Topics, Sophistical Refutations*. This tradition was followed by their Syriac and Islamic successors (Vagelpohl 2008, 56; Fakhry 2014, 8). Matta, an heir to the Greco-Syriac traditions of the School of Alexandria, translated *Posterior Analytics* and wrote exegeses on both *Posterior Analytics* and *Prior Analytics* (Yousif 1997, 118; Endress 1991, 844). He firmly situated his translation of the *Poetics* within this framework. It fell to Islamic philosophers after him to explore the philosophical side of the *Poetics*, especially the connection of poetry to philosophy and the position of the book within the other works of the *Organon*, which provide a more systematic and direct engagement with logic.

Translation without a Shared Frame of Reference

This conception of the *Poetics*, classifying it as a philosophical rather than a literary work, had a significant impact on the reception of the book in Arabic. However, the real difficulty for the translator lay in the differences between Greek and Arabic literary traditions—above all the fact that the genre which Aristotle's work examines had no equivalent in the Arabic literary canon of the time. Neither Arabic translators and scholars, nor their Syriac predecessors, were aware of the principles, or even the basic nature, of the theater, as this art did not exist in these cultures (at least not as an officially recognized member of the literary pantheon). In his attempt to convey the concepts and terms of Greek literature, the (seemingly unsurmountable) barrier facing Matta was the absence of cultural counterparts through which the source text could be conveyed to the receiver in a different context, or at least approximated. In fact, the translator was obviously not even aware of this absence. Had he been, he might have looked for equivalent terms (using such techniques as borrowing, semantic expansion, or coinage), further employing explanation and paraphrase as necessary. This was the practice in the contemporary translation of philosophical works; and indeed in the nineteenth-century translation of the same theatrical terms into Arabic. However, the title of the book was somewhat deceptive. Given that the contemporary Arabic literary canon (i.e., the literature of the elites, as opposed to popular forms) recognized only poetry and a limited number of narrative prose genres, the translator was inevitably led to the conclusion that the aim of Aristotle was to elucidate the laws governing Greek poetry. Considering that Arabic literature followed the same universal principles, these laws could be projected onto it.

It would be facile to dismiss this approximation as a simple case of misreading. Nor is it accurate to attribute it to uncritical reverence for Aristotle, whose judgments could be taken to apply wholesale to any literary context. For one thing, Matta was only following the common translation methods of his time, which relied on adapting source texts into the receptive Islamic setting, infusing them with local color, and eventually integrating them as naturalized products.

As Hasan Hanafi describes the practice of Classical Islamic translators, "the entire text is rewritten by the translator (rather the second author) from the perspective of the receiver . . . in its own terms and expressions" (2000, 1:393). In fact, this cultural adaptation "may go beyond linguistic to conceptual transfer" (2000, 2:101). What made such practices acceptable was what Hanafi calls "Islamic universalism," which, he argues, formed the intellectual foundation of translation in the Classical age of Islam; it was part of the process of assimilating foreign knowledge, as a prelude toward the expansion, and eventually the creation, of new knowledge (2000, 1:319 ff) (Hanafi 2000:20–25). Islamic universalism, Hanafi argues, derives from the belief in the unity of wisdom (of which Greek philosophy was a single, though a prime, example), as drawing on the same primary human nature common to all nations. As the Quran says: "God bestows wisdom on whomever He chooses" (2000, 2:269). Thus, wisdom, it was believed, notwithstanding its different manifestations, draws on one divine source, which could be granted by God to anyone, even before Islam. In fact, the Quranic term *hikma* (wisdom), and its derivative *hakim* (wise man/sage), were the standard translations of philosophy/philosopher, allowing the identification of divinely bestowed wisdom, extolled in the Quran, as the same formulated by Greek philosophers, albeit under a different name. In this respect, translation is practically the restoration of the wisdom of other nations to its divine, and specifically, Islamic source, as Islam is the faith of *fitra* ("original nature"). This naturalization was made possible by the Quran's assertion that it is the inclination of all humans, when left in their *fitra*, that is, natural state without prejudice of local upbringing or tradition, to find the wisdom of faith in a monotheistic God. Consequently, the translator's textual practices went beyond even the most flexible parameters of translation practice, which distinguish, under different terms, between sense-for-sense and word-for-word translation. These practices involved restructuring the texts and the concepts they conveyed. As Hanafi argues, "[W]e cannot talk about word for word transfer (regardless of the sense), nor of sense for sense transfer (regardless of the words): the entire text is transported from the old into the target culture" (2000, 2:46).[1]

Therefore, Matta approached the *Poetics* with the aim of acculturation, rather than homology or equivalence. And if this transformative method was the preferred practice for his fellow Arabic translators, it was virtually the only one for Matta, who was encountering a totally alien literary tradition for the first time. Given these circumstances, the translator arguably demonstrated remarkable ingenuity in adapting Aristotle's terms into the Arabic context of reception, at least on the conceptual level, as his translation choices have sometimes been branded unidiomatic and stylistically awkward (Kilito 2002, 110; 'Aiyad 1967, 179).

The main challenges facing the translator were the basic terms and definitions of the new art, specifically the foundational terms of "tragedy" and "comedy," introduced among arts that rely on mimesis. The absence of equivalent terms in Arabic was only compounded by the translator's assumption that the *Poetics* dealt exclusively with poetry. It was not only that the canonical Arabic literature of the time was dominated by this genre; the title of the book is "poetry" and its purpose, as defined by Aristotle, "is to discuss both poetry in general and the capacity of each of its genres; the canons of plot construction needed for poetic excellence" (Aristotle 1995, 29). This conviction was only reinforced by Aristotle's inclusion of "epic and tragic poetry, as well as comedy," together with poetry, and "most music for aulos and lyre," which "are all, taken as a whole, kinds of mimesis" (Aristotle 1995, 7). Matta translated "mimesis" unproblematically into *al-muhakat* ("imitation"/ "simulation"), which remains the standard Arabic term to this day. Having used the lexical borrowing *dithrambo* for "dithyramb" and translated the musical arts into roughly equivalent Arabic terms, he had to deal with "tragedy" and "comedy." These were terms specific to an art known neither to the Arabs nor to other ethnic groups of the Islamic empire of the time, in a text almost 1,300 years old, produced in a practically extinct culture, from which only a limited number of texts had survived into Matta's time. As he had assumed that the book dealt with poetic genres, Matta had to look for equivalents for these terms in contemporary Arabic poetry. He settled on what he found closest to Aristotle's description, that is, *madih* ("panegyric") for tragedy, and *hija'* ("satire") for comedy.

Farfetched as it may seem, the choice was not random. In fact, one could argue that it demonstrated an enterprising reading of the source text. In defining the difference between tragedy and comedy, Aristotle writes:

> Since mimetic artists represent people in action, and the latter should be either elevated or base (for characters almost always align with just these types, as it is through vice and virtue that the characters of all men vary), they can represent people better than our normal level, worse than it, or much the same . . . Clearly, each kind of mimesis already mentioned will manifest these distinctions, and will differ by representing different objects in the given sense. (Aristotle 1995, 33)

This is also how tragedy and comedy are distinguished—"the latter tends to represent people inferior, the former superior, to existing humans" (Aristotle 1995, 35). The translator seized on this primary distinction in the way poetic forms represent the moral nature of people, as either better or worse than they are, in order to establish the—necessary—link between the two literary traditions in question. Arabic poetic genres were defined by their "purpose" (غرض), including, among others, love poetry, satire, elegy, and panegyric. Surveying the established genres of the Arabic poetry of his time, Matta found a possible (one may say natural) parallel in satire and panegyric, to which Aristotle's definitions of tragedy and comedy can be applied almost entirely. So he translated as follows:

> As those who imitate or liken do so with regard to voluntary actions, then those [imitated] have by necessity to be either good or bad (as customs and morals have to belong to either these two). Since all their customs and morals would be distinguished by virtue or vice, so would narration and imitation: people who are virtuous, unvirtuous, or just like us . . . So it is clear that any imitation or narration has to be as described above . . . It is this difference that distinguishes satire from panegyric—that the one imitates the unvirtuous, while the other imitates and the good and likens to them. (Aristotle 1953, 88–89)[2]

The Arabic *Poetics* in Context

Little information can be found concerning the reception of Matta's translation. The philosophers who discussed and commented on the work did so much later; there are also only brief references in the context of cataloging Arabic translated works from the Greek or in biographical notes of the translator himself (Ibn al-Nadim 1971, 309, 324; e.g., al-Qifti 2005, 242). The only related commentary of any substance on the translation can be found as part of a scholarly debate in which Matta defended logic against grammar, represented by the contemporary linguist Abu Sa'id al-Sirafi (al-Tawhidi 2004, 89–101). The debate has been referenced and analyzed in several modern studies, which have usually focused on its philosophical side (e.g., Kemal 1991, 45ff). However, Matta's opinions on language, translation, and culture as expressed in this debate would certainly help us understand the intellectual background of his translation methods. No less significantly, we may draw valuable insights into the context of reception of Matta's translation from a close analysis of the arguments about logic and grammar put forth from the two sides, focusing specifically on why these particular disciplines should have been pitted against each other as the main rivals for scholarly primacy. The discussion will further shed light on the approaches to the *Poetics* among later scholars, and specifically Averroes.

Before looking at this exchange, the introduction by Abu Hayyan al-Tawhidi (the eminent tenth- to eleventh-century belletrist who reproduced the debate in one of his major works) gives us important clues about its purpose, and how it was viewed at the time. Al-Tawhidi cites the debate in the context of a discussion of the best methods of attaining wisdom. Specifically, the question is whether intellectual inquiry should be based on scholarly research—"reading hefty books with numerous pages, and expending laborious efforts in studying and analyzing questions and answers"—or on independent intellectual inquiry, employing nothing but "original nature" (*fitra*), whereupon "the best path would be the knowledge of nature, the self, the mind, and God Almighty" (2004, 89, 88). While al-Tawhidi, generally supporting the latter viewpoint, acknowledges that one can learn, to a certain extent, from previous scholars, he condemns philosophers, and especially logicians, for having unduly complicated their methods—his primary example being Matta himself, the leading logician of the time (2004, 89).

As al-Tawhidi's unflattering view of Matta runs counter to contemporary evaluations, which tend to be quite positive, one has to locate its motivation (as will become clear from the debate) in his attitude toward logic itself (see Ibn Khallikan 1994, 153; al-Qifti 2005, 241–42).[3] An imported science that emerged in Arabic as a result of translating Greek philosophy, logic was seen in direct opposition to grammar, which occupied a central position among what came to be known as the Arabic (or traditional) sciences, together with rhetoric, literary criticism, jurisprudence, hadith (the collection and study of the Prophet's sayings), and history. These disciplines, known as "*naqliya*" (literally, "transmitted," i.e., from tradition), were opposed to the "rational" (*'aqliya*) sciences, including above all philosophy and logic, which developed through the influence of translation (Meehan 2013, 35–36; Nasr 2006, 251; Ibn Khaldun 1988, 550–51). In fact, grammar (a discipline that was closely linked to Islamic sciences, especially as it was perfected mainly in the context of Quranic exegesis), was seen as the epitome not only of native sciences, but also of *fitra*, the original nature, which Islam postulated as the source of true faith. It is this conflict between the traditional and rational sciences, between what is native (and hence "natural") and what is imported though translation, that underlies the debate between Matta and al-Sirafi.

Language versus Thought

In the beginning of the debate, Al-Sirafi rejects Matta's definition of logic as a tool with which to distinguish truth from falsehood in thinking and language use, on the grounds that truth and falsehood can be distinguished through reliance on "familiar patterns and established conjugations if we speak Arabic," and "with reason, if reason is what we use" (al-Tawhidi 2004, 90). Language and reason are at the heart of the debate; the former is, of course, al-Sirafi's domain, and he will try to demonstrate that it is the only decisive standard. Reason, on the other hand, is also cited by al-Sirafi, but only in the sense of *fitra*, the exercise of pure intellectual inquiry, free from the artificial methods contrived by philosophers. Consequently, al-Sirafi argues, the principles of thinking do not need to be borrowed from other nations, for "if logic had been devised by a Greek man, following the idioms, features and characteristics of their own language, then why would the Turks, Indians, Persians, and Arabs be bound to consider it, or to use it as a judge for them and against them?" (al-Tawhidi 2004, 94). Here, it can be argued, lies the crux of al-Sirafi's argument, for his objections are not directed at the principles of logic as such, but at the mere fact that they had been conceivably borrowed from another nation. On his part, Matta does not reject pure reasoning; indeed, he maintains that this is what makes it universal, unlimited to one nation: "When it comes to what is recognized by reason people are one and the same" (al-Tawhidi 2004, 92). Thus, if the Greeks have achieved any special distinction in this area, it is merely because "of all nations, they have given special attention to philosophy, and the investigation of the visible and hidden truths of the world" (al-Tawhidi 2004, 92). To this, al-Sirafi responds with what is arguably one of the loci of the argument, one that is most intimately connected with the central problem of translation. While the basic substance and principles of rational inquiry are indeed, as Matta explains, "spread amongst all people of the world," a fundamental distinction lies in the way this knowledge is expressed: "If the objects of rational inquiry and meanings recognized by the mind cannot be comprehended save with a language that contains nouns, verbs, and particles, does it not become necessary to know this language?" (al-Tawhidi 2004, 91). Therefore, rational inquiry and logical proofs being necessarily fashioned in the mold of the language in which they are articulated, what Arabic logicians actually practice is, at root, the translated grammar of Greek: "So you are not actually inviting us to [practice] logic, but to study the Greek language" (al-Tawhidi 2004, 91).

In response, the logician insists that there is a common basis to reasoning that transcends linguistic difference; indeed, he argues that logic does not need grammar at all, "for logic considers meaning, while grammar concerns itself with utterance: it is only incidentally that the logician addresses the utterance, or the grammarian the meaning. Truly meaning is higher than utterance, and utterance is lower than meaning" (al-Tawhidi 2004, 93). This firm separation between language and thought is not confined to Matta; it can be seen as a primary principle in Muslim approaches to Greek philosophy. For example, al-Farabi (a major Islamic philosopher, known as the "second teacher," Aristotle being the first) presents this distinction in his *A Survey of the Sciences* within a universalist perspective: logic, he says, "shares a common ground with grammar in that it postulates the laws governing utterances; it diverges from the latter in that, while grammar lays down the laws of the utterances of one nation, logic lays down common laws that apply to all nations" (1998, 34–35).

Al-Sirafi and Matta stand at the two ends of the controversy about the relationship between language and thought, summed up by the two opposing metaphors of language as a "cloak" or a "mold." In modern linguistic terms, their positions can be described, respectively, as embracing linguistic relativity and linguistic universalism. Furthermore, Matta's insistence on the separation of meaning and utterance, and the former's superiority to the latter, underlies a "logocentric" view which relies, as translation theorist Vicente Rafael argues, on "a belief in the existence of a signifying hierarchy, with language subordinated to thought and thought originating from a thinking subject. It regards thought to be distinct from language, closer to the soul, and thus of a higher order than its linguistic representation" (2015, 86).

Within their immediate intellectual environment, these two perspectives lead to opposing positions on the translation of the Greek heritage and its transmission in Arabic. On the one hand, linguistic relativity (at least in its extreme form espoused by al-Sirafi) conceives of cultures as separate islands demarcated by the boundaries of their own languages, whose vocabulary, grammatical structures, and rhetorical devices formulate their worldview, and even their thinking habits. This view naturally results in a highly skeptical attitude toward translation, as linguistic differences underlie separate intellectual operations, accessible only through the language in which they are expressed. Translation, in this viewpoint, is practically impossible, for as al-Sirafi puts it, "no one language is identical to another in all its features . . . So how can you trust something that was translated under these conditions?" (al-Tawhidi 2004, 94). By contrast, Matta belittles the impact of linguistic difference on utilizing Greek logic, as this process would only require the basic ingredients of language: "From language, I only need the noun, the verb, and the particle. These are enough for me to attain the meanings which have been refined by the Greeks" (al-Tawhidi 2004, 116).[4] Thus, similarity to Matta is more predominant than difference; even different forms of linguistic expression do not invalidate the shared foundation of common human truths, as they rely on fundamental principles common to all languages. A similar view of linguistic universals is found again in al-Farabi, reinforcing his humanist outlook and echoing Matta, who was among his teachers: "Utterances have categories common to all nations, such as the fact that words are either simple or compound, and that the simple ones are nouns, verbs, or particles" (Ibn Khallikan 1994, 154; Fakhry 2014, 39; 1998, 35).

Beyond the (im)possibility of translation, the two views on language and thought lead to different methods of translation. According to the relativist position, if translation is possible at all, it should be literal and strictly accurate, so as to convey as closely as possible the original linguistic modes which are indispensable to the authentic understanding of the Other. The universalist position, on the other hand, allows considerable leeway in translation. Indeed, fashioning the meanings of the source texts into the molds of the target language is not only permissible, but possibly even desirable, as the basic underlying truths are the same. As embraced by Matta, as well as by the translators and exegists of Greek philosophy, this adaptive approach is not merely "domesticating." Rather than implement a forced transformation of the Other into the terms of the self, their approach aims to reveal fundamental universal truths that can be uncovered beneath the facade of linguistic and cultural difference.

While deployed as (more or less natural) offshoots of theoretical positions on the relationship between language and thought, these opposing views of the possibility and methods of translation have to be seen in their historical contexts as reflecting, and rationalizing, conflicting contemporary attitudes toward the reception of Greek, and generally foreign, sciences in Arabic. This is why al-Sirafi's insistence on natural knowledge, acquired though pure reason rather than logic, though seeming to allow some possibility of shared universal wisdom, draws more narrowly on the concept of Quranic *fitra*. Hence, while one can attain knowledge through the exercise of pure reason, this can be done only when his judgment and discrimination are "enlightened by God's generous gifts and His exalted bounty, which he bestows upon whom he chooses from among his creatures" (al-Tawhidi 2004, 98). In this way, natural knowledge is reduced to divine knowledge as defined by one religion, and while wisdom is indeed spread among all nations, it still has to be weighed with one, Islamic measure. In other words, al-Sirafi's theorization of language and translation is at root motivated by his rejection of imported knowledge as such, in favor of the native traditional sciences.

By contrast, Islamic scholars who sought to apply foreign sciences to their own intellectual practice had to discern a basis of shared humanity with the original texts. Therefore, even as they recognized that the ultimate source of knowledge was divine, with its truest manifestation in Islam, they still allowed the possibility that this knowledge could be acquired by people in non-Muslim cultures through the exercise of natural reason. It is this attitude that enabled translators in the Classical age to minimize cultural, and even religious, differences in the source texts, which they dismissed as inessential, in their effort to stress what is universal. In this way, non-Islamic, even anti-Islamic, practices, were mitigated or Islamicized: "the First Cause" (or even polytheistic gods) became "God Almighty" (الله تعالى), and references to alcohol and gambling were usually removed (see, for example, Hanafi 2000, 1:393–94, 304–5; 2:46, 100–1). Even more, Aristotle was sometimes described as "divine" (الإلهي), as he managed through his rational philosophy to arrive at intimations of wisdom whose primordial fountainhead cannot be but divine. Pursuing this line of thought, it should not be surprising that Aristotle and some other Greek sages were seen as prophets. For if the Quran had declared that God had sent a messenger to every nation, then the Greeks should have had their own prophet (16: 36). And who else would deserve this status but their greatest sage? In this context, we can understand the significance of the saying attributed to the Prophet of Islam stating that "Aristotle was a prophet who was neglected by his own people" (al-Daylami 1999, 117). There were also claims that other Greek thinkers, such as "Hipparchus and Ptolemy were prophets, as were most sages—except that people were confused by their Greek names" (al-Daylami 1999, 117). In short, then, the wisdom of foreign sages was restored, as it were, to its original sources, making it possible for Muslims to choose what is compatible with their faith without fear of contradiction.

From Theatrical Laws to Literary Ethics: Averroes' Reading of the *Poetics*

Ibn Rushd, known in the West as Averroes (1126–1198), was an Islamic philosopher who lived in Islamic Spain (Al-Andalus). Besides his status, in the Muslim world as well as in Europe, as one of the most celebrated and influential Islamic philosophers, Averroes' commentary on the *Poetics* merits special attention as the most substantial study of Aristotle's book in Classical Arabic. To be sure, Averroes was not the first thinker to tackle or even comment on the *Poetics*. Some sources mention a lost early commentary by al-Kindi, the first major Islamic philosopher, although it is not clear whether al-Kindi relied on a translation or the original Greek text (Ibn al-Nadim 1971, 309; Badawi 1953, 51). Next was al-Farabi, who, in his *A Treatise on the Principles of the Art of Poetry*, built on "statements attributed to the sage Aristotle about the poetic art, as well as to Themistius and other ancient sages and exegists" (1953, 155). However, al-Farabi does not reference the *Poetics* by title; in fact, his only direct involvement with Aristotle is the concept of mimesis, using the same Arabic term coined by Matta (المحاكاة). Finally, completing the list of major Islamic philosophers who studied the *Poetics* was Avicenna, who produced a complete summary in his philosophical and scientific encyclopedia *The Book of Healing*, with the general purpose of discussing "poetry as such, methods of poetic compositions, and forms of Greek poetry" (Avicenna 1953, 161). Averroes, however, was unique: not only did he provide a detailed exegesis, striving to explain the entire text and dispel any obscurities caused by translation; his main goal was to apply Aristotle's literary concepts as a critical tool to generate new insights into Arabic poetry, which he subsequently deployed in the construction of his own philosophical and political theories.

Averroes addressed the *Poetics* in two commentaries, separated by a time span during which his conception of the book and its value apparently evolved. The first was a brief summary, which limited itself to explaining the nature of "poetic statements," Aristotle's reason for their study being mainly their persuasive function (1977, 203). In this shorter commentary, Averroes places the *Poetics* at the bottom of the hierarchy of the *Organon*, preceded by *Rhetoric* and *Topics* in that order, depending on their proximity to the logical sciences, which occupied the top of the hierarchy (Butterworth 1977, 22–23). The second, far more comprehensive exegesis is classified in the category of "middle commentaries," which do not follow the original sentence by sentence, but give a detailed summary, using select quotations (Badawi 1953, 52). Averroes cites Aristotle's text one extract at a time, explaining what he understood it to mean and substituting Greek examples for extensive ones taken from Arabic poetry. In addition, his commentaries are interspersed with his own reflections on Arabic poetry, especially its ethical value, which, it will be argued, seems to be the main goal of the exegesis.

In order to understand Averroes' translation, it is necessary to investigate what the *Poetics* meant to the Islamic philosopher and how he situated it within the context of his own philosophical concerns. The point, in other words, is what Averroes was trying to do with the text, which went far beyond retrieving the truth-value of Aristotle's arguments. From the very beginning of his exegesis (and reminiscent of Avicenna before him), Averroes makes it clear that he is not interested in the specific characteristics of Greek literature, but in what he calls "totalities" (الكليات): "our purpose here is to summarize what can be found in Aristotle's book of the total laws that are common to all, or most nations. For much of this book concerns laws that are specific to their poetry. Their poetic practices either exist to varying extents in Arabic, or in other languages" (1953, 201). This is why Averroes is content with brief summaries of those parts of the *Poetics* dealing with literary forms that seemed specific to the Greeks, even skipping some parts, as when Aristotle lists Greek poets who represented particular literary genres. Averroes emphasizes throughout that he is confining himself to what is shared between Arabic and Greek poetry, and, broadly, to what is common to all, or most, nations.

As Averroes starts inserting extended examples from Arabic poetry into his exegesis, and reflecting on its ethical functions, it becomes clear that his aim is to incorporate Aristotle's terms, as filtered through the translation that was available to him, into Arabic literary criticism and his own philosophy. Specifically, he uses this commentary as a vehicle to express his own ethical views of some poetic forms in Arabic, and poetry in general, relying on the authority of the "First Teacher." For Aristotle was not only seen as a learned authority in himself, but, more importantly, as an expositor of common laws—a vehicle for "timeless wisdom" (as described in the title of a famous book by tenth- to eleventh-century Islamic philosopher Miskawayh), which combines the greatest wisdom of all nations, Islamic and non-Islamic, beyond linguistic and cultural differences.

Averroes' standard for assessing poetry is its truth-value (the extent to which it communicates the truth about the world). He argues that poetry can be judged by its representational function, thereby introducing mimesis into the discussion. For good poetry uses mimesis to provide true pictures of the world, without exaggerations or fantasies, elements of Arabic poetry that merit his disapproval, especially as exemplified in the traditional pre-Islamic Arabia, by then already canonical. He criticizes poetic hyperboles that amount to falsehoods, using a strictly philosophical standard: the "lies" of some poets, he states, are "to the truth what sophistries are to logical proofs," and so he rebukes what he brands "sophist poets" (Badawi 1953, 228, 227). Good poetry is, in fact, closer to philosophy than to parables (Badawi 1953, 214).

Having established this strict form of mimesis as the criterion of poetic function, Averroes links it to a normative ethical standard. He invokes a dichotomy of ethical judgment that was introduced by Islamic philosophers, and later incorporated into literary studies as an aesthetic measure: *Al-tahsin wa al-taqbih* (التحسين والتقبيح), literally "beautifying" and "uglifying," and, more broadly, representing, or evaluating, something as either good or bad. Combining the ethical and aesthetic sides of the *al-tahsin wa al-taqbih* dichotomy, Averroes argues that the aim of poetic mimesis is chiefly ethical: making virtue attractive, equating it with the good (*al-tahsin*), and making vice repulsive, equating it with evil (*al-taqbih*), or else avoiding its imitation altogether. So, mimesis can serve one of two purposes; "it seems every simile or narrative is intended either for the good or the bad" (1953, 204). Accordingly, Averroes defines what he calls "virtuous poetry" (الشعر العفيفي) (1953, 238). The ultimate purpose of this kind of poetry is improving virtuous conduct by encouraging moral actions and discouraging immoral ones. Specifically, Averroes views the moral function of poetry within a pedagogical system whose aim is to help the proper upbringing of the young. Therefore, when he condemns love poetry (النسيب) as inciting wickedness, he concludes that "it should be kept away from the young" (1953, 205). On the other hand, he notes with approval that Arabic poetry does celebrate some virtues, especially bravery and generosity (though he still objects that these two are usually extolled in the context of pride, rather than moral persuasion), which makes some of it conducive to the edification of children (1953, 205).

The criteria of morality are, of course, determined by Islamic laws, and especially by the Quran, which is, among other things, a literary book. Hence, Averroes' indictments of the moral shortcomings of some Arabic poetry (exaggeration, falsehood, debauchery, especially in erotic poetry) are complemented throughout not only with the edifying purposes that Aristotle supposedly identifies in Greek poetry, but, more importantly, with counterexamples from the Quran (showing how the holy book commends virtuous deeds and condemns unvirtuous ones); indeed, Averroes attributes the Quran's famous condemnation of poetry to this very reason, that pre-Islamic poetry was mostly devoid of ethical purpose, while emphasizing that the holy book made an exception for the kind of poetry he calls for (26: 224; 1953, 216). By establishing this ethical aim of poetry, Averroes explains that his discussion is meant to set examples for contemporary poets. Citing some edifying samples from Arabic poetry, he concludes: "It is this praise of virtuous human acts, and denunciation of unvirtuous ones, that we need" (Badawi 1953, 216).

For a full appreciation of Averroes' reflections on poetry, it is important to place them within the general framework of his philosophical practice, where they form an important part of his ethical system. Averroes' views on the general moral and social function of poetry can be found in his commentary on Plato's *Republic* (usually known in Arabic as *What Is Necessary in Politics*, الضروري في السياسة).[5] There, Averroes examines the role of education in promoting virtue. Following Plato, he holds that there are two ways of imbuing virtue in the people of the city: rhetoric and poetry (1974, 10).[6] This method, it should be noted, is limited to the "multitude of humans," as opposed to the "elect few," whose moral education is based on "the true ways," derived from logical proof (1974, 10). The type of poetry that is effective for this instruction of the multitude is exactly the one he advocates in his commentary on the *Poetics*, that is, that which praises virtue and denounces vice, or ignores its imitation. Thus, Averroes stresses the necessity of removing all examples encouraging the pursuit of money and pleasure, which, he claims, abound in Arabic poetry (1974, 24). For these, he argues, are inappropriate for moral education. As he says time and again in the *Poetics*, he emphasizes in his discussion of Plato's *Republic* that Arabic poetry (specifically that of pre-Islamic Arabia), is "filled with these evil things. It would therefore be more harmful than anything else to accustom youths to them from the outset" (1974, 24–25).

It becomes clear, then, that Averroes' view of poetry, and more precisely Arabic poetry, which seems to be the focus of his exegesis of the *Poetics*, should be seen as an element of his general ethical philosophical system. Irrespective of the true nature of Greek literature, and what we may call Aristotle's particular (as opposed to universal) theories of literature, Averroes' project was to domesticate the *Poetics* into Arabic literature; in the same way he domesticates poetry to philosophy, that is aesthetic values to truth and morality—all under the auspices of Islamic law.

Toward a New Horizon

The picture that emerges is one that challenges the standards of comprehension and miscomprehension that are usually used in the assessment of translation, often derived from a textual comparison between source and target. Indeed, it could afford a new perspective on the questions of faithfulness, adaptation, and the transformation of the Other. For it is obvious that Averroes' intention in his commentary on the *Poetics* was not merely to recover the meaning of the original text (although he undoubtedly tried to do that), but, more importantly, to engage the Greek text in contemporary debates, and rely on it to work through moral and philosophical questions that preoccupied him. Nor does our analysis of his interpretation of Aristotle's text, and his resourceful integration of it into his intellectual pursuits, support Dimitri Gutas's claim that Averroes, part of a movement to "return to the original Greeks works," "sought a return to the understanding of 'pristine' Aristotle" (1998, 153). In fact, in spite of the factual errors that resulted from the translation, and the cultural gaps beyond the confines of his historical moment, Averroes' reading, I would argue, holds some truth of its own, one that is validated by the limitations of transmission and the necessities of his place and time. His integration of the terms of the *Poetics* into Islamic philosophy and literature can be seen, in Gadamer's terms, as a "fusion of horizons," allowing the assimilation of the unfamiliar or culturally different, "making what is alien our own" (Gadamer 1977, 19). In this process of negotiation between the familiar and the different, the self and the Other, the receiver's horizon of interpretation unavoidably limits the possibilities of understanding; yet, it is enriched and transformed, even as it simultaneously transforms the Other.

While the case of the *Poetics* in Classical Arabic seems to present an extreme instance of cultural difference, intercultural barriers of all kinds will always exist. We need to recognize that there are at least some cases that transcend the precepts of faithfulness and accuracy, usually derived from a comparative reading of source and target texts. This claim certainly does not discount the importance of such assessments. However, although a comparative study is an important first step, limiting our analysis to that will make us unable to go beyond dichotomies of either/or, meaning versus distortion. Instead, in a situation such as that of Averroes' commentary, we need to explore the complex and often interesting ways in which foreign texts speak to other cultures across the limitations of time, place, and literary tradition. Texts can be creatively transformed and expanded in this process—their meanings enhanced and multiplied.

Notes

1. For the practices of translators in Classical Islam, see also Shamma, 81–84.
2. All translations are by the author unless otherwise stated.
3. It is worth noting also that al-Tawhidi was al-Sirafi's student and a great admirer of his (e.g., al-Tawhidi, 20).
4. Matta here follows the standard categorization of the parts of speech in Arabic grammar: noun, verb, and particle (i.e., function word). See also al-Sirafi above.
5. This book has survived only in a Hebrew translation, which has been translated into English by Ralph Lerner. This is the version used here.
6. "Hymns to the gods and eulogies of good people are the only poetry we can admit into our city" (*Republic*, 311).

Works Cited

'Abdallah, Ibrahim. 2014. *Al-Tarjama min Su' al-Fahm ila Su' al-Ta'wil (Hawla Qadiyat Fan al-Shi'r li Aristo)*. [Translation from Miscomprehension to Misinterpretation: On the Question of Aristotle's *Poetics*]. In al-Imam, Mujab, and 'Abd al-'Aziz, Muhammad, *Fi al-Tarjama wa Ishkaliyat al-Muthaqafa*. [On Translation and the Problematics of Interculturation]. Doha, Qatar: Forum for Arab and International Relations, 355–66.

'Aiyad, Shukri. 1967. *Kitab Aristotales fi al-Shi'r, Naql Abi Bishr Bin Yunus al-Qina'i*. Cairo, Egypt: Dar al-Kitab al-'Arabi.

Al-Daylami, Qutb al-Din. 1999. *Mahbub al-Qulub*. [The Beloved of the Hearts]. Tehran, Iran: Ayna Mirath.

Al-Farabi, Abu al-Nasr. 1953. *Risala fi Qawanin al-Shi'r*. [A Treatise on the Laws of Poetry], edited by 'Abd al-Rahman Badawi, 147–58. Cairo, Egypt: Maktabat al-Nahda al-Masriya.

———. *Ihsa' al-'Ulum*. 1998. [Survey of the Sciences]. Beirut: Dar Al-Hilal.

Al-Musawi, Muhsin J. 2001. "Arabic Rhetoric." In *Encyclopedia of Rhetoric*, vol. 1, edited by Thomas O. Sloane, 29–33. Oxford, UK: Oxford University Press.

Al-Qifti, Jamal al-Din. 2005. *Ikhbar al-'Ulama' bi-Akhbar al-Hukama'* [Informing Scholars of the Narratives of Sages]. Beirut, Lebanon: Dar al-Kutub al-'Ilmiyya.

Al-Tawhidi, Abu Hayyan. 2004. *Al-Imta' wal Mu'anasa*. [Enjoyment and Companionship]. Beirut, Lebanon: al-Maktaba al-Asriyya.

Aristotle. 1953. *Kitab Aristotales fi al-Shi'r.* [Aristotle's Book on Poetry], edited by 'Abd al-Rahman Badawi, and translated by Matta Bin Yunus, 83–145. Cairo, Egypt: Maktabat al-Nahda al-Masriya.

———. 1995. *Poetics.* Edited and translated by Stephen Halliwell. Cambridge, MA: Harvard University Press.

Averroes (Ibn Rushd, Abu al-Walid). 1974. *Averroes on Plato's Republic*, edited and translated by Ralph Lerner. Ithaca, NY: Cornell University Press.

———. 1953. *Talkhis Kitab Aristo fi al-Shi'r.* [Middle Commentary on Aristotle's *Poetics*], edited by 'Abd al-Rahman Badawi, 199–250. Cairo, Egypt, Maktabat al-Nahda al-Masriya.

———. 1977. Jawami' Kitab al-Shi'r. [Short Commentaries on the *Poetics*]. In *Three Short Commentaries on Aristotle's "Topics," "Rhetoric," and "Poetics,"* edited by Charles Butterworth. Albany: State University of New York Press.

Avicenna (Ibn Sina, Abu 'Ali). 1953. "Fasl fi al-Shi'r" fi Kitab al-Shifa.'" [A Chapter on Poetry in *The Book of Healing*], edited by 'Abd al-Rahman Badawi, 159–98. Cairo, Egypt: Maktabat al-Nahda al-Masriya.

Badawi, 'Abd al-Rahman. 1953. *Fan al-Shi'r, ma'a al-Tarjama al-'Arabia al-Qadima wa Shuruh al Farabi wa Ibn Sina wa Ibn Rushd.* [Poetics, with the Ancient Arabic Translation, and the Commentaries of al-Farabi, Ibn Sina, and Ibn Rushd]. Cairo, Egypt: al-Nahda al-Masriyya.

Butterworth, Charles (ed., trans.). 1977. *Averroës' Three Short Commentaries on Aristotle's "Topics," "Rhetoric," and "Poetics."* Albany: State University of New York Press.

Endress, G. 1991. "Matta Bin Yunus." In *The Encyclopedia of Islam*, vol. VI, edited by C. E. Bosworth et al., 844–46. Leiden, the Netherlands: Brill.

Fakhry, Majed. 2014. *Islamic Philosophy, Theology and Mysticism: A Short Introduction.* Oxford, UK: Oneworld.

Gelder, G. J. H. van. 1989. *The Bad and the Ugly: Attitudes towards Invective Poetry (Hijā) in Classical Arabic Literature.* Leiden, Brill.

Gutas, Dimitri. 1990. "On Translating Averroes' Commentaries." Review. *Journal of the American Oriental Society*, 110, no. 1: 92–101.

———. 1998. *Greek Thought, Arabic Culture.* London and New York: Routledge.

Hanafi, Hasan. 2000. *Mina al-Naql ila al-Ibda'* [From Transmission to Creation], Part 1: al-Naql [Transmission], 3 vols. Cairo, Egypt: Dar Qiba'.

Ibn al-Nadim, Abu Al-Faraj. 1971. *Kitab al-Fihrist* (The Index). Tehran: n.p.

Ibn Khaldun, 'Abd al-Rahman. 1988. *Tarikh Ibn Khaldun*, 2nd ed. [The History of Ibn Khaldun], vol. 1. Beirut, Lebanon: Dar al-Fikr.

Ibn Khallikan, Shams al-Din. 1994. *Wafiyyat al-A'yyan* [Notable Deaths]. vol. 5. Beirut, Lebanon: Dar Sader.

Kemal, Selim. 1991. *The Poetics of Alfarabi and Avicenna.* Leiden, the Netherlands: Brill.

Kilito, Abd a-Fatah. 2002. *Lan Tatakalama Lughati*. [You Will Not Speak My Language]. Beirut, Lebanon: Dar al-Tali'a.

Miskawayh, Abu 'Ali. 1983. *Al-Hikma al-Khalida*. [Timeless Wisdoms]. Beirut: Dar al-Andalus.

Meehan, Mark W. 2013. *Islam, Modernity, and the Liminal Space Between*. Cambridge, UK: Cambridge Scholars Publishing.

Meisami, Julie Scott. 1998. "Literary Criticism, Medieval." In *Encyclopedia of Arabic Literature*, vol. 2, edited by Julie Scott Meisami and Paul Starkey, 472–74. London and New York: Routledge.

Nasr, Seyyed Hossein. 2006. *Islamic Philosophy from Its Origin to the Present: Philosophy in the Land of Prophesy*. Albany: SUNY Press.

Plato. 2004. *Republic*, translated by C. D. C. Reeve. Indianapolis, IN: Hackett Publishing.

Rafael, Vicente L. 2015. "Betraying Empire: Translation and the Ideology of Conquest." *Translation Studies* 8, no. 1: 82–106.

Shamma, Tarek. 2009. "Translating into the Empire: The Arabic Version of *Kalila wa Dimna*." *The Translator: Studies in Intercultural Communication*, 15, no. 1: 65–86.

Vagelpohl, Uwe. 2015. "The *Rhetoric* and the *Poetics* in the Islamic World." In *Aristotle and the Arabic Tradition*, edited by Ahmed Alwishah and Josh Hayes. Cambridge, UK: Cambridge University Press.

———. 2008. *Aristotle's Rhetoric in the East: The Syriac and Arabic Translation and Commentary Tradition*. Leiden, the Netherlands: Brill.

Yousif, Ephrem-Isa. 1997. *Les philosophes et traducteurs syriaques: d'Athènes à Bagdad*. Paris: L'Harmattan.

Chapter 2

Lost in Transliteration

Morisco Travel Writing and the *Coplas del hijante de Puey Monçón*

Benjamin Liu

Their story begins on ground level, with footsteps.

—Michel de Certeau

Travel, Translation, and Transliteration

In her 2013 critique of world literature, Emily Apter interrogates various modes of untranslatability and argues for among other things, a "linguistic pluralism" and a comparative practice that takes "full measure of linguistic constraints, in an investigation of singular modes of existing in the world's languages" (Apter 2013, 27). In one chapter, Apter considers a meditation by the Moroccan writer and critic Abdalfattah Kilito—in dialogue with Jorge Luis Borges, Ernst Renan, and the medieval Andalusi philosopher Ibn Rushd or Averroes—that circles around an apparently untranslatable Arabic phrase "loughatu-na l-'ajamiyya," which is immediately translated, of course, into French as *"notre langue étrangère,"* or "our foreign tongue" (Apter 2013, 254).

The word *'ajamiyya*, the foreign part here, means not-Arabic, the language of non-Arabs, historically often applied to Persian, a category of opposition that would seem to confound the plural possessive, *-na, notre*, "our." But it also gives rise, centuries later within the contact zone of Averroes' Iberian Peninsula, to one of Apter's "singular modes of existing in the world's languages," called precisely *'ajamiyya* or *aljamiado*, the mixed language system employed by Spanish Mudejars and Moriscos for writing their native Castilian or Aragonese in Arabic script. To be precise, *aljamía* refers to the (foreign) Iberian Romance languages, while the Spanish adjective *aljamiado* originally referred to a bilingual subject capable of reading Arabic script, most notably Cervantes' Morisco translator of *Don Quixote*. As Jacques Lezra has pointed out, the earliest English translations of *Don Quixote*—Shelton's—render his "morisco aljamiado" first as a "more translated Spaniard," later emended to "any Moore turned Spaniard" (Lezra 2015, 171). In an earlier period, the *Poem of the Cid* similarly speaks of a "moro latinado," a Muslim versed in Romance, but by the seventeenth century, a "morisco aljamiado" is a former or crypto-Muslim still able to read and translate Arabic script.

The Mudejars, Muslim subjects of Christian lords, and the Moriscos, "translated" Spaniards or nominal Christians after their forced conversions from 1499 to 1526, used this clandestine strategy of diglossic writing in transliteration to mediate their dual linguistic affiliations to Spanish and to the language of the Quran. For the Moriscos, transcribing "our" *'ajamiyya* (Spanish) into *aljamiado* (Arabic script) is a writing practice through which they maintained a covert cultural memory within a Spanish state that sought actively to erase it. The eventual expulsion of the Moriscos from Spanish territories, ordered in 1609 and carried out over the following years, is testimony to how persistent—and how dangerous—that memory work was seen to be. Fernand Braudel saw the "radical" solution of the Morisco's mass deportation as a limit case of what he called "overlapping civilizations," and ultimately a consequence of their cultural "inassimilability" (Braudel 1995, 776, 780, 796), though scholars such as Bernard Vincent perceive in Braudel's writings an evolution of his views on the subject of the Moriscos (Vincent 2010, 298–301). In more recent times, scholars such as Luce López Baralt have eschewed a civilizational model to view the Morisco rather as "a hybrid being and a cultural mestizo, at once deeply Muslim and fully Spanish" (López Baralt 2009, 19).

My argument here is that for the Moriscos, writing about their travels between the greater Muslim world and their non-Muslim home, between the distant *dār al Islām* and the local *dār al ḥarb*, reenacts a movement that crosses between translation and transliteration. If translation brings the world closer to home, makes it more familiar, then *aljamiado* transliteration seeks somehow to render it once again more strange—and less translatable—that is, to put the foreign back into Kilito's paradoxical "our foreign language." In advancing this argument, I am drawing on an incomplete and enigmatic suggestion made by Carroll Johnson, from his posthumous book *Transliterating a Culture: Cervantes and the Moriscos*, that "transliteration, as opposed to translation, [is a] perfect metaphor—two different versions of the same language" (Johnson 2009, 21).

The tensions that Johnson described between translation and transliteration can be illustrated by two sixteenth-century works that showcase the special translational status of sacred texts. Francisco Ximénez de Cisneros, around 1502, began the humanist enterprise of compiling and printing the Complutense Polyglot Bible, in Hebrew, Greek, Latin, and Aramaic. If, in Walter Benjamin's dictum, "the interlinear version of the Scriptures is the prototype of all translation," then Cisneros's massive Bible project is a kind of Rosetta Stone for reading scripture simultaneously and multilingually. But it is worth noting that Latin remains the common denominator here, the privileged target language into which scriptural meaning is ultimately transferred via the substitutive process of *translatio studii*. The Greek Septuagint is mediated with an interlineal translation in Latin and Jerome's Latin Vulgate occupies the very center of the page between the Greek and Hebrew versions.

At nearly the same time that he sets into motion the Polyglot Bible project, Cisneros was also the intellectual author of the forced conversion of the Moriscos of Granada (1499–1500) and of Castile (1502), and of the public burning of Arabic manuscripts and books in Granada in the same year (Eisenberg 1992). One Morisco Quran with interlinear aljamiado "translation" that managed to escape the inquisitorial scrutiny comes from the largest trove of aljamiado-morisco found manuscripts, fortuitously discovered by workmen in Almonacid de la Sierra, near Zaragoza, in 1884, stashed under floorboards in a house under renovation. Many of these unreadable manuscript codices were discarded, burned or destroyed by the workmen or local children (Montaner Frutos 1988, 119–20). These documents so carefully transliterated, written out by hand, preserved and concealed for centuries after the expulsion, present us with a view of Spanish Islam in its last phases, as it finds itself increasingly isolated from the larger Muslim *umma* or faith community and its linguistic and cultural practices.

The Quran, as a revealed text, is considered to be inimitable, under the doctrine of *i'jāz*, and its chosen language, Arabic, is considered to have a special eloquence that renders it resistant to translation. One version of Kilito's injunction against translation ("Thou shalt not translate me!") concerns the untranslatability of poetry and, specifically, of Arabic poetry, which, following al-Jāḥiẓ, "can only be read or recited in its original language" (Kilito 2008, 42, 25–42). If this applies to Arabic poetry, it does so even more regarding the sacred language of the Quran through its inimitability, a form of what Apter terms "linguistic monotheism" (Apter 2013, 260; Apter 2010, 251). Anwar Chejne describes how the very "prohibition of committing the Quran to any foreign language [. . .] presented a dilemma for non-Arabic-speaking Muslims, and particularly for the Moriscos, unwilling to compromise their faith, and yet unable to maintain a knowledge of Arabic . . ." (Chejne 1983, 52–53; quoted in Johnson 2009: 175–76). This difficulty eventually leads them to the in-between practice of interlineal aljamiado translation.

One Quranic chapter from Almonacid has an interlineal aljamiado version that occupies this in-between space between translation, commentary, and transliteration (Gil 1888, 162). The *sūra* or chapter of the Fig is one of the early revelations from Mecca, a place that is explicitly referenced in the Arabic words of the *sūra*, "wa hadha l-baladi l-amīni" (and by this secure city). Chejne once again suggests, in the context of this very passage, that "in light of the religious injunction against translation, the Moriscos thought that rendering the Quran in the form of explanation rather than straight translation would do less violence to the Holy Book. Thus, for them translation and commentary may be one and the same thing" (Chejne 1983, 55). The Quranic verses in the chapter of the Fig stand out in a larger script, while the aljamiado translation/transliteration is written right-to-left in a smaller script above each of the lines. The aljamiado version is not Arabic, nor fully Spanish, but rather a translation and commentary that renders the meaning of the verses while trying to do so with the utmost respect for the original language that lies immediately beneath it. For example, after the initial *basmala* of the first line, the Arabic construction "wa-t-tīni wa-z-zaytūni" grammatically conveys the swearing of an oath, and it is translated in aljamiado as "Juro [a] Allah por" (I swear to God by . . .). Then the four substantives of the next verses are interpreted within a geographical frame of reference, "por el monte de" (by the mountain of Tīn and by the mountain of Zaytūn and by the mountain of Mount Sinai). In fact, the aljamiado version reads it as "by the mountain of Watīn," instead of at-Tin, "the mountain of the fig tree," because its cues are as much graphical as they are phonetic. At a very basic level, one advantage of aljamiado transliteration is that both texts move in the same direction, from right to left, leading the eye downward toward the original Arabic text, which it resembles without being identical to it. Nor do substantives like *tīn* or *zaytūn* "fig and olive trees" require much work of translation, since they would presumably already be understood by any reader able to decipher aljamiado script, and may be partially built in to Spanish through its numerous Arabic loan words such as *aceituna* (olive). But by inserting the words "el monte de," "the mountain of," the commentary leads us to a geographical and prophetic interpretation of the *sūra*: the Mount of the Olives, meaning Jerusalem and Jesus, Mount Sinai and Moses, and finally to "al-baladi l-amini" (the secure city) of Muḥammad. The aljamiado translation spells it out for us: "la villa de seguridad que es Meca" (the city of security which is Mecca). Even in translation, however, the word used is the Spanish *villa* (town) rather than *ciudad* (city), which is usually used for major world capitals such as Mecca (as, for example, in the Catalan Atlas's "ciutat de Mecha"). The choice of *villa* here is, in my view, driven by the graphical and consonantal resemblance between the aljamiado *villa* (*bā' - lām*) and the Arabic *balad* (*bā' - lām- dāl*), with the corresponding consonants neatly aligned one above the other in a sort of visual, calligraphic rhyme. Once again, the literalness or hyperliteralness of this interlinear "translation" directs the reader's gaze toward the original text, leading us in parallel to the movements of the larger Quranic script, reading almost as if in Arabic but not quite.

This does not reach the extreme of Pierre Menard's exact translation of *Don Quixote*, but it is approaching it. It does not try to accommodate the original's meaning into the target language, but rather reshapes the target language to fit around the meaning and form of the original. It is a kind of Spanish that only makes sense in the particular diglossic and bilingual contexts of aljamiado, the context of Kilito's "our" (*'ajamiyya*), our own linguistic foreignness. One feature of this linguistic hybridity is a verbal fecundity that produces many neologisms through morphological derivation, reshaping Spanish to fit Islamic meanings. For example, in the last line, the phrase "khalaqna l-insan" (We created man ex nihilo), is translated and transliterated as "khalaqamos a la persona," adapting to the grammar, but not to the vocabulary, orthography or linguistic theology of Spanish.

Other aljamiado texts similarly forge a new and singular vocabulary that includes words like *poemança* (poetic eloquence), *muslimadamente* (in Muslim fashion), or *aljamàlmente* (collectively, as Muslims) (López Morillas 1995, 204) or the word *hijante*, the Spanish Muslim pilgrim from Puey Monçón to Mecca of my title.

At the very beginning of the *Coplas del hijante de Puey Monçón*, or verses of the pilgrim to Mecca from Puey Monçón, the anonymous Aragonese Morisco author announces that he has left behind his home and family to travel to "tierra de moros" (Muslim territories) (Khedr 2004, 363; Pano y Ruata 1897, 36, stanza 2).

The expression in earlier texts such as the *Poema de Mio Cid* is synonymous with *tierras extrañas*, strange or foreign lands, and in that traveling motion of crossing between home and away, near and far, here and there, familiar and strange, *fort* and *da*, *dār al-islām* and *dār al-ḥarb*, I think that the Morisco travel writer performs the same ambiguous gesture that the aljamiado interlineal translator enacts between translation and transliteration. Travel writing, the "relaçión," or account that he promises in the partially illegible first stanza, becomes a site both of translation, in which the wider Muslim world as experienced and recounted through the travel narrative is drawn closer in, and of transliteration, through which the ordinary is defamiliarized, relocated and reinscribed as a sign of cultural distinction.

Besides these *Coplas*, Morisco aljamiado travel writing is not extensive. While Arabic has several well-developed genres of travel literature, especially that of *riḥla*, this is not the case for aljamiado (Chalmeta 1997, 107). L. P. Harvey calls them "a few scattered Morisco jottings" and Anwar Chejne attributed their paucity to a general lack of mobility and literary sophistication among the Moriscos, though I hope to suggest below that there may be alternative forms of geographical knowledge that provide practical ways of rendering movement legible and mobility accessible (Harvey 2005, 170; Chejne 1983, 111). There are also, of course, notable exceptions such as the Mancebo de Arévalo, as well as a few other first-person *riḥla* accounts of Mudejar pilgrimage travel to Mecca, including one by Omar Patún in 1495 from Ávila, just after the fall of Granada and just a few years prior to the Moriscos' forced conversions in Castile. Patún's account was discovered in 1988 inside the wall of a demolished house in Calanda, and shows the high cultural value placed by Moriscos on travel lore from earlier, preconversion times (Cassasas Canals 2015, 221–23).

There must have existed a similar appetite for hearing about travel in fiction, as evidenced by a popular and widely translated and circulated chivalric novel from the early fifteenth century, *Los amores de Paris e Viana*, transliterated for a Morisco audience into aljamiado. What is the peculiar attraction this tale might hold for a crypto-Muslim public? In my view, there are two specific reasons beyond the usual ones for the appeal of popular fiction. The first is a desire for knowledge about the wider Muslim world. The protagonist Paris undertakes a Byzantine overseas journey to Ultramar, traversing the Mediterranean and the Middle East, through Muslim lands, even reaching China and India. His is a journey of escapist adventure, to be sure, but also of *talab al-ʿilm*, the quest for knowledge that should lead, says the hadith, as far as China. Second, in Constantinople, Paris and his companion disguise themselves by growing beards, changing their dress and spending a few years learning Greek and "morisco," that is, Arabic, in order to "appear" Muslim ("parescia moro") and so to pass undetected through Islamic territories, including such major centers of commerce and Islamic culture as Tabriz, Baghdad, Damascus, and Jerusalem (Baranda and Infantes 1995, 160).

This familiar scenario of disguised identities, ever present in the so-called Moorish novels, must have been irresistible to a Morisco audience, well versed in daily practices of dissimulation. But the prospect of vicarious, narrative travels through the geographies of the *dār al-Islām* must have been as attractive to Morisco audiences as they were to old Christian ones, to judge by the demand for medieval and modern accounts of such real undercover travelers to Mecca as Niccolo di Conti, Pero Tafur, Ludovico Varthema, Ali Bey, Jean Louis Burkhardt, or Richard Burton.

The Mancebo de Arévalo, writing after 1526, undertakes his own quest for knowledge throughout Spain to gather accounts about how Islam was practiced before the forced conversions. Elsewhere, the Mancebo describes his own plans to perform the Haj, receiving advice and funds for the journey from the crypto-Muslim community, who emphasize the significant costs of such a voyage: "Your *doblas* will become *reales* and your *reales* will become *maravedies*," in a systematic devaluation of coinage through expenditure (Harvey 1987, 19). But, at a time when performing the Haj must have been quite rare, such an expenditure in coin and effort would also confer a high degree of spiritual and cultural distinction on the men and women who returned to tell of their firsthand experience, though it remains uncertain whether the Mancebo de Arévalo himself ever managed to undertake the overseas journey (López Baralt 2009, 441n60; Harvey 1987, 20–21).

Travel Bans and the *Kamino*

It is perhaps an accident of scholarship that a number of scholars in dialog about the historical experience of the Moriscos adopt geographical and chiefly aquatic metaphors: Galmés de Fuentes's *orilla* (shore), Márquez Villanueva's *laderas* (slopes), or Bernard Vincent's *río* (river), which Márquez Villanueva rhetorically turns into a sea (Márquez Villanueva 2009, 279). Mercedes García Arenal (2008) astutely contrasts this aquatic turn with the more stable ground of plodding *caminos* (roads). The *kamino* represents the ordinary, daily mode of Morisco mobility. The *hijante* from Puey Monçón calls himself a "caminero" (stanza 75), an archaic way of identifying himself as foremost a walker. In the sixteenth-century drawings and etchings of northern European travelers like Hoefnagel and Weidetz, Moriscos are most often depicted in motion, sometimes barefoot or shod in a wide variety of sandals, shoes, or platform *chapines*. Even when traveling by water, one Morisco exile describes the sea as an overland *camino* "road," a meadow strewn with green flowers: "en el mar camino, que stá de berdes flores prado hecho" (Galmés de Fuentes 1981, 440).

In terms of their practical knowledge of geography, Moriscos had extensive overland transportation networks, because driving mule trains was a profession most frequently linked to Moriscos (Lea 1901, 247), to such an extent that contemporary literary works stereotypically associated them with Moriscos, such as the wealthy *arriero* (muleteer) from Arévalo in *Don Quixote* I, 16 (López Baralt 2008, 254). This mode of land transport was a principal industry, for example, of numerous Morisco communities such as Arévalo or Hornachos (Harvey 2005, 371–72). And it is from this ground-level position that Morisco travelers develop strategies for circumventing the increasingly oppressive restrictions on mobility imposed by the "Faraón de Spaña" (Pharaoh of Spain), the Spanish monarch (Galmés de Fuentes 1981, 440).

Ricardo Padrón makes an important distinction between two cartographic forms: on one hand, the professionally gridded maps in two dimensions whose most expansive example is the *mappa mundi*, and on the other, the one-dimensional amateur itinerary, whose aim is linear way-finding from place to place (Padrón 2004, 84). The former visually encodes an "imperial optic" (Jay and Ramaswamy 2014, 25), a privileged vantage point that allows noncontiguous colonial territories to be apprehended in a single view from above, "seeing the whole"—the aerial view, the "celestial eye," the cinematic God's-eye view—while the latter instead resembles what Michel de Certeau calls "an opaque and blind mobility," or an "operational," "migrational," "pedestrian speech act" enunciated from the ground level (De Certeau 1984, 92–93, 97–98).

As Padrón, Barbara Fuchs and others have discussed, the second book of Alonso de Ercilla's epic poem *La Araucana*, dedicated to Phillip II in 1578, paints in words just such an imperial optic of the Iberian world in several rather cinematic cantos. Ercilla frames the naval battle of Lepanto as a global civilizational contest for geopolitical power that spans from "the Ganges to Chile and from pole to pole" between European Christendom—Spain, Italy, and Germany—and an ethnically diverse Ottoman Empire (Ercilla 1986, 333–39; Padrón 2004, 198–210;

Fuchs 2001, 39–46). This 1571 battle of Lepanto followed the suppression of the Morisco revolt of the Alpujarras; both campaigns were led by King Phillip's half-brother Juan de Austria. The world at stake is further depicted in a shamanic vision seen through a translucent, spherical *mappa mundi*, a glowing orb variously called an apple, a crystal ball, a globe, a luminous circle, a sphere, and a world. Ercilla describes Fitón's magical orb through an expansive enumeration of place names from around the globe to be "viewed" in a worldwide inspection from the "beginning of Asia" in Turkey, to the "limits of Spain and the Crown" (Ercilla 1986, 376–81) in its overseas colonies.

Coincidentally, in 1576, right around the time of Ercilla's writing, Phillip II issued new edicts to regulate and restrict the movements on the ground of Moriscos from Granada. Already in 1571, after the rebellion of the Alpujarras, the Granadan Moriscos had been expelled and resettled throughout other communities. These new revisions to the Morisco "travel ban" respond to several petitions from Morisco *arrieros*, or mule drivers, whose ordinary trade directly involved transportation and geographical mobility, being on the road. In one successful petition before the King, a Morisco muleteer from Granada named Miguel Rodriguez, resettled in Osuna, and who "generalmente andaba por toda España" (generally traveled throughout Spain) sought explicit permission to carry a small, blunt, pointless knife, necessary for his trade, but which was frequently confiscated from him under the general ban on weapons for Moriscos from Granada, and on account of which he received constant harassment (Janer 1987, 250–51). A month later a neighbor of Miguel Rodriguez named Miguel Fernandez, also a Morisco muleteer from Granada resettled in Osuna, and, perhaps emboldened by the success of the earlier request, similarly complained about the theft of his mules, damage to the tools of his trade, and like Miguel Rodriguez, general harassment. Both Miguels habitually traveled with their *recuas* or pack trains between the court at Madrid, Toledo, Granada, Seville, Osuna, and throughout all of Spain (Janer 1987, 246–49). In this instance, however, the King reaffirms and intensifies the existing travel ban. Even though Miguel Fernandez already possesses a legal travel document, a *pasaporte*, the new law now requires a special, individualized permit for each journey away from the Morisco's registered domicile, absolutely forbids any transit to Granada, and requires that each licensee be safe and free of suspicion, a kind of character or background check. Though the declared intention is to promote the Moriscos' livelihood and commerce, these enhanced restrictions no doubt imposed a significant new burden on these displaced Morisco muleteers and their itinerant brethren, accustomed to traveling all throughout the Peninsula. The enhanced travel ban was in part an attempt at control of international travel, export and emigration: "If the aforesaid Moriscos were freely able to come and go from their places of resettlement, then some might attempt, as indeed some have done, to pass abroad to foreign kingdoms or to return to Granada . . ." (Janer 1987, 247).

There are a couple of very brief aljamiado itineraries, studied by Luce López Baralt, that do confirm the existence of some of these prohibited clandestine international travel routes, and give us a glimpse into the strategies and practices adopted by Morisco travelers in the face of travel prohibitions. They are entitled *avisos* or *memorias del kamino*, pragmatic advice for the road and records of roads traveled, practical, one-dimensional itineraries for way-finding on the ground.

These short travel guides collect experiences and advice from prior Morisco travelers along these paths. They describe precise routes, costs, locations, lodgings, modes of transport, how many supplies to buy for how many days of travel, where to buy them, at what price, how to negotiate with innkeepers and Turkish and Jewish ship captains in Venice, and numerous other such minute particulars of the voyages from northern Aragon to Salonica, in one text, and home again from Venice to Mollet del Vallès, outside Barcelona, in another. These routes are by no means direct, and in this they resemble the circuitous paths taken by sixteenth-century Protestants around Catholic areas in northern Europe, as journeys that are simultaneously geographical, social, and spiritual. Instead, these roundabout itineraries give practical advice meant to facilitate mobility in disguise by Moriscos unable to travel under official identities. In part, the indirect courses are determined by the clandestine purposes of the voyagers; these are secret routes which can be followed by Moriscos posing as merchants, relatives, Christian pilgrims, or anything that can help them conceal their underlying identities and the ulterior motives for their journeys: "From here on you will say that you are going to visit the shrine of St Mark in Venice . . ." (López Baralt 2009, 406–7).

The Morisco guidebooks are continually aware of transiting, touching, entering or exiting Spanish territories, repeatedly called the lands of the emperor, or the lands of King Philip. What strategies do Morisco travelers adopt in the face of this on-and-off contact with Spanish jurisdictions? Do they, like Ozmín and other fictional Muslim characters in so-called Moorish novels, disguise themselves in language, name, dress, and manner? Or do they simply adopt a certain gait, a way of walking, a certain idiom of pedestrian speech act? These documents of advice for the road suggest the latter. When approaching the duchy of Milan, travelers are advised to make a four- or five-league-wide circle around the city, passing instead on the other side of the mountain from the lands of the Emperor. Once past Milan, they are instructed to go with the flow of foot traffic as Christian pilgrims. In the port of Venice, they are directed to seek out Ottoman and Jewish merchants, with whom to seek passage to Salonica, saying that they have relatives waiting there.

But on more than one occasion, this prosaic migrational advice seems to become metaphorical: one *memoria*, barely legible, describes an alternative route that leads to a dead end: "A record of where we strayed from the path to seek out another path, but we did not find it suitable to our purpose." Or even downright metaphysical: "A record of the road we have walked in search of a better road by which we would be better off, and be happier, and more secure, and under the protection of Him who can do all things, being the powerful Lord of great power who is most powerful" (López Baralt 2009, 417–21). But the same passage also takes pains to describe, still with repeated adjectives, the very material economic bounties of certain Italian territories that lie outside the domains of the Spanish monarchy. "It is a happy land, with many provisions, and abundant in all things, and full and plentiful in all things." Or the Duchy of Savoy, which is a "land abundant in every provision which you can ask for from any type of provision and everything that is conducive to a person's sustenance" (López Baralt, 420–21). The juxtaposition of the material and the spiritual roads illustrates the point that Morisco travel outside the Spanish territories confers a freedom of movement but also a freeing of the imagination to contemplate alternative abodes beyond the *encerramiento* or confinement that crypto-Muslims experience within the Peninsula. Lamentably, of course, this half-imagined, utopian possibility of resettlement would become all too much a harsh and practical necessity after the 1609 order of deportation.

The *Hijante*'s Pilgrimage

Material and metaphysical roads converge most closely in the pilgrimage route, like that of the unnamed Morisco *hijante* (pilgrim to Mecca) hailing from Puey de Monçón, a locality in the mountains of Aragon. The seventy-nine *coplas*, or stanzas, make it one of relatively few works in verse in the aljamiado corpus. This poet may be "no master poet" but neither are his verses "rather doggerel," as L. P. Harvey describes them (Harvey 1987, 21–22). Its somewhat "irregular" syllable count and a "very free" rhyme scheme attest to the idea that this is popular poetry in ballad form, eight-line stanzas with rough octosyllables. The verse form, like the style, is oral, not graphical, since the aljamiado lines do not end on the rhyme words, but rather continue over the width of the page (Khedra 2010, 222; Zúñiga López 1989, 454).

The language is Castilian strongly inflected with Aragonese, Catalan, and Spanish-Arabic formations. The *hijante* (pilgrim to Mecca) also calls his trip a "romeaje" (pilgrimage to Rome), redirecting or translating the Christian's customary pilgrimage to Rome instead toward the holy cities of Islam. The first and last stanzas state the explicitly spiritual reason for the arduous and expensive trip, "por gran perdón" (to seek divine forgiveness) (stanzas 1, 76, 79). The Haj, though one of five pillars of Islam, is often overlooked in Morisco devotional instructions, due to the limitations on Morisco mobility in their particular Peninsular context. In the Mancebo de Arévalo's *Tafsira*, or commentary, he includes sections on four of the *deudos*, or obligations, but does not address the Haj as an obligatory pillar. Even some of the other obligations could be discharged through mechanisms of dissimulation and inner intention, under the "relaxation of the rigours of the pillars of Islam which extended to the four other pillars" (Harvey 1987, 13). Travel, by contrast, is not so easy to conceal. Nevertheless, the *hijante* from Puey Monçón does call the Haj a "deudo principal" (a major obligation).

I have already mentioned the extreme attention to costs and payments of the journey in the Morisco itineraries and in the Mancebo de Arévalo's preparations for the Haj. The *hijante* shares—almost obsessively—those very material concerns. He frequently mentions money, taxes, the availability of provisions, the companies of "mercandantes" (merchants) who travel the pilgrimage roads. He dwells on the size, wealth, and luxuries of populous cities like Tunis, but notes that, lacking means, he and other pilgrims were forced to sleep outside the city walls.

The route taken by our pilgrim from Puey Monçón is an indirect one, like those recorded by his Morisco brethren in the *avisos del kamino*, following Mediterranean commercial routes of land transport and the cabotage of commercial ports by sea: "cuando por tierras, cuando por mares," (now by land, now by sea). On the Tunisian coastline alone his ship will stop in the ports of Tunis, Hammamet, Hergla, Sousse, Monastir, Mahdia, and Sfax, where, suffering from three days of hunger, they manage to buy a lamb, but prepare it without sauce, garnish, or bread. He quotes the exact price: "por siete nasrines" (stanza 11). Lacking the precise instructions given in the *avisos del kamino*, he has neglected to put in the recommended fifteen days' store of water, firewood, a pot, rice, oil, vinegar, olives, garbanzos, beans and fresh bread for the first week, biscuit for the second (López Baralt 2009, 406–7). Fortunately, they resupply in Djerba before heading to Alexandria. The captain of the ship is called Çebití, presumably hailing from Ceuta though said to be born in Venice. In the port of Valencia, our Morisco pilgrim calls him Patrón, but in Tunis he starts to call him Raiç, reverting once in the high seas to Patrón, possibly for reasons of rhyme, before shifting definitively to Raiç, an example of the overlapping linguistic spaces operating both on board this Mediterranean transport vessel and within the author's own code-switching.

After suffering a storm at sea and losing their goods and provisions, they reach Barqa (better known today as Benghazi), then travel on to Alexandria and Cairo. At this point the tone of the account changes significantly. Instead of hardships, natural hazards, hunger or expense, the focus shifts to describing the ancient monuments and modern marvels of Cairo in superlatives. The *hijante* visits important mosques and other religious sites, but also notes the inscrutable and untranslatable hieroglyphic "letters" that Muslims, Jews, and Christians are all equally incapable of reading: "No las sabe leir moro / Ni jodio, no cristiano" (stanza 33). A repeated phrase is "I will tell you what I saw," the descriptive function of the first-person narrative telling of wonders. He joins up in Cairo, with an army of 100,000 other pilgrims from diverse parts who travel on foot ("caminando," stanza 37) and by horse or camel, led by the *amīr al-hajj*. Upon their arrival in Mecca, the marvels are so wondrous that they can hardly be described ("Esta fue mira tan gran / que no sería de decir," stanza 42), or can hardly be believed ("Salieron tan ricamente . . . / que creer no se podría," stanza 43). Everywhere there is silver, gold, and every form of wealth, "oro y plata y riqueza," and the adjective "rich" is thrown about in excess. Of the four schools of *fiqh* (jurisprudence), he particularly notes "Málic, nueso doctor" (Mālik, our teacher), the founder of the Mālikī school that held sway in the Al-Andalus and the Islamic West, and whose tomb he will later visit in Medina.

Though hitherto loquacious and prone to repetition, words now fail the *hijante* entirely upon reaching the Great Mosque: "Quien más quisiese escrebir / Ni lo podría acabar / Ni de palabra decir, / No lo podría contar; / Casa tan singular, / las cosas qu' están en ella, / Noble, gran, rica y bella / Qu'en en mundo no hay su par" (If anyone tried to write on, he would be unable to finish, nor say anything in words, nor tell of it. It is such a unique house—the things that are in it!—noble, great, rich and beautiful, that there is no equal in the world) (stanza 53). The collapse of language marks the very center of his journey, and the emotional core of his tale. He will continue on, of course, describing the rituals of the Haj, his subsequent visit to Medina, and the holy places of Islamic history, but he has already reached the desired destination and the narrative zenith of the trip. The last few stanzas are full of regrets. His heart is broken as he leaves the land of blessings. He feels bad that he did not make it to Jerusalem, a city so holy that both Muslims and Christians visit it. His account ends, somewhat abruptly, at "Toriciné," Mount Sinai, where he again regrets that he did not climb the mountain of Moses.

The unnamed Morisco traveler's account closes with the same holy sites alluded to in the *sūra* of the Fig: the Mount of Olives, Mount Sinai, and the City of Security. The traveler who left his happiness and all his family in the second stanza ("partí de mi gozo / Y de todo mi linaje") seems in no hurry to return, and his *riḥla* concludes on a bittersweet note full of longing and doubt. He will bring back his Spanish verse record of his travels, experienced firsthand, in the flesh, in the original and in Arabic, now translated and transliterated into "our" *'ajamiyya* for his Morisco audience, so that they can partake at a distance of the perils and rewards of his quest for knowledge and his journey for salvation ("gran perdón") to a land at once foreign and familiar.

This Morisco traveler from Puey Monçón is not Cervantes' or Shelton's "more translated Spaniard," or "Moore turned Spaniard," but a Spanish Muslim living in transliteration, whose cultural artifact will remain secreted in a space of confinement (under floorboards, behind walls) until it is nearly as unreadable as the hieroglyphs of Cairo, while its community of "linguistically plural" potential readers, diglossic or bilingual, disperse by terrestrial and maritime *kaminos* in the footsteps of this hopeful and remorseful pilgrim: "cuando por tierra, cuando por mares."

Works Cited

Apter, Emily. 2006. *The Translation Zone: A New Comparative Literature*. Princeton, NJ: Princeton University Press.

———. 2013. *Against World Literature: On the Politics of Untranslatability*. New York: Verso.

Baranda, Nieves, and Víctor Infantes. 1995. *Narrativa popular de la Edad Media: Doncella Teodor, Flores y Blancaflor, París y Viana*. Madrid, Spain: Akal.

Braudel, Fernand. 1995. *The Mediterranean and the Mediterranean World in the Age of Philip II*, translated by Siân Reynolds. Berkeley: University of California Press.

Cassasas Canals, Xavier. 2015. "La riḥla de Omar Patún: el viaje de peregrinación a la Meca de un musulmán de Ávila a finales del siglo XV (1491–1495)." *Espacio, Tiempo y Forma* 28, 221–54.

Chalmeta, Pedro. 1997. "El viajero musulmán." In *Viajes y viajeros en la España medieval*, edited by Miguel Angel García Guinea, 97–107. Madrid, Spain: Polifemo.

Chejne, Anwar G. 1983. *Islam and the West: The Moriscos*. Albany: State University of New York Press.

De Certeau, Michel. 1984. "Walking in the City." In *The Practice of Everyday Life*, translated by Steven Rendall, 91–110. Berkeley: University of California Press.

Eisenberg Daniel. 1992. "Cisneros y la quema de los manuscritos granadinos." *Journal of Hispanic Philology* 16: 107–24.

Ercilla, Alonso de. 1968. *La Araucana*. Mexico City, Mexico: Porrúa.

Fuchs, Barbara. 2001. *Mimesis and Empire: The New World, Islam, and European Identities*. Cambridge, UK: Cambridge University Press.

Galmés de Fuentes, Alvaro. 1981. "Lengua y estilo en la literatura aljamiado morisca." *Nueva Revista de Filología Hispánica* 30, no. 2: 420–40.

García Arenal, Mercedes. 2008. "Ríos y caminos moriscos: el islám tardío español." *Revista de libros* 134: 10–15.

Gil, Pablo, Julián Ribera, and Mariano Sánchez. 1888. *Colección de textos aljamiados*. Zaragoza, Spain: Litografía de Guerra y Bacque, Tipografía de Comas hermanos.

Harvey, L. P. 1987. "The Moriscos and the Hajj." *Bulletin* (British Society for Middle Eastern Studies) 14, no. 1: 11–24.

———. 2005. *Muslims in Spain: 1500 to 1614*. Chicago, IL: University of Chicago Press.

Jay, Martin, and Sumathi Rawaswamy, eds. 2014. *Empires of Vision: A Reader*. Durham, NC: Duke University Press.

Johnson, Carroll B. 2010. *Transliterating a Culture: Cervantes and the Moriscos*, ed. Mark Groundland. Newark, DE: Juan de la Cuesta.

Khedr, Tarek. 2004. *Códice aljamiado de varias materias (manuscrito no. XIII de la antigua Junta para Ampliación de Estudios)*. Madrid, Spain: Instituto Universitario Seminario Menéndez Pidal (Universidad Complutense de Madrid).

Khedr, Tarek. 2010. "Las Coplas del Alhichante de Puey Monçón." In *Memoria de los Moriscos: Escritos y relatos de una diáspora cultural*, 222–23. Madrid, Spain: Sociedad Estatal de Conmemoraciones Culturales.

Kilito, Abdalfattah. 2008. *Thou Shalt Not Speak My Language*, translated by Waïl S. Hassan. Syracuse, NY: Syracuse University Press.

Lea, Henry Charles. 1901. *The Moriscos of Spain: Their Conversion and Expulsion*. Philadelphia, PA: Lea Brothers.

Lezra, Jacques. 2015. "On Contingency in Translation." In *Early Modern Cultures of Translation*, edited by Karen Newman and Jane Tylus, 15–174. Philadelphia: University of Pennsylvania Press.

López Baralt, Luce. 2008. "El sabio encantador Cide Hamete Benengeli: ¿Fue un musulmán del al-Andalus o un morisco del siglo XVII?" In *Cervantes y las religiones: actas del coloquio internacional de la Asociación de Cervantistas (Universidad Hebrea de Jerusalén,*

Israel, 19–21 de diciembre de 2005), edited by Ruth Fine and Santiago López Navia, 339–60. Madrid, Spain: Iberoamericana.

———. 2009. *La literatura secreta de los últimos musulmanes de España*. Madrid, Spain: Trotta.

López Morillas, Consuelo. 1995. "Language and Identity in Late Spanish Islam." *Hispanic Review* 63: 193–210.

Mancebo de Arévalo. 2003. *Tratado [Tafsira]*, edited by María Teresa Narváez Córdoba. Madrid, Spain: Trotta.

Márquez Villanueva. 2009. "Carta abierta a Bernard Vincent." *Sharq al-Andalus* 19: 279–93.

Montaner Frutos, Alberto. 1988. "El depósito de Almonacid y la producción de la literatura aljamiada (en torno al ms. Misceláneo XIII)." *Archivo de filología aragonesa* 41: 119–52.

Padrón, Ricardo. 2004. *The Spacious Word: Cartography, Literature, and Empire in Early Modern Spain*. Durham, NC: Duke University Press.

Pano y Ruata, Mariano de. 1897. *Las Coplas del peregrino de Puey Monçón: viaje a la Meca en el siglo XVI*. Zaragoza, Spain: Comas hermanos.

Vincent, Bernard. 2006. *El río morisco*, translated by Antonio Luis Cortés. Valencia, Spain: Universitat de València, Universidad de Granada, Prensas Universitarias de Zaragoza.

———. 2010. "Carta abierta a Francisco Márquez Villanueva." *Sharq al-Andalus* 19: 295–304.

Zúñiga López, Ramón. 1989. "Las coplas del alhichante de Puey Monçón: Peregrinación a la Meca de un morisco aragonés a finales del siglo XVI." *Miscelánea De Estudios Árabes y Hebraicos* 37–38: 449–79.

Chapter 3

Modern Hebrew Literature as "World Literature"

The Political Theology of Dov Sadan

Hannan Hever

Dov Sadan, Modern Hebrew Literature, and the "Jewish Question"

Dov Sadan (Brody, Ukraine, 1902–Jerusalem, 1989), perhaps the greatest scholar of Jewish literature in the twentieth century, immigrated to Palestine in 1925, and quickly became a prominent figure in the field of literature in the Yishuv.[1] Sadan described his basically Eurocentric theoretical work, *Avnei bedek* (1962), as a book "intended to survey the house of our literature by surveying its foundation and its wings [. . .] exploring the relationship between our literature today and all of Jewish literature over the generations on the one hand, and *world literature*, particularly European literature, on the other hand" (Sadan 1962, 5; emphasis added).

Sadan's view regarding the connection between Jewish literature, and world literature may be described as "catholic," to borrow Dan Miron's characterization of Sadan's historiographical approach; that is, an all-embracing approach comprising every text ever written by Jews. This includes the belletristic and the nonbelletristic genres of Jewish literature, and more specifically, modern Hebrew literature. According to Sadan, the correct approach to the study of modern Hebrew literature begins with the elimination of the boundaries between its component parts.

> Now, from the distance of time [. . .] we see that the three main streams of literature—Maskilic, Hassidic, and Mitnagdic—despite their differences, draw from common roots or, more precisely, from a single root, and ultimately come together in the crown of a single tree, and modern Hebrew literature is therefore the literature of all three. (Sadan 1962, 9–10)[2]

The central question I will address in this chapter is whether, on the basis of Dov Sadan's literary approach, we may consider modern Hebrew literature to be a part of the phenomenon of world literature. The answer to this question, as I will show, is *essentially negative*. According to Sadan's literary theory, unsurmountable political theological boundaries separate Hebrew literature and *world literature*. Hebrew literature cannot transcend its own theological or—in light of its overall Jewish nature—ethnic and racial boundaries. The theology of the territoriality of modern Hebrew literature by definition written in the sacred territory of the Land of Israel, even if in the diaspora it merely imagines itself as an adequate alternative to the Holy Land, prevents it from escaping the confines of Hebrew as a sacred language. As is well known, the sacred is a product of separation and a clear-cut distance from the profane, and at the same time, modern Hebrew literature is written in the sacred letters of the Hebrew alphabet (Gross 2004, 116–18; Weiss 2014). Regularly, the Hebrew language is perceived as sacred. According to the Jewish *Sefer Yetsira*, God nominated every Hebrew letter to take part in Creation. According to Judaism, the option that in a Jewish context the sacred tongue is not identified as Hebrew is absurd. Judaism does not affirm the possibility that any Hebrew text will not be defined as a Jewish religious text. And in addition, there is not a dispute regarding that the language of God is identical with the language of the people of Israel, and the holy scripts as well (Dan, 113–15).

As I will show later, the common definition of world literature as a product of a movement of a literature beyond its national and prenational identities does not fit the political situation of Hebrew literature. The study of Hebrew literature requires an approach unlike the universalism of Goethe, who began to identify signs of a connection between the foreign literary knowledge that was new to him, and the colonies in which it was created.

As for Sadan he was involved in pointing out the theological detachment between Hebrew literature, written in a sacred tongue, and world literature. For him, the most profound identity of Hebrew literature is its religiosity; unlike other contemporary literary critics of his time he did not think of it as "secular," since for him it is literature anchored in the Jewish religion.

Following Moshe Halbertal, in his essay "*Al kedushah u-gevulot ha-yitzug ha-omanuti ve-ha-leshoni*" (On Holiness and the Boundaries of Artistic and Linguistic Representation), it may be argued that the sacred is that which cannot be manipulated, as holiness imposes rigid external boundaries. Thus, in order to pose insurmountable obstacles, violating the prohibition against a nonmediated relationship to holiness is perceived as sacrilege. And indeed, like the Jewish prohibition against the visual representation of God, the subordination of holiness to human control is sacrilege (Halbertal 2002, 30). Accordingly, we may conclude that the movement from Hebrew literature to world literature is an act of sacrilege, that is, a sin against God. Again following Halbertal, it may be argued that the sin precipitated by the aspiration to integrate Hebrew literature into world literature in itself serves as an impediment to such integration, due to the aversion it inspires. In other words, of the two contrasting movements—desire to appropriate the sacred, on the one hand, and aversion to doing it, on the other hand—the determining factor is aversion, that is, the curtailing of human authority and thus human control over the sacred. This signifies the theological prohibition against the integration of Hebrew literature into world literature (Halbertal 2002, 31).

A striking example of the existential and theological imperative that compels the Hebrew writer to write in the sacred Hebrew tongue can be found in the words of Y. H. Brenner, one of the greatest Hebrew authors of the twentieth century.

> We write nothing but Hebrew, because we cannot but write Hebrew, because the divine spark within us spontaneously bursts only into this flame, because this scintilla does not ignite, does not fully realize itself in any other language but this one—not even in that dear mixed [Yiddish language], our spoken mother tongue. (Brenner [1985] 1906, 107–8)

What looks very clear is that Hebrew, as a sacred language, which cannot be manipulated, is a static phenomenon. Anyway, its materiality stands in opposition to the Marxist historical materialism. While Marxist theory includes a movement toward a revolutionary emancipation, the sacred stops any movement and suppresses any hope for a change that can be seen, besides mysticism, and a very long waiting for the Messiah. The materiality of the sacred Hebrew language, and its eternity, prevents any option of a materialistic movement. Nevertheless, Sadan, who was influenced by R. Nachman Krochmal, the most important Jewish philosopher in the nineteenth century, and used dialectic for describing the ongoing spiritual essence of the eternal People of Israel, stayed with an ahistorical concept of the Hebrew language.

Well-known lines from the *Communist Manifesto* exemplify how Marxist historical materialism stands in contrast to the static, ahistorical, affirmative, and sacred Hebrew language.

> All fixed, fast-frozen relations, with their train of ancient and venerable prejudices and opinions, are swept away, all new-formed ones become antiquated before they can ossify. All that is solid melts into air, all that is holy is profaned, and man is at last compelled to face with sober senses his real conditions of life and his relation with his kind.
>
> [. . .]
>
> And as in material, so also in intellectual production. The intellectual creations of individual nations become common property. National one-sidedness and narrow-mindedness become more and more impossible, and from the numerous national and local literatures, there arises a *world literature*. (Marx and Engels [1848] 2005, 10)

On the subject of Jewish literature in languages other than Yiddish, and especially other than Hebrew, Sadan wrote, "Jewish literature that is written in a non-Jewish language [but] in a context of full national Jewish consciousness and activity is self-contradictory" (Sadan 1962, 91). He proceeds to characterize non-Jewish-languages national writers as follows:

> [They] are not representatives of their people in *world literature*, and internal complications render them potential enemies to our literature. There is a greater problem, however, and that is that [the idea of] Jewish literature in non-Jewish languages attests to the inherently illusory belief in the coexistence, as a single unit, of two types of literature: the one in the people's

own language and the other in a language that is not theirs." (Sadan 1962, 82; emphasis added)

Sadan uses the *theological singularity* of Hebrew to identify the dialogue between Hebrew canonical and noncanonical literatures, hereby subsuming aesthetically marginal texts, if only to fulfill the condition of catholic "holism," which Sadan saw as the role of modern Hebrew literature. Jews viewed their literature as an instrument for the creation of political identity that would enable them to contend with the "Jewish Question," that is, the dangerous situation of persecution, discrimination, and physical danger that culminated in the Holocaust, a murderous solution to that "Question." Jewish efforts to resolve the "Jewish Question" through "normalization" have had to contend with anti-Semitism and with colonialism, which persist inversely even when the Jews themselves are sovereign and the persecutors of others.

Many years earlier, beginning in the early eighteenth century and over the course of the nineteenth century, Hebrew Haskalah (Jewish Enlightenment) literature played a central role in the struggle of European Jews for the political emancipation capable of protecting them against violence from non-Jews, as citizens who enjoy universal standing. The Hebrew literature that migrated to Palestine during the period of the Yishuv, on the other hand, can be, by following Robert Young, defined as Zionist postcolonial literature (Young 2011, 215). It allowed the literature of European—especially Eastern European—Jews to import the "Jewish Question" to Palestine and to seek to resolve it there.

Hebrew Literature and Jewish Sovereignty

The role of Zionist Hebrew literature was, and remains to participate in the constitution of Jewish sovereignty in Palestine through its Hebrew symbolism and political imagination. It thus sets the political and cultural agenda of the Jewish people that shapes Zionist identity in anticipation of the political and violent struggles it faces, in the framework of the "Jewish Question." In Zionist Hebrew literature (and sometimes in non-Zionist Hebrew literature as well), the goal of Jewish sovereignty is the aspiration to authority charged with defending its subjects against external violence, and to control Jewish violence directed at non-Jews, particularly in the context of the expulsion of 750,000 Palestinians during the events of the Nakba of 1948 and the occupation regime that, since June 1967, has been maintained by Jews over the Palestinians.

In 1897 the Zionist movement was established with the intention of resolving the "Jewish Question." Zionism sought to create a sovereign territorial authority that would remove Jews from diasporic European space in order to settle them in Palestine, and later in the State of Israel. The foundational text of the Zionist movement is Leo Pinsker's *Auto-emancipation* ([1882] 1906), which starts from the premise that emancipation, that is, civic equality for the Jews of Europe, had reached an impasse. Pinsker therefore argued—citing the famous adage attributed in the *Mishna* to Hillel the Elder, "If I am not for myself who will be for me? And if not now, when?"—that the only recourse was auto-emancipation, which entailed the relocation of the Jews of Europe to a neutral and uninhabited place.

Pinsker effectively blamed the Jews for the creation and spread of the illness he called Judeophobia. He attributed the spread of this illness to the liminal existence of European Jews, that is, the in-between existence as a specter that frightens non-Jews, who responded with anti-Semitism. The fact that the Jews, over the course of their struggle for emancipation, refused to assimilate and insisted on preserving their religious identity rendered their identity liminal—a frightening specter, an identity located both within and beyond the boundaries of the empire.

Pinsker was convinced that relocating the Jews to a neutral place would put an end to pogroms, inasmuch as it would eliminate European Jewish liminality, thereby resolving the "Jewish Question" (Pinsker [1882] 1906). According to this global approach, the Hebrew literary text would be present in a territory inhabited exclusively by Jews, where they could live as protected citizens and enjoy universal rights.

However, the difficulty Pinsker faced was theological as well as political. The fact that he had failed to name the destination to which he believed European Jews should be relocated brought political pressure to bear on him from members of the Jewish "Hovevei Zion" (Lovers of Zion) movement. They demanded that he designate Zion, the "Holy Land," according to Jewish political theology as the only possible destination for such a program.

The question of the national context of the Hebrew literary text according to Sadan's catholic sacred approach may actually serve as a theological point of departure for understanding Zionism's protestant nature—defined as such by Akiva Ernst Simon, in his seminal article *"Ha-im od Yehudim anahnu?"* (Are We Still Jews?, Simon 1983). In this article, Simon addressed the profound crisis that modernity provoked within Judaism, leading to the development of Zionist Judaism, which he described as "protestant." According to Simon, the fundamental difference between the two theological positions is the difference between total, catholic theology, which leaves no room for anything outside of sanctity, and a protestant theology that distinguishes between the sacred (generally in private space) and the profane, and through negotiation between the domains, establishes a process of secularization (Simon, 1983, 9–10). The premise that the modern change in Jewish literature was from a religious, rabbinical ethos to a humanistic ethos is a baseless one (Miron 2005, 18). It is rooted in the uncritical acceptance of the protestant demand expressed in J. L. Gordon's poem "Awake, My People" (1866) by the line: "Be a man when you go out, and a Jew in your tents." Gordon, the most important Maskilik Hebrew poet in the nineteenth century, followed the erroneous Mendelssohnian perception that the public space in which Jews existed was religiously neutral, a neutrality which later became Zionism's mainstream position. Sadan's catholic Zionist position, on the other hand, is based on the correct observation that Christian public space in Europe, and Jewish space—essentially in the Land of Israel and in the State of Israel—are by no means neutral. According to Sadan, the idea of the secularization of Jewish public life, and, by extension, Hebrew literature, is absurd.

The theological shift from Jewish catholicism to Jewish protestantism that Simon identifies in modernity derives from the fact that Protestant theology subjugates the sacred end to the sacred means required for its achievement—contrary to Catholic theology, which views sanctity as an end that justifies the means to its realization. And indeed, from Sadan's catholic perspective, the total and sacred end nullifies the protestant sanctity of means. Thus, if the political theology espoused by Sadan is catholic, the historiography of Hebrew literature according to Sadan is not diachronic or subject to changes due to contingent historical constraints. Sadan's catholicity establishes religion—the realization of which is eternal—as the supreme goal of Hebrew literature, with nationalism serving as the means to that realization. And indeed, Sadan's catholicity, which opposes the protestant distinction between the sacred and the profane, invalidates the theory of secularization, and, in so doing, precludes any attempt to link the nonexistent secularity of Hebrew literature to the secularity of world literature.

The inability to distinguish between the Jewish nation, and the Jewish religion accords with the all-encompassing totality of Dov Sadan's catholic Zionism, including the catholicity of Hebrew literature. Thus, according to Sadan, the dominant catholic political theology in the field of Hebrew literature affords the Hebrew author writing in the sacred tongue a monopoly, that is, complete sovereignty over Hebrew national culture, reflected in the writer's public standing and authority, even when that culture appears weak. Consequently, we may assert that secular Hebrew literature, according to Sadan, is little more than a fiction, and it is the sanctity of Hebrew literature, founded on catholic and Zionist political theology, that realizes the national literature of the chosen people (Sadan 1962, 28).

In objecting to the term *National Jewish Literature*, Dan Miron notes that every conceptual definition creates liminal areas that exist, at once, both within and beyond the area delineated by the concept (Miron 2005, 159–61). A typical literary example is the hyphenated identity "Arab-Jew," coined by the Iraqi-born Hebrew writer Shimon Ballas. "Arab-Jew" is a liminal concept that joins the Jewish identity of a partner and ally with the Arab identity of the enemy, thereby acting as a locus of opposition to the Zionist orientalism that separates the two. The aspiration to eliminate Zionist orientalism is in fact the aspiration to eliminate the gap between the universal civic standing of the inhabitants of the State of Israel, and the nonuniversal materiality of its Palestinian inhabitants, that is, the elimination of their liminal citizenship. The eradication of the liminality of the Palestinian inhabitants of Israel, that is, the elimination of the gap between their universal citizenship, and their noncivic materiality, is impossible.

In contrast, in the field of Hebrew Literature it is quite clear that Hebrew literature's refusal to dedicate itself to a colonialist translation, that is supposed to eliminate the gap is based on Jewish ghosts and is, therefore, a theological refusal. It is a refusal based on the signified Jewish body, created as a result of the structuring of sacred discourse, that is, discourse that does not allow its sanctity and the sacred Hebrew it produces to be transferred to other languages. The sanctity of the Hebrew text that prevents the inward elimination of the liminality of the Jewish body is the same sanctity that prevents the Hebrew text's outward translation, leaving as the only option the sacralization of the profane.

Dov Sadan in the Footsteps of Nahman Krochmal

According to the historiographical theory of "literatures of the Jews" developed by Dov Sadan, there is no way to transcend the boundaries between the various national literatures and sacred Hebrew literature, thereby allowing it to become universal world literature. As a national literature written and read in the Jewish diaspora or in the Land of Israel, Hebrew literature should be able find its way to the universality of world literature, transcending the material boundaries of the conditions of its own creation. However, according to Sadan's historiographical theory, rooted in Hebrew literature's constant commitment to Jewish political theology, such universal transcendence of the extreme particularism of Hebrew literature, which would allow it to take its place within world literature, is simply impossible.

Miron characterized relations between Jewish secularism and religion as "re-sacralization," or the sacralization of the profane and the profanation of the sacred that ultimately gave rise to the ambivalence of what he called a "version of secularism," following the years in which the labor movement (of which Sadan was one of the spiritual leaders) had espoused a "version of religion"—the religion of the nation and the state (Miron 2005, 88, 93). Rather than ambivalence, however, with regard to the essentially protestant signifier of "secularism" (a stable signifier characterized by its existence between two dichotomous signifiers), I would suggest a movement in time that both connects and separates the signifier "secularism," and the signifier "apostasy." In effect, what we see before us is a historical act of apostasy that, in itself, becomes the object of apostasy.

The title of Sadan's theological work *Elkhah ve-ashuvah* (I will go and return) reflects the historical motion of legitimate "apostasy," which does not repudiate the covenant between God and his people through circumcision, but acts rather as a Gnostic repudiation that seeks to accord vitality to a collective that exists within the duality of the evil, transcendent God and the good, immanent God (Sadan 1971, 45). A good example of apostasy against apostasy is the Zionist apostasy of M. Y. Berdychevski, a giant of modernist Hebrew literature, against the transcendent God (the diaspora), in favor of the immanent God that is materialized in the land of Israel (Hotam 2013). Indeed, Zionist apostasy serves as a source of energy to negate negation, in order to eliminate the theological duality based on the movement from sanctity to an absence of sanctity, to which considerable political significance is ascribed. The aspiration to unify the two Gods is the aspiration for an immanent Palestinian Zionism, which is permeated with Gnostic sanctity and that will eliminate transcendent, diasporic Jewish existence, and replace it with an authentic Hebrew vitality, which prefers nature rather than religious law (Hotam 2013).

The Zionist apostates of the evil, diasporic God thus went to the Land of Israel, realm of the good God, where they repudiated the evil God who ruled over the diaspora they had abandoned. It is the apostasy against apostasy that makes it possible to envisage the prospect of the Zionist elimination of dualism. Sadan's Jewish position stresses the fact that the apostle Paul never completed his mission, while Marcion, founder of the Gnostic sect, was unable to persevere. Nonetheless, the Zionist Sadan, writing in 1941, hoped for the Gnosis of the apostasy against apostasy, in which the good would contain some evil and the evil some good, thereby allowing the Jewish collective to fight the Nazi evil and realize its national aspirations as a result (Sadan 1971, 13–47). Writing it in 1941, before the systematic destruction of European Jews became a known fact, Sadan based his argument on Gnostic duality, separating the Jewish people from the Nazi pure evil (Sadan 1071, 9). Identifying the Nazis as the anti-Christ, "the perverse revolution monster," known as the ultimate enemy of Jesus the Messiah, Sadan defines a double Gnostic heresy. It relates to the trajectory whose point of departure is the Jewish heretical denial of Jesus followed by the heresy of the Nazi anti-Christ, the pure evil, in the denial of the Jews, and thus bringing evil to its utmost stage, which denies Jesus through his cruel heretical denial of the Jewish heretics. It is, then, a theological mega-duel between the Jews and the Nazis that delivers Zionist Gnosticism to heights never known until then for their utter horror.

Sadan developed his thesis under the influence of the Galician *maskil* and philosopher Nahman Krochmal (Brody, Ukraine, 1785–Tarnopol, Ukraine, 1840), who, in the nineteenth century, exerted considerable influence on the philosophical thought of the Hebrew Haskalah and Jewish modernity. The goal of Krochmal's book *Moreh nevukhei ha-zeman* (*Guide for the Perplexed of the Time*), published posthumously, was to address the perplexity of the believer at the seeming contradiction "between recognition of the principle that God is just and personal experience that cries out the contrary," which lay at the heart of the perplexity elicited by the "Jewish Question" (Amir 2010, 19). Krochmal believed that Jewish religious tradition, and reason are influenced by Jewish history, as an all-encompassing common point of departure for Hebrew literature (which, for Krochmal, comprised the written and oral Torah), and that the Jewish people should strive to spiritual nationalism commensurate with its historical condition.

Krochmal's philosophy is spiritual and idealistic, and argues that the spirituality of the Jewish people was chosen by God as unique among the nations, since "spiritual matter is born in a people by means of the great affinity between its component parts in time and place, generation after generation" (Krochmal [1924] 2010, 36). The spiritual essence of the Jewish people is identical to the absolute spirituality that is God, who reveals himself to the Jewish people through prophecy. Therefore, contrary to other peoples that appear on the stage of history only to disappear after a time, the Jewish people are eternal. Krochmal's metaphysical point of departure was the source of Jewish historical development—a principle to which he was committed, despite the ahistoricity of Jewish religious law (Halakhah), which he observed meticulously (Rawidowicz 1924, 42).

Krochmal's influence on Sadan's "eternity of Israel" approach allays the fear that the failure of Zionism to eliminate Jewish liminality would result in the disappearance of the Jewish people. As noted above, Zionism would thus appear, according to Sadan, the faithful Zionist, to be no more than a passing episode in Jewish history, able to fulfill its national therapeutic role only on the basis of the eternity of religious belief, like that of Sadan, in the "sacred history" of the Jewish people (Miron 1990, 87, 91). Indeed, according to Sadan, the identity of Hebrew literature is defined by a necessary and absolute condition that its creators must be members of the Jewish religion. Sadan writes,

> I am absolutely convinced that Jewish culture in its latter phase will be as it was at the beginning; just as it was essentially a faith, and a religion, so too it will be a faith and a religion, even if we are, at present, in the midst of an interregnum. But I have no reason not to admit that the focus of our current historical dynamic now lies within an interregnum. (Sadan 1962, 167)

Krochmal explains the eternal reality of the Jewish people by means of the existence of God, who is the spiritual absolute, as realized in the Jewish religion. In light of Krochmal's Hegelian argument that the goal of spirituality is self-consciousness, however, Sadan viewed Jewish literature, including Hebrew literature, as literature that progresses through history as reflective spirituality that, in turn, recognizes itself. Krochmal, the *maskil* and philosopher, believed that while self-recognition had, in the past, been realized through Jewish religion, it was realized in the present through the universalism of reason.

Krochmal, who sought to resolve the dualistic contradiction within the concept of religion, highlighted the importance of the "national spirit," which develops in three stages. The first stage is the formation of the people and its institutions, the second is the creation of its unique culture, and the third is its extinction and return to materiality. Krochmal traces these three stages in Jewish history, explaining them as the historical process of the growth and decline of patterns of Jewish sovereignty. Ultimately, however, Jewish history rests on a foundation of absolute spirituality, which ensures the eternity of the Jewish people. The set pattern of Jewish historical development necessitates exile and diaspora, but since the "eternity of Israel" had not yet been achieved in Krochmal's time, he believed, influenced by Fichte, that it was the nation that was of essence and not a Jewish state that had once existed, in the distant past, of which he makes no mention in his book (Rawidowicz 1924, 179).

Following Krochmal's concept of the "eternity of Israel," Sadan developed his own view that the many different facets of Jewish literature, including modern Hebrew literature, can be reduced to an eternal Jewish theological principle.

> Even if the concept of God has changed and even if the reality of the people has changed, the relation between God and the people has not changed throughout history, and this relation, the life of the Torah and the continuity of its precepts, are not merely its secret, but also its foundation. (Sadan 1962, 80)

And indeed, like Krochmal, who knows both the past and the future of Jewish history, the catholic Sadan knows the past of Jewish literature and predicts its future. This is the meaning of the term "Literature of Israel" (*Sifrut Israel*) coined by Sadan, which derives from Krochmal's view regarding the eternity of the Jewish people.

Like Krochmal, Sadan believed that the role of Jewish religion in Jewish history was not over. However, as a Zionist he espoused the modernist Jewish political theology of Zionism, which viewed the materiality of the new and healthy Jewish body as an important and permanent stage in the development of the Jewish religion toward a Gnostic theology. Indeed, Krochmal's discussion of Gnosis as a national phenomenon, in the penultimate section (sec. 15) of *Moreh nevukhei ha-zeman*, is later reflected in the Zionist political theology, and in the thought of the laborite Sadan. Sadan's remark, that "[w]e have no real tradition of [secularization;] it is an absolute innovation," suggests his participation in the Gnostic theological process of apostasy against apostasy (Sadan 1962, 80). He describes it using Krochmal's spiritual dialectic, as "[a] Torah [i.e., doctrine] of life, so that the secularity of our literature in recent generations, which they engendered or by which they themselves were engendered, will not be merely a temporary dialectic" (Sadan 1962, 84). This view may be compared to the Gnosis described by Krochmal in section 15 of *Moreh nevukhei ha-zeman* (citing Marcion). It is also very possible that Sadan found in chapter 12 of the above-mentioned *Guide of the Perplexed of Our Time* fascinating discussions on the issue of the Gnosis.

The major article about Dov Sadan's method of studying literature was written by Dan Miron. He characterizes Sadan's method as one that does not uproot "the problem from its live dialectic context in order to catalogue it and summarize it according to its kind and its focus of interest in a minimizing language while rejecting anything that is less than absolutely relevant" (Miron 1990, 85). In fact, it seems that it is Miron who detaches Sadan from traditional dialectic such as Hegel's and definitely Marx's—a dialectic that has a defined trajectory and leads exactly to "the architectural-summation tradition," the existence of which Miron negates in Sadan's writing altogether. Sadan, who absorbed the metaprinciple of his dialectic studies in Hebrew literature from Krochmal's teachings, stayed faithful to the philosophical principle of the spiritual national development that would finally bring about the eternal spiritual totality of Am Israel (the People of Israel). Through his faithfulness to the theo-political aspect characterizing Krochmal's teachings, Sadan sought to present his dialectic interpretation of the literary text as a dynamic process that promotes and advances the fulfillment of a well-defined political target, at the center of which stands the reenactment of the sovereignty of the People of Israel.

This dialectic continuity can be understood in accordance with Marcuse's discussion of the question of identity. At its very core, dialectic continuity is founded on the notion that something exists that is turned, in fact, into something other than itself. Therefore, identity is the continuous negation of inadequate existence (Marcuse, 65).

Miron notes that Sadan, while pointing out the contradictions within the Hebrew literary text, cannot prove the relations between the particular and the general, even as he oscillates between one and the other. But Miron then claims that from this failure Sadan leaps to a "belief in Zionism as a single Modern spiritual political Jewish movement, that has in its power, if it will not get caught in internal limitations that might have a way to be relieved of, to bring the bifurcated Jewish personality to cultural national re-integration."

But if one holds on to the dialectic characteristic of Sadan's literary way of thinking, it seems that, along with Marcuse's argument in the name of Hegelian dialectic, it is possible to assert that Sadan is not so much concerned with a leap beyond all limitations or with a release from internal limitations that will bring about reintegration; rather, he is concerned with a detailed, graded dialectic struggle that will open up a continuous advancement creating a consciousness of freedom. In this example it is national freedom, Zionist, which, following Leo Pinsker's famous book title, can be defined as national auto-emancipation (Marcuse 65).

Miron, who rightly asserts that Sadan was dialectic and that his mind constantly moved back and forth between negation and acquiescence, did not notice that—following Krochmal—the force guiding Sadan has been a methodical effort that will enable him to develop through dialectics an idealist historical narrative based on the striving to total materialization of the eternal spirituality of Am Israel that turns each of its stages into an episode. One should also understand Sadan's commitment to "the coherence of the general space of the literature of Israel" (Miron, 84) as the same dialectic effort toward the total spirituality of the eternal existence of Israel.

It seems, then, that Miron's claim that Sadan, who refrained from developing a proof and a short, one-directional argument connecting center and periphery, did not justify the unexplained jump from the specific interpretations to the synthesis, behind which stands that Zionist and religious faith is wrong (Miron 1990, 85, 87, 90).

The dialectic process of Hebrew literature's identity is entangled also with his active participation in that which is dubbed "the republic of Hebrew literature," within which he apparently perceived himself as one of its sovereigns, maybe even its most prominent one. And, indeed, his books, which deal with Hebrew literature's public standing, and much more beyond that, can attest to the fact that it is within the power of dialectic thinking that through its struggle with contradictions it advances toward creating a correspondence between concept and reality, and that it is entangled also in the change that it creates in reality, which includes contradiction within it (Marcuse, 66).

This change of reality is also expressed in Marcuse's assertion that if, according to Hegel, progress in the scale of freedom is inseparable from progress in thought, then Marx's subversive materialism is entwined with the recognition that "the establish[ed] forms of life were reaching the stage of their historical negation" (Marcuse, 70).

Marcuse provides a brilliant phrasing of the character of the paradox that exists at the basis of any totality in his assertion that, on the one hand, there is no method that can claim monopoly on cognition, but on the other and at the same time, there is no method that seems authentic which does not acknowledge the fact that both of the following assertions are meaningful as a description of the situation within which we find ourselves: "the whole is the truth, and the whole is false" (Marcuse, 71).

A revealing example of dialectics searching to change reality through education and showing the right way to achieve, at the end of a long dialectic process, a total spiritual situation can be found in the manner in which Sadan identifies contradiction between the writers of the history of Hebrew literature.

In his dialectic way, Sadan profiles the writers of the history of Hebrew literature by their neglect to include, that is—their negation—of all that has been created in literature. This reproach is addressed to all who failed to write the total literary history, who excluded from the discussion, that is—negated the existence of sizable parts of modern Hebrew literature.

And indeed, the histories of reality-changes that can occur in each of the historical episodes one can explain by following Marcuse's phrasing according to which Marxist materialism at the subversive foundations Marx points at Hegel is dependent on the understanding of "a recognition that the established forms of life were reaching the stage of their historical negation" (Marcuse, 70).

This argument stands in contrast to the radical duality, of the universal significance, highlighted in Erich Auerbach's *Mimesis*, the ultimate model of the study of world literature. In his book, Auerbach expressed his commitment to humanistic universalism through the epigraph taken from a poem by Andrew Marvell: "Had we but world enough, and time . . ." (Auerbach [1953] 2003, v).

Sadan was commissioned to write the introduction to the Hebrew translation of *Mimesis*. As one might expect, in his introduction Sadan addresses the universality of translation of foreign literature into Hebrew. Sadan first notes the fact that interest in world literature is on the rise among readers of Hebrew literature, and goes on to discuss the concern that words may not be understood in another language. Here is how Sadan characterizes Auerbach's great talent.

> [His] dedication to the analysis of currents, ideas, and themes [which] is tireless, to the point that each and every voice is given its full due on the field of battle and in the great campaign. The danger, that the meaning of words in another language will be misunderstood is averted by a wealth of quotations in the original language. The selection of the quotations is excellent. (Sadan 1969, 9)

The martial metaphor ("the field of battle") that Sadan uses to characterize the field of translation, serves to underscore what he identifies as Auerbach's political goal: that "each and every voice is given its full due." The reference is to the autonomy of translations as texts in their own right. This autonomy allows the translated text to act independently or, as Bialik put it, in such a way that "its extraneous origin is unrecognizable" (Bialik, 1935). In order to serve the universalistic goals of world literature Sadan ascribes to Auerbach the intention to defend these goals against those who would destroy them, having written his book during the Second World War, in the service of a humanistic agenda and against Nazi philology (Zakai 2017). In Sadan's words,

> We would not be fulfilling our duty, however, if we were to make do with a reference to his journey from the center to the periphery, without addressing the periphery-consciousness he acquired during the course of his journey, which served him in the writing of the present volume, and for which purpose it was written. [. . .] The point of departure for his inquiry is the fact that the earth, which is the stage of world literature is becoming smaller, losing the multifacetedness that is its very heart and soul. The homogenization of life, the undermining of distinct traditions, the convergence of ways of life, the proliferation of standardization, whether in keeping with the American-European model or with the Russian-Bolshevik one, will ultimately result in a single culture—a process that seems to be well underway. Also imminent is the reduction to a few languages or even a single language. Consequently, the idea of world literature will be realized and destroyed all at once. (Sadan 1969, 11)

The universalism of world literature, argues Sadan, may be achieved through philology, which in addressing a small part radiates to and allows us to understand the whole (Sadan 1969, 13). We may draw an analogy between the universalism of Auerbach's world literature—which he defended in a time of emergency, the Second World War, by means of the autonomy of translation, which, in Sadan's words, exists "on the battlefield"—and Bialik's well-known essay "*Shiratenu ha-tze'irah*" (Our Young Poetry), published also in a time of emergency—four years after the Kishinev pogrom, and two years after the pogroms of 1905. It was indeed a time of Jewish emergency, in which the "Jewish Question" presented itself in all its gravity. The similarity between the universalism of the national poet Bialik, and that which Sadan saw in Auerbach's work lies in the act of translation in a time of emergency, which demands the autonomous existence of the translated text, that it might defend universalism against the chauvinism and the totalitarianism of Nazi Germany and the Soviet Union.

The Political Theology of the Sanctity of the Language of Hebrew Literature

The thesis that Sadan developed following Krochmal is thus rooted in a Zionist territorial reading of *Moreh nevukhei ha-zeman*. Despite the differences between Krochmal's nonterritorial, spiritual approach, and Sadan's national-Zionist and territorial position, they share a common view on the Hebrew language of Hebrew literature, as a sacred tongue. Krochmal asserts that when something is spiritual the symbols lose their physicality and the letters become voice, speech, utterance, and especially revelation (Krochmal 2010, chapter 6, 176; about the sacred in Hasidism see Gross 2004, 118–16). If Sadan's historiographical thesis regarding the place of language in Hebrew literature is examined in this light, the main reason that Hebrew literature is unable to be a part of world literature would appear to be the sacred materiality of its language, in which writing literature is a kind of sacred ritual.

As noted above, the Hebrew language is the language of what Krochmal defines as the people chosen by God among all the other peoples (*am segulah*, or "treasure people," in Hebrew). The fact that the people was chosen by God determines that its language is not one of ordinary communication but of communication in a sacred tongue. For this reason, the Jewish sovereignty constituted through Hebrew literature is a sovereignty for which the material, linguistic, determinant moment is a theological moment that the Jew can identify in the giving of the Torah at Mount Sinai. The instant at which the modern Jewish subject determines that the materiality within which the Jews exist is what Carl Schmitt called a state of emergency keenly arouses the "Jewish Question" (Schmitt 2005). Hebrew literature is thus a sacred material articulation of the language that constitutes its sovereignty through Hebrew political theology.

A particularly trenchant formulation of the messianic political theology of the Hebrew language can be found in a well-known letter that Gershom Scholem wrote to his friend Franz Rosenzweig in 1926. In the letter, Scholem describes the dangerous theological energy within the Hebrew language, liable to rise with great force to the surface of the ostensibly secular speech of the Jewish inhabitants of Palestine.

> What about the actualization of Hebrew? Must not the abyss of a sacred language [. . .] break out again? [. . .] The secularization of language is only

> a *façon de parler*, a ready-made phrase. [. . .] Will we [. . .] have a youth capable of withstanding the uprising of a sacred language? [. . .] Often, out of the ghostly shame of our language, the power of the sacred speaks out. [. . .] A generation that takes upon itself the most fruitful in our sacred traditions—our language—cannot live, were it to wish it a thousand fold, without tradition. The moment the *power* stored at the bottom of the language *deploys itself*, the moment the "said," the content of language, assumes its form anew, then the sacred tradition will again confront our people as a decisive sign of the only available choice: to submit or to go under. In a language in which he is invoked back a thousand fold into our life, God will not stay silent. (Scholem 2002, 226–27)

The paradox of the presence of sanctity in ostensibly secular Hebrew speech attests to the theological forces that threaten that which is mistakenly perceived as the secularity of the Hebrew language.

It seems, then, that as far as Hebrew is concerned, Emily Apter's discussion of the untranslatability of sacred languages is partial and unfitting (Apter 2013). Her point about the prohibition of vernacularization of sacred texts and the sacred language is irrelevant, as Hebrew's secularization is, as Scholem puts it, only a *façon de parler*. And it should be remembered that Bible translations into Latin, English, and especially German, even when existing within nonsecular contexts, are based on a clear theological distinction, which does not exist in Hebrew, between the sanctity of Biblical Hebrew, that of the Hebrew of prayer, Mishnah, Midrash, and contemporary Hebrew.

In fact, even Sabah Mahmoud, who wrote extensively about the politics of piety, does not do full justice to the special case of the Hebrew language. It is evident that she is right in stating that piety is always-already political. But when she interprets Talal Assad's claim, she misses the fact that the sacred materiality of the Hebrew letter has nothing to do with any practices of manipulation, or of power relationships.

> Assad shifts from an understanding of scripture as a corpus of authoritatively inscribed scholarly opinions that stand for religious truth, to one in which divine texts are one of the central elements in discursive fields of relations of power *through which* truth is established. Thus the process by which a particular interpretation of a canonical source comes to be authorized

depends not only upon one's knowledge of the scholarly tradition, but also upon the practical context of power relations (including hierarchies of age, class, gender, and knowledge), under which textual authority is invoked (Mahmood 2005, 116).

As was noted above, it may be argued that the sacred is that which cannot be manipulated, as holiness imposes rigid external boundaries.

And indeed, like the Jewish prohibition against the visual representation of God, the subordination of holiness to human control is sacrilege (Halbertal 2002, 30). A direct result of this argument is that the very act of signification of the sacred is contradictory. On the one hand, there is no other way than signification to get any meaning out of sacred text, but on the other hand, and by the same token, it is clear that signification is also an act of manipulation. According to this internal contradiction we can point out that any act of producing sacred textual meaning will bring us to a dead end. Accordingly, as was noted above, we may conclude that the movement from Hebrew literature to world literature is no less than an impossible mission. This theological dead end not only bars Hebrew literature from inclusion in world literature, but also defines this possible inclusion as an act of sacrilege, that is, a sin against God. Again, following Halbertal, it may be argued that the sin precipitated by the aspiration to integrate into world literature in itself serves as an impediment to such integration, due to the aversion it inspires.

This ostensible secularity of Hebrew creates a false impression of the possibility of translation from Hebrew, which, dialectically, also clearly indicates the impossibility of its translation into any other language. The idea that the powerful theological energy within the Hebrew language threatens to rise to the surface of the ostensibly secular speech of the Jewish inhabitants of Palestine is precisely the postsecular Gnostic mechanism of apostasy against apostasy.

Scholem cautions against the danger of the Gnostic duality of the theological forces that threaten the secularity of the Hebrew language (Scholem 2002). It is these threatening forces that give rise to the dialectic, theological conflict between the good, sacred God and the evil secular God or, in Zionist terms, between the Israelite homeland and the Jewish diaspora (Hotam 2013).

The catholic Sadan's aspiration to combine the two extremes through Zionist "fulfillment" (Jewish relocation to Palestine) is thus also a process of striving to realize monotheism through the elimination of Zionist Gnostic duality. Zionist Gnosticism is divided between the diaspora and its evil God, and the Land of

Israel and its good God, who hinders the translation of the sacred Hebrew language until the arrival of the Messiah. Then Zionism will complete its fulfillment, and all Jews will return to the Holy Land. It is only Sadan's catholic immanence that enables the future completion of the Zionist redemption narrative.

Like other Zionist thinkers, Sadan adhered to the Gnostic immanence that derives from the political and material theological necessity of the Zionist engagement with the "Jewish Question." Anyway, it looks like Sadan perceived Gnosticism as a temporary belief that will be eliminated only in the Jewish future. In other words, he believed that the Gnostic duality created by Jewish liminality will be transcended in the future.

But in accordance with Derrida's claim that the logocentrism of monotheistic religions is what imposes translatability as a basis for sovereignty (Derrida 2009, 455), it is clear that only when the Gnostic dualism of Zionism—that is, the heresy of the heresy—is replaced by logocentric monotheism, will it be possible to translate Hebrew as the language of sanctity. This is Jewish Messianism, that its full materialization, always ahead of its time, will import non-Jewish political theology to the Jewish people via the translation of the sacred language.

It is this normative sovereignty of the peoples of the world, the result of translating the sacred language into non-Jewish languages that will bring about the sanctity of Jewish sovereignty, that is—violent Jewish fascism, the presence of which can be detected in the acts of the settlers in the Israeli occupied territories, who are certain they are living in the Messianic era. But unlike them, Sadan, who followed Krochmal, does not believe that the Messiah is coming, but believes, rather, in the eternal narrative of eternal Israel.

Sadan defines Scholem's linguistic approach as a search for national, that is, Zionist truth that will eradicate its Gnostic duality—for example, the fulfillment of Zionism as overcoming the global contrast between the diaspora and the Land of Israel. In effect, Sadan argued that it was Scholem's interest in Kabbalistic Gnosis—as someone who came to his homeland from a geographical and emotional distance—that brought him to a Zionist engagement with the Hebrew language. Through the language of Zionist political theology, Sadan manages to articulate the dramatic link that Scholem created between the cosmic dualism of the Hebrew language and Hebrew literature, which lies at the heart of his academic truth as a Kabbalah scholar, and his own desire to overcome this dualism through Zionist fulfillment in the Zionist political reality of the Hebrew of the Yishuv.

For some reason, the solution to the "Jewish Question" by means of a return to Zion was rolling in the streets, and was picked up by those who were closest to it, who did so as amateurs in every sense of their name *Hovevei Zion* movement. And one day, someone came from afar, who did not know what to do when called up to the Torah, just as he did not know how to save the orphaned Hebrew word from being mangled in his utopian novel [Theodor Herzl's *The Old New Land*]. And it was he who bent down and picked up the truth and made it a reality. (Sadan 1963, 341)

Hebrew Literature as World Literature

A critical reading of the Zionist Sadan's "post-Gnostic" and postsecular, future theological dimensions of worldliness, and a nonsecular literature, in which the good and the evil God will converge, raises a material contradiction within the apostasy against apostasy, due to the presence of non-Jewish inhabitants within the sacred territory (Apter 2014, 347). The expression of this contradiction can be found in the fact that the institutional canon of "Hebrew literature," ostensibly defined on purely linguistic grounds, within a State of Israel defined by its Jewish citizens as "Jewish and democratic," is in fact a canon of "Jewish literature," entailing a contradiction between the democratic identity of the state and its definition as having a religious identity that is also an ethnic and racial identity.

The distinction can be further refined by comparing Arab literature in Hebrew to Jewish literature in Hebrew. The distinction thus becomes biopolitical, determined by the difference between the Jewish body and the Arab body, with the Hebrew language each produces, giving rise to a political comparison between sacred and nonsacred Hebrew rooted in the materiality that signifies the antagonism between the Jewish body and the non-Jewish Palestinian body. In the rebirth of the Hebrew language realized in the establishment of the State of Israel, Sadan saw the fulfillment of the aspiration to national unity, entailing the potential to eliminate Jewish liminality (Sadan 1962, 266). Despite his enthusiasm, however, Sadan, as a student of Krochmal, was not convinced of the permanency of this new reality. That is why he viewed the political theology of the Zionist state as a brief event of little import in comparison to the eternity of the Jewish religion (Sadan 1971, 139). He thus, of course, exceeds political theology's temporality that, according to Carl Schmitt, is based on the sovereign as he who declares a state of emergency without time-limit and sharply divides between friend and foe (Schmitt 2005).

The muscular, vital Zionist body that is bound to the soil of the homeland, as an immanent and political model contemptuous of the spiritual diasporic Jewish body, detached from the materiality of the soil of the homeland, lies at the heart of the duality of the protestant Zionist Gnosis that Sadan seeks to overcome with his catholic approach (Gluzman 2007). The discourse that constitutes the Zionist body that writes Hebrew literature constructs the identity of the Jewish subject as a racial, biopolitical identity that, in turn, constructs the biopolitics of the male Jewish body by indelibly marking it as born to a Jewish mother. The converted male subject is constructed by the biopolitics of Jewish discourse by indelibly marking his body with circumcision, while biopolitics construct the identity of the body of the female convert as a Jewish woman whose descendants will be Jewish.

The "Jewish Question" will be resolved by means of the sacred language, which will restore the covenant between God and the Jewish people that was broken at the time of the destruction of the Second Temple. Indeed, use of the sacred language affords Jewish sovereignty the authority to rule by sacred rhetoric, both actual and potential; and it is by means of this sovereignty that the Jewish people will contend with the modern "Jewish Question."

A very telling example of Sadan's dialectic reading, which marks on the far horizon the totality of national sovereign political theology, is his dialectic thesis regarding the fateful meetings that Bialik, the national poet, had and that formed his standing.

Following his discussion of the contradiction between the depths of Bialik's soul and its expression in his texts, Sadan struggles with the issue of the poet's national sovereign status. Basically, Sadan portrays Bialik as a bifurcated sovereign. Bialik's fatal meeting with Ahad Ha-am constrained him and would not let him reach the pinnacle of his status; but as a dialectic, Sadan also points to Bialik as he who exists within the immense tradition of the leadership and kingship of the Jewish people. He finds this leadership in the history of Hebrew poetry and points to the synthesis of them both—leadership and poetry—for example, in King David. But a more scrutinizing reading of his claim shows that the link between the Sacred Spirit and political leadership exists throughout the entire history of Hebrew poetry, that it is possible to conclude from his total and dialectic stance that Bialik is the one who materializes in a very complex manner his being, the spiritual sovereign as an integral part of the great tradition of response to the nation's demand for the presence of poets and leaders on the shoulders of whom rises the sacred soul (Sadan 1962, 7). Sadan doubts the definition of Bialik as a national poet; nevertheless, again dialectically, he negates this very term and replaces it with the concept of the poet of the nation. Still, ongoing in his dialectic manner, he undermines this concept, but finally he criticizes the literary critics who could not perceive the totality constituted by the duality of his personality. Therefore, finally he points at Bialik as the pinnacle of the Hebrew literature of his time, and to the totality that carries with it sovereign force as it marks his greatness as he who gave life "the self recapitulation of the Israeli human being." Again, via dialectics, Sadan constructs Bialik as the leader and in fact the sovereign who enables his readers among the Jewish people to merge together the national pragmatism and profound internal being. There is no doubt that through the total merger between the individual poetry and the public poetry, Bialik positions himself in the literary-political tradition of the sovereignty of the poet in the Eastern European culture (Sadan 1962, 12).

Bialik gained his sovereign authority based on national political-theology, thanks to the saturation of his poems with the sacredness of the Hebrew language, to which he also related in his essays. Sadan discusses Bialik's literary sovereignty turned into a national one as it took form via his meetings with the Volozin Yeshiva, where he studies with the most important Zionist thinker and ideologue, Ahad Ha-am, and with Mendele Mocher Sforim (Abramovitz), one of the greatest Yiddish and Hebrew writers of the second half of the nineteenth century. According to Sadan these meetings can, indeed, help understand Bialik's greatness, and hence his sovereignty; but through his dialectic Sadan also points to the utopian totality of the national poet, which, at a certain biographical and nationally historic stage, has been negated due to the great threat he felt from the results of these meetings (Sadan, 163).

Indeed, according to Sadan (and many others), the ultimate sovereign in the domain of Hebrew literature, in the Land of Israel and around the world, that is, in the domain of national discourse, is the national poet Chaim Nahman Bialik. Bialik's statement from 1926 that the spoken Hebrew should be developed toward a holy tongue (1935, 129), is similar to Sadan's explanation of the national discourse that constitutes Bialik as the sovereign who contends with the theology of the materiality of the "Jewish Question."

> If we were to view the structure of the literature of recent generations as a dual system of conquest [of depth as well as breadth], and we were to seek within it a point of reference, we would choose the greatest focal point, and

that is Ch. N. Bialik, in whom the overt and covert forces at work within an entire era are defined, without his being defined by them, since he possesses that quality of uniqueness that marks a phenomenon. (Sadan 1962, 59)

Sadan therefore criticized those who failed to grasp the totality of Bialik's sovereignty through psychoanalysis and Gnosticism.

In Bialik, all of the literary endeavors of recent generations attain completion—the self-recapitulation of the Israelite; a recapitulation that descends from the highest layers of the [human] spirit to the lowest layers of the [animal] soul, from the façade of programmatic consciousness and its surface to the foundation of physical passion and its depth; [a recapitulation that, rather than] placing Bialik in two opposing circles, takes the contrast into [Bialik] himself, placing [the poet's] essence in the great field of conflict between Jewish antiquity and its embodiment in the ancient tradition the content and form of which are religious, and the new reality embodied in the new secular experiences (Sadan 1962, 64–65).

Bialik is the Jewish sovereign who extends his authority over the entire Jewish domain, protecting it and separating it from the global non-Jewish domain. Although Bialik was the poet who gave expression to Jewish weakness in the diaspora, he was also the author of the long poem *"Be-ir ha-harigah"* (City of Slaughter) in which he blamed the Jewish victims of the Kishinev pogrom (April 1903) and, by manipulating the facts, attacked what he presented as Jewish cowardice. Bialik thus delineated the boundaries of legitimate Jewish power, the theological foundation of which—based on the helpless God who speaks in the poem—allows us to draw a clear line between the literary Hebrew sacred text and the textuality of the world literature. Indeed, Bialik, the national poet, replaces God's helplessness with his own theological authority as the sovereign who brought about the formation of Jewish military units against the violence of the pogroms.

Translation from Hebrew as the Sacred Language

Sadan makes a fascinating distinction between two types of translation: *ha'atakah* and *targum*. It is an old Jewish textual distinction: "And that is what is known as the *ha'atakah* of the seventy sages" (Krochmal 1961, 61). In essence, it is the difference between the method employed in the great translation project of the Tibbonides in the Middle Ages, and the modern concept of translation. The *ha'atakah* of the Tibbonides—whose founder, R. Yehuda Ibn Tibbon, was known as the "father of the *ma'atikim*"—consisted in the creation of Hebrew texts to parallel the Arabic texts of the medieval Jewish philosophers, by replacing every Arabic word or expression with a Hebrew one, to the point that "its foreignness is forgotten" (Even-Shmuel 1973, 56). When it came to syntax, however, they sought to remain faithful to the original, "removing the Hebrew sentence from its natural environment and subjugating it to the foreign sentence, and its structure" (Even-Shmuel 1973, 58). Ultimately, however, in word as well as syntax, the Tibbonides' desire to remain faithful to the original outweighed their desire to produce a comprehensible translation (Even-Shmuel 1973, 62–63).

In the introduction to his translation of Ibn Paquda's *Hovot ha-levavot* (Duties of the Heart), from Arabic to Hebrew, the translator R. Yehuda Ibn Tibbon explained his method (and doubts) as follows: "Wherever I have managed to translate word for word, even if the language is not as beautiful as I would have liked, that is what I have done" (Ibn Pakuda, 1973, 31). And indeed, a large part of the Tibbonides' work lay in inventing Hebrew philosophical terminology to replace the Arabic terminology, often with insufficient sensitivity to the textual context. Here are Sadan's considerations regarding this issue.

> It thus seems that we were justified in explaining the position of the reader who is unable to read world literature in the original and requires a translation. Indeed this position, which requires considerable reinforcement, may be explained in terms of the state of our literature and language, in which the passage from the method of *ha'atakah* to the method of *targum* is still very young. It thus goes without saying that its approach to translation is equally young, although the weaknesses and shortcomings of that approach are manifest when the reader has before him a book such as the present one, which is more non-fiction and textbook than literature. (Sadan 1969, 18)

The weak approach to which Sadan refers is the failure to complete the passage from *ha'atakah* to *targum*, that is, the detachment or autonomy of the translation from the source text, which is the basis of the universalism of world literature within Hebrew literature. Contrary to *ha'atakah*, which requires that the translated text be read together with the source, the autonomous translation requires detachment from the source. The practice of *ha'atakah*, on the other hand, does not create an autonomous text capable of acting in an independent fashion, as a text translated by *targum* does. Sadan goes on to cite examples of successfully translated literary texts, that is, translations that stand in their own right (Sadan 1969, 19). Indeed, it is this autonomy of the translation that creates a universal text. The fact that these translations are written in the sacred tongue attests to their ultimate political role, which is to justify Zionism as Jewish national particularism.

The political significance of the act of translation thus creates an autonomous and universal text that is, at the same time, also imbued with theological significance that affords translation theo-political authority. Contrary to *ha'atakah*, which is characteristic of a political situation in which Jews accept the fact that they are a national minority, that is, subject to foreign sovereignty, a political theology of the kind evoked by Bialik serves as the foundation for the constitution of Jewish sovereignty, contending with the Jewish state of emergency (Schmitt 2005). It is interesting that when Even-Shmuel sought to praise Sadan's initiative as a member of the Knesset, the Israeli parliament—that is, as sovereign—to impose voweled script on Hebrew literature, he did so in terms that revealed his view that the matter at hand was one of Zionist political theology. He affirmed that Sadan had, "raised the question of imposing voweled script as the only script in our literature before the Knesset, the only institution that possesses 'the power and the dominion' to enact this fundamental change in our spiritual lives" (Even-Shmuel 1973, 73). By "our spiritual lives," Even-Shmuel, of course, meant Jewish spiritual lives, which he claimed demand "reaffirmation of the holiness of our times" and which he defined as the opposite of Christianity (Even-Shmuel 1973, 73).

Concerning his own attempt to turn a *ha'atakah* of an Arabic text like Yehuda Halevi's *Kuzari* into Hebrew, Even-Shmuel remarked, "One who seeks to translate from this source into Hebrew feels as if he is returning a lost object to its owner, as he discovers the Hebrew foundation of the *Arabic source*"—that is, the holiness hiding within the Arabic text, which translation into Hebrew reveals and puts on display for all to see (emphasis in the original; Even-Shmuel 1973, 43). The following is a further example of the modern dismissal of *ha'atakah* and its transformation into *targum*, as a result of what appears to be the realization of Zionism:

> In recent generations, we have become increasingly alienated from the style
> of the foundational texts of medieval Jewish philosophy in general, and from

the works of their translators in particular. This alienation is felt especially keenly in our generation, in our land, in the teaching of the masterpieces of our literature to a generation for which Hebrew is a spoken language. Hence the need for a new translation of this literature in general and of the *Kuzari* in particular. The work here presented to the members of our generation is an attempt to meet this need. (Even-Shmuel 1973, 59)

While the desire to incorporate the literature written in Hebrew into world literature is, in practice, impossible to realize, due to the holiness of the Hebrew letters, which serve as an impenetrable barrier between Hebrew literature and other literatures, movement in the opposite direction is possible. Krochmal notes one exception to this rule.

The *ha'atakah* of the seventy sages, considered holy by all the Greek Jews, as if it had been done in the spirit of God that descended upon the translators, and this is also the opinion of the rabbis, recounted in the Aggadah and the Midrash. (Krochmal 1961, 61)

So too is the work of Akilas (Aquila) the proselyte, who translated the Torah into Aramaic and converted to Judaism: "and it is he who translated the Torah, according to [the teachings of] R. Eliezer and R. Joshua." However, over time "the Septuagint became corrupted, unintentionally, and intentionally by the heretics, who cited this *ha'atakah* extensively, and they vociferously decried the *ha'atakah* of Akilas, which denied them many of their prooftexts." Despite the heretics' misinterpretations, the *ha'atakah* from the sacred tongue to Aramaic did not lose its theological significance. On the contrary, Akilas the proselyte reaffirmed the theological significance of the translation from the sacred tongue to Aramaic, "translating only the words that Moses uttered [as he received them] from the Almighty" (Krochmal 1961, 449).

The realization of the theological significance of the translated text depends, however, on the holiness of the Hebrew translation—achieved through its creation as an autonomous textual alternative. Nevertheless R. Yehuda Ibn Tibbon expressed his fear that the Hebrew translation might lack the theological dimension of holiness: "And on a number of occasions, some of our noble friends among the scholars of our communities have beseeched me to translate for them some of the writings of the Geonim in Arabic to the sacred tongue" (Ibn Tibbon 1949, 58). After citing the difficulties faced by a translator from Arabic, Ibn Tibbon concludes by expressing his faith that God will guide him, ensuring that his translation will possess the dimension of holiness.

> And as we ask our God to save us from any stumbling block or fault in our work, so ask him to save us from the stumbling block of our words, and the sin of our mouths, as His anointed one asked of Him: "Place, O Lord, a watch on my mouth, a guard at the door of my lips." (Ps. 141:3; trans. R. Alter). And with this I shall begin to translate the words of the author, with the help of the Lord God, amen.

Indeed, the impossibility of integrating Hebrew literature into world literature also pertains to the question of translation. In his classic essay about world literature, Goethe expressed his hope that the best literature written beyond Europe could join in with European literature (Goethe, 2013). Goethe's enthusiasm about the poetry of the Persian poet Hafiz—Orientalist enthusiasm, sparked by the translations of William Jones, a judge who worked for the East India Company—was a colonialist act that enabled him to transcend the boundaries between non-European aesthetic tastes and ostensibly universal European taste (Young 2011, 213–14).

Translation from Hebrew and other oriental languages into European languages and American English always entails an act of colonialism. In the case of Hebrew literature, however, the situation is considerably more complicated. The material Jewish body of the Hebrew writer, which produces Hebrew literature written in the sacred tongue, does not surrender to the semantics of colonialism, just as it carefully maintains the religious liminality that prevents it from completely joining social movements—like the communist revolution that embraced the idea of world literature in Marx and Engels's *The Communist Manifesto* as an expression of the universalism of class (Young 2011).

It goes without saying that Goethe and his followers did not pay attention to the colonialist power relationships that were involved in their reading and producing translations. In any event, this kind of universalism opposes any translation of Hebrew as a sacred language. And indeed the sacred Hebrew language blocks any option for its participation in the literary space of world literature.

This structure of power relations undergoes a marked change in the case of translation of a Hebrew text without losing its holiness. A more detailed explanation of the fact that the holiness of the Hebrew language precludes the possibility of the integration of Hebrew literature into world literature should begin with an examination of the power relations between the reader of a sacred text and the sacred text itself. The first element that allows us to interpret this power-relation dynamic is, as noted above, the fact that holiness cannot be manipulated by the reader of the sacred text (Halbertal 2002, 31). Therefore, every human action that attributes holiness, which originates from God, to place, time, territory, or language, establishes a stable, inflexible, and immutable boundary between the sacred and the profane. It thus follows that, in accordance with the theological foundation at the basis of holiness, one who manipulates the sacred object for political ends, that is, changes the boundaries between the sacred and the profane, is immediately defined as a sinner. Therefore, and as I have noted, according to this Jewish theological approach, anyone who seeks to integrate Hebrew literature into world literature may be defined as a sinner and violator of God's will. This refers, of course, only to Jews or, more precisely, to Hebrews, who thereby abrogate their obligation to the covenant forged between the patriarch Abraham and God and to the subsequent, Sinaitic covenant between God and the Israelites. The Jewish collective is defined by its covenant with God, whether as the enlightened Jews of Mendelssohn's day, or, for example, as Zionist Jews, who have never renounced their political theology, which remains, to this day, the common denominator of their shared national existence, indistinguishable from its Jewish religious foundation. In other words, the implication of these definitions is that the theological significance of the integration of Hebrew national literature into world literature is no less than the religious sin of violating the covenant forged between God and His chosen people.

The Jews were relegated to "exilic time," in which they exist, whether in the Holy Land of Israel or in nonsacred diasporic space, as they await the coming of the Messiah.[3] Until the Messiah comes and redeems the Jewish people from exile, however, the sacred Hebrew tongue, that is, the language of Scripture, the Mishnah, liturgy, and Midrash, as well as Hebrew literature throughout the ages, has been assigned the practical role of safeguarding holiness against sin—such as the sin of making the sacred tongue part of the multilingual phenomenon known as world literature.

The holism of Jewish sanctity according to Sadan, that is, of the language of the Jewish body of the Hebrew writer, is the sacred language.

> the one language, the Hebrew language, which, since it was the founding language of the nation and its vitality never departed from [the nation] over

the course [of time] and was the solid foundation [on which it was built], is at the end just as it was at the beginning. (Sadan 1962, 125)

The sacred history of Hebrew literature has also known times of crisis, however, to which Sadan gives expression in his remarks about members of the younger generation, who consider it a bore.

Not only criticism that they should find such a flaw in it, but also a degree of astonishment that it can be said to possess such [a flaw], for the way of sanctity is that of the tablets and the broken tablets that lay in the holy ark. (Sadan 1962, 158)

Following this trajectory, it is possible to portray how Sadan constitutes sacred Hebrew as the political Jewish theology as the basis of Jewish sovereignty through the dialectics of the atheist nationality of the Hebrew language. He portrays the Jewish state and the Hebrew language as follows:

courageous attempts to maintain our existence on a new basis the power of which is a given and its power of life is yet to be examined, as the basis of atheism as is found ruling culture; or on renewed foundations, that the interruption between their beginning and their continuation is the major bulk of the road of the history of Israel, such as the founding national independence and as the founding of Hebrew language as the vehicle for the expression of all the needs of life. These are immense and defining processes, and one cannot discuss each and every one of them separately." (Sadan 1962, 110)

To describe the next stage in the relationship between sacred Hebrew and its secular uses, Sadan employs nationalistic and Gnostic terms of apostasy against apostasy.

The previous generation approached the language with reverence, purifying itself as it were, before the act of writing and even before the act of speaking—borrowing from its attitude toward it in its youth, that is, to a sacred thing, according that very same sanctity to its every expression, as secular as that might be. (Sadan 1962, 162)

The failure of efforts to normalize Hebrew literature after the establishment of the State of Israel (Miron 2005, 11–12), that is, the literary failure that preserved its diasporic liminality as a national majority acting like a national minority (Hever 2002) is apparent in the fact that the sacred liminality of the chosen people served as a barrier to translation for fear that it would subvert its sanctity. This is the Janus face of nationality, as it is materialized by the language of Hebrew sovereignty (Nairn 1977).

The sacred tongue of Hebrew literature is at once the language that constitutes colonialist Jewish sovereignty and the language of the diasporic tradition, in which modern Hebrew literature was born as postcolonial resistance to its oppression at the hands of European colonialism. In other words, Hebrew literature is used by both the oppressor and the oppressed. Robert Young defines postcolonial literature as literature that exposes and challenges asymmetric power relations and the injustices to which they give rise. It can be argued that the preference of the sacred language and form of the Hebrew literary text over its thematic reading, which lacks theological commitment, attests to the postcolonialism of the sacred language of modern Hebrew literature, which is incapable of dealing with reality that lies beyond itself (Young 2011, 217).

By adopting a materialist perspective, it is a clear that a translation from Hebrew into a foreign language that maintains its holiness is an impossible mission. Franz Rosenzweig was particularly sensitive to the paradox in the possible impossibility of rendering the sanctity of Hebrew into another language. Sadan, like Rosenzweig, characterized translations of Hebrew literature as caricatures that will always remain so, "unless translators are capable not only of perceiving its multiple underpinnings and hidden meanings, but also of sustaining them in translation, something that is, given their general level of training, like trying to square the circle" (Sadan 1962, 84).

In a letter to Gershom Scholem (March 10, 1921), Rosenzweig explained this paradox of translating sanctity, and defined its source by citing the example of the definitive Protestant translation of the Bible into German.

> Only one who is profoundly convinced of the impossibility of translation can really undertake it. Not by any means of the impossibility of translation in general (that isn't the case at all; rather, all life beyond one's own soul is conditioned by the possibility of this miracle, as you so rightly call it), but of the impossibility of the particular translation he is about to embark on. This special impossibility is different in every case. In this case its name is: Luther. [. . .] If I happen to have a Jewish guest who can just read Hebrew—even if he cannot understand a sentence and, so to speak, not a word—I conceal

the existence of the translation from him. The uncomprehended Hebrew gives him more than the finest translation. There is no getting away from it. Jewish prayer means praying in Hebrew. (Rosenzweig 1998, 101–2)

Here, Rosenzweig seems to have embraced the idea of the Jewish body as holy, deriving its holiness from God—an idea expressed in Leviticus 19:2: "You shall be holy, for I the Lord your God am holy" (Shinan 2002, 11). In light of this, the discussion of the boundaries of holiness would appear to be contradictory. Since holiness flows from God, who fills the entire world, and there is no place in which He is not present, holiness may be said to be everywhere, and in every person, that is, in what may be identified as a Jewish body (Sperber 2002, 104). Contrary to the protestantism of Zionist literature, which distinguishes between sacred and profane, the catholic Sadan chose an alternative path, whereby all of Hebrew literature is sacred. As in the writings of Krochmal, the sharp distinction between sacred and profane does not apply to the chosen and holy people. Thus, the Jewish Havdalah prayer, which distinguishes between the holy Sabbath and the other days of the week, attests to the internal tension within holiness, but not to the possibility of eliminating it (Sperber, 2002, 104). The question of the translation of Hebrew literature in order to allow it to be included in world literature may be examined from the perspective of Emily Apter's theory that translated texts do not constitute world literature.

Apter views the global literary market as the circulation of literature within a transnational, that is, a trans-civic market. Translations from specific languages, which enable the constitution of world literature, may thus be characterized as a mechanism for the dissemination of national literature through the erasure of its particularity. Apter, therefore, concludes that comparative literature based on translation is, in its inclusivity, even more exclusionary of non-Western cultures than national literatures. Dov Sadan, in asserting the impossibility of integrating the holiness of Hebrew literature in world literature, appears to be far more radical than Apter. For the catholic Sadan, it is not merely a matter of theology defining the problem of world literature; rather, it is the absence of any distinction between the holiness of national literature in Hebrew and the political theology of the Hebrew text that makes its integration into world literature impossible. Thus, we can conclude that there is no way to separate Jewish identity into Jewish nationality, on the one hand, and Jewish religion, on other. The reason for such a conclusion is that the Jewish identity is based on a permanent conflation of the Jewish national imagined community, with the religious imagined community.

In order to understand the political theology at the basis of this Gordian knot, that is, at the basis of Hebrew Zionist discourse, we must examine the concept of Jewish sovereignty. Jewish sovereignty is founded on the impossible distinction between Jewish religion and Jewish nationality, fully present in Hebrew literature, and which may only be resolved by recognizing their inseparability. In so doing, however, one must also give up on the idea of the universality of Jewish citizenship, constituted, inter alia, by Hebrew literature. This problem also appears in Giorgio Agamben's note on "an intention to signify that cannot be identified with any particular signification" (Agamben 1999, 66). It also appears to have been Benjamin's intention to delineate this difficulty, when in his essay "The Task of the Translator," he suggests that it is in fact the untranslatable text, because it is not subject to mediating sense, that reflects the true language of the Dogma ["Torah"], (Benjamin 1969: 140).

For Rosenzweig, in Hebrew the spirit of God is "poured into the vessel of the language created to receive it," and the divine revelation of the Torah "speaks in the language of human beings" (quoted in Mendes-Flohr 1993, 229). According to Mendes-Flohr's discussion, Rosenzweig does not regard Hebrew as divine speech; unlike the divine language of the Kabbalah, Hebrew is "sanctified by God's gracious decision to sound His word through it. Detached from the divine word, Hebrew would presumably forfeit its sanctity" (Mendes-Flohr 1993, 229). For Rosenzweig, "Hebrew is the language of the prophets, for whom the future is not a somewhere, but *not yet to be*. . . ." It is "the language that bears both God's revelation and prophetic promise of redemption" (quoted in Mendes-Flohr 1993, 229). Rosenzweig's insight is crucial to our understanding of the fundamental way in which the sanctity of language functions. It is clear that when we speak of theology and political theology, there is no place for the essential demarcation of the boundaries of the sanctity of literature's language, as if we were referring to a homogeneous body of text.

By using a longer quotation we can follow Benjamin's thoughts on the ability to express without conveying meaning.

> For this very reason Hölderlin translations in particular are subject to the enormous danger inherent in all translations; the gates of a language thus expanded and modified may slam shut and enclose the translator with silence. Hölderlin's translations from Sophocles were his last work; in them meaning plunges from abyss to abyss until it threatens to become lost in the bottomless depths of language. There is, however, a stop. It is vouchsafed

to Holy Writ alone, in which meaning has ceased to be the watershed for the flow of language and the flow of revelation. Where a text is identical with truth or dogma, where it is supposed to be "the true language" in all its literalness and without mediation of meaning, this text is unconditionally translatable. In such case translations are called for only because of the plurality of languages. Just as, in the original, language and revelation are one without any tension, so the translation must be one with the original in the form of the interlinear version, in which interlinear and freedom are united. For to some degree all great texts contain their potential translation between the lines; this is true to the highest degree of sacred writings. The interlinear version of the Scriptures is the prototype or ideal of all translations. (Benjamin 1969, 81–82)

But in the meantime, silence and silencing, that is the act of ceasing speech, are ahistorical threshold points that do not depend on those who speak them. And in the meantime, beyond them there is nothing, and only through them can a broad range of phenomena be signified. The fact that materiality precludes communication is also a clear, unequivocal, and inessential signifier of the inability to transcend the division between the translating and the translated language, and the threshold from which, only ostensibly, communication may occur between Hebrew literature and world literature.

This brings us to the matter of temporality, generally formulated in terms of continuity, in relation to which Baruch Kurzweil, one of the greatest scholars of Hebrew literature, asked whether modern Hebrew literature constitutes a continuation or a revolution in Hebrew literature. As was mentioned above, Kurzweil argued that, with a handful of exceptions marked by internal contradictions, the passage is one of dramatic revolution, from sacred Hebrew literature to secular Hebrew literature (Kurzweil 1959). Clearly, Kurzweil's view on the subject of world literature contrasts with that of Sadan, who saw no point in Kurzweil's binary question, and preferred to speak of an "arduous journey" (Sadan 1971, 127). For Rosenzweig, who did not approach the issue in historical terms of continuous or discontinuous narrative, the answer to Kurzweil's question would always include both possibilities, as striking as the contrast may be. Kurzweil's question invites a teleological response that establishes the various turning points in accordance with the end to which they point. An answer based on silence or silencing, on the other hand, hinges on a threshold or liminal point, that is, one that preserves diasporic Jewish existence, that creates the turning point without incorporating it into a preexisting narrative. This offers the possibility of creating inessential discourse that inherently includes communication and the impossibility of communication. This threshold allows us to point to the political theology of the Hebrew language as an existing and accessible signifier, which, even if immediately erased, can still serve scholars as a guide in their quest to distinguish between the text they have before them, and its framework as political theology.

Even when Sadan describes the narrative of the development of the new Hebrew literature, he rejects the kind of development that allows for contemporary Hebrew writers who represent a multiplicity that, aesthetically speaking, is fundamentally no different from Western literature. Contrary to local writers who write in Hebrew as an indigenous language, these Hebrew writers write, for the Western reader, literature that can be termed "post-national" (Young 2011, 214).

Notes

1. The political framework of the Jewish community in Palestine prior to the establishment of the State of Israel.
2. The terms Maskilic, Hasidic, and Mitnagidic refer, respectively, to the Jewish Enlightenment, the Jewish Pietist movement founded in Eastern Europe in the late eighteenth century, and the Orthodox Jewish opposition to Hasidism.
3. I would like to thank Elchanan Reiner for his explanations on this subject.

Works Cited

Agamben, Giorgio. 1999. *The End of the Poem: Studies in Poetics*, translated by Daniele Heller Roazene. Stanford, CA: Stanford University Press.
Amir, Yehoyada. 2010. "Introduction to Nahman Krochmal." In *Moreh nevukhei ha-zeman*. Jerusalem, Israel: Carmel.
Apter, Emily. (2013) 2014. "Against World Literature." In *World Literature in Theory*, edited by David Damrosh, 345–62. Malden MA; Oxford, and West Sussex, UK: Wiley Blackwell.
———. 2013. *Against World Literature: On the Politics of Untranslatability*. London and New York: Verso.
Auerbach, Erich. (1953) 2003. *Mimesis, The Representation of Realty in Western Literature*, with a new introduction by Edward W. Said; translated by Willard R. Trask. Princeton, NJ and Oxford, UK: Princeton University Press.

Benjamin, Walter. 1969. *Illuminations*, edited by Hannah Arendt; translated by Harry Zohn. Schoken Books: New York.

Bialik. H. N. 1935. "Al Kodesh Ve-Hol Balashon," *Dvarim Shebealpe*, vol. 2, Tel Aviv, Israel: Dvir.

Brenner, Yosef Haim. (1906) 1985."Dapim, mipinkaso shel sofer ivri." In *Ketavim*, vol. 3, 104–9. Tel Aviv, Israel: Hakibbutz Hameuhad and Sifriyat Poalim. [*Hame'orer* 1 (January 1906), signed H. B. Zalel.]

Casanova, Pascale. 2005. "Literature as a World." *New Left Review* 31: 71–90.

Damrosch, David. 2003. *What Is World Literature?* Princeton, NJ: Princeton University Press.

Derrida, Jacques. 2009. *The Beast and the Sovereign*, translated by Geoffrey Bennington. Chicago, IL: University of Chicago Press.

Even-Shmuel, Yehuda. 1973. Introduction to his translation of *Sefer Ha-Kozar* [the *Kuzari*] by R. Yehuda Halevi. Tel Aviv, Israel: Dvir.

Fleischmann, Jacob. 1956. "Franz Rosenzweig ke-mevaker ha-Tziyonut." In *Al Franz Rosenzweig bi-melot 25 shanim le-moto*, 54–73. Jerusalem, Israel: Magnes.

Goethe, Johan Wolfgang v., 2013. *World Literature, A Reader*, edited by T. D'haen, C. Dominguez and M. R. Thomsen, 9–15. London: Routledge.

Gluzman, Michael. 2007. *Ha-guf ha-tziyoni: Le'umiyut u-migdar u-miniyut badifrut ha'ivrit ha-hadashah*. Bnei Brak, Israel: Hakibbutz Hameuhad.

Gross, Benjamin. 2004. *Berit Lashon, Hadibur Be-Machshevet*. Israel, Jerusalem, Israel: Reuven Publishing House.

Hever, Hannan. 2002. *Producing the Modern Canon, Nation Building and Minority Discourse*. New York & London: New York University Press.

———. 2007. *Ha-Sipur Ve-Haleom Be-Kanon Ha-Siporet Ha-Ivrit*. Tel Aviv, Israel: Resling.

Halbertal, Moshe. 2002. "Al kedushah u-gevulot ha-yitzug ha'omanuti ve-ha-leshoni." In *Gevulot ha-kedushah: Ba-hevrah, ba-hagut u-va-omanut*, edited by Emily D. Bilski and Avigdor Shinan, 30–41. Jerusalem, Israel: Keter.

Hotam, Yotam. 2013. *Modern Gnosis and Zionism: The Crisis of Culture, Life Philosophy and Jewish National Thought*, translated by Avner Greenberg. London: Routledge.

Ibn Tibbon, R. Yehuda. 1949. Introduction to his translation of *Hobot HaLebabot* [Duties of the Hearts] by R. Bahya Ben Joseph Ibn Pakuda. Tel Aviv, Israel: Machbarot Lesifrut.

Kurzwiel, Baruch. 1959. *Sifrutenu ha-Hadaha, Hemshech O Mhapecha*. Tel Aviv: Schocken Books.

Krochmal, Nahman. (1961) 2010, *Moreh nevukhei ha-zeman*. Jerusalem, Israel: Carmel.

———. (1924) 2010. *Moreh nevukhei ha-zeman*, ed. Yohayada Amir. Jerusalem, Israel: Carmel.

Mahmud, Saba. 2005. *The Politics of Piety, the Islamic Revival and the Feminist Subject*. Princeton, NJ and Oxford, UK: Princeton University Press.

Marx, Karl, and Friedrich Engels. (1848) 2005 Introduction and notes by Martin Puchner, *The Communist Manifesto, and Other Writings*. New York: Barnes and Noble Classics.

Mendes-Flohr, Paul. 1993. "Hebrew as a Holy Tongue: Franz Rosenzweig and the Renewal of Hebrew. In *Hebrew in Ashkenaz: A Language in Exile*, edited by Lewis Glinert, 221–41. New York and Oxford, UK: Oxford University Press.

Miron, Dan. 2005. *Harpayah le-tzorekh negi'ah: Likrat hashivah hadashah al sifruyot ha-Yehudim*. Tel Aviv, Israel: Am Oved.

———. 1990. "Bein hekef le-merkaz: Al mif'alo shel Dov Sadan." *Jewish Studies* 30: 83–92.

Nairn, Tom, 1977. *The Break-Up of Britain*. 2nd ed. London: Verso.

Pinsker, Leon. (1882) 1906. *Auto-Emancipation*, translated by B. Y. Blondheim New York: Maccabean Publishing House.

Rawidowicz, Simon. 1924. Introduction to Nahman Krochmal, *Moreh nevukhei ha-zeman*. Berlin, Germany: Ayanot.

Rosenzweig, Franz. 1998. *Franz Rosenzweig: His Life and Thought*, presented by Nahum N. Glatzer. Indianapolis, IN and Cambridge, MA: Hackett.

Sadan, Dov. 1962. *Avnei bedek*. Tel Aviv, Israel: Hakibbutz Hameuhad.

———. (1957) 1963. "Be-sod ve-atah tehezeh: Al Gershom Scholem." In *Bein din le-heshbon: Masot al sofrim u*-sefarim, 335–41. Tel Aviv, Israel: Dvir.

———. 1969. "Introduction" to Erich Auerbach's *Mimesis*, translated by Baruch Karu. Jerusalem, Israel: Mosad Biakik.

———. 1971. *Elkhah ve-ashuvah: Devarim be-inyanei emunot ve-de'ot*. Tel Aviv, Israel: Don.

Schmitt, Carl. *Political Theology: Four Chapters on the Concept of Sovereignty*, translated by George Schwab. Chicago, IL & London: University of Chicago Press, 2005.

Scholem, Gershom. 2002. "Confession on the Subject of Our Language" [*Bekenntnis über unsere Sprache*], 226–27. In Jacques Derrida, *Acts of Religion*, edited by Gil Anidjar; translated by Gil Anidjar. New York and London: Routledge.

Shinan, Avigdor. 2002. "*Gevulot shel kedushah—Sippurah shel taharut*," 8–13. In *Gevulot ha-kedushah: Ba-hevrah, ba-hagut u-va-omanut*, edited by Emily D. Bilski and Avigdor Shinan. Jerusalem, Israel: Keter.

Simon, Akiva Ernst. (1950) 1983. "*Ha-im od Yehudim anahnu?*" In *Masot*, 9–46. Tel Aviv, Israel: Sifriyat Hapoalim, Hebrew University, and The Jewish Theological Seminary.

Smolenskin, Peretz. (1882) 1982. *Nekam Brit*. tr. Steven Adams. Hebrew Union College.

Sperber, Daniel. 2002. "Gevulot shel kedushah ba-halakhah u-va-minhag," 102–11. In *Gevulot ha-kedushah: Ba-hevrah, ba-hagut u-va-omanut*, edited by Emily D. Bilski and Avigdor Shinan. Jerusalem, Israel: Keter.

Spivak, Gayatry Chakravorty. 2003. *Death of a Discipline*. New York: Columbia University Press.

Steinsaltz, Adin. 2002. "Al ha-kedushah u-gevulot ha-kedushah," 18–22. In *Gevulot ha-kedushah: Ba-hevrah, ba-hagut u-va-omanut*, edited by Emily D. Bilski and Avigdor Shinan. Jerusalem, Israel: Keter.

Weiss, Tzhahi, 2014. *Letters by Which Haven and Earth Were Created* [*Otiot Shenivreu Bahen Shmaim VeAretz*]. Jerusalem, Israel: Magnes Publishing House.

Young, Robert, 2011. "World Literature and Postcolonialism," 213–22. In *The Routledge Companion to World Literature*, edited by Theo D'haen, David Damrosch, and Djelal Kadir. London and New York: Routledge.

Zakhai, Avihu. 2017. *Erich Auerbach and the Crisis of German Philology of the Humanities: The Humanist Tradition in Peril*. Switzerland: Springer.

Chapter 4

Islam in the Theory and Practice of World Literature

Translating *Adab* in the Middle Eastern Novel

Karim Mattar

Once upon a time, they had all lived together, and their lives had had meaning, but then, for some unknown reason, they had lost that meaning, just as they'd also lost their memories. Every time they tried to recover that meaning, every time they ventured into that spider-infested labyrinth of memory, they got lost; as they wandered about the blind alleys of their minds, searching in vain for a way back, the key to their new life fell into the bottomless well of their memories; knowing it was lost to them forever, they felt the helpless pain known only by those who have lost their homes, their countries, their past, their history. The pain they felt at being lost and far from home was so intense, and so hard to bear, that their only hope was to stop trying to remember the secret, the lost meaning they'd come here to seek, and, instead, hand themselves over to God, to wait in patient silence for the hour of eternity.

—Orhan Pamuk, *The Black Book*

Introduction: Critical Valences of *The Medieval Islamic Republic of Letters*

In his recent study *The Medieval Islamic Republic of Letters: Arabic Knowledge Construction* (2015), Muhsin al-Musawi, professor of Arabic Literature at Columbia

University, sets out to map a world literary system radically alternative to that proposed by Pascale Casanova (al-Musawi 2015; Casanova 2004). Stretching from Andalucía to Anatolia to South Asia, spanning the twelfth to the nineteenth centuries, and structured primarily around Arabic as the language of the Quran, this model of world literature posits Islam—Islamic theology, metaphysics, epistemology, logic, law, rhetoric, and poetics—as the *episteme* or condition of possibility for knowledge production as manifest in the *adab* of the Middle East throughout the postclassical period. While al-Musawi acknowledges the Cairo of the Fatimid Caliphate (909–1167) as a Casanova-esque capital of the Islamic republic of letters, suggesting that "it stood to the postclassical Islamic world as Paris stood to Europe," he also takes pains to emphasize that "centers at any given time may be replaced by other centers," that the Islamic "cultural sphere [. . .] was greater than any single territorial center" (al-Musawi 2015, 7, 2). Pulled variously toward Mecca, Baghdad, Damascus, Aleppo, Isfahan, Istanbul, Mashhad, and elsewhere as the political and cultural influence of these centers rose and fell, his model is therefore fundamentally deterritorialized. Permeated by Islam, it is enacted by a vast network of itinerant scholars, thinkers, and poets such as Ibn Khaldun, Ibn Battutah, Ibn al-Arabi, and Rumi, whose intellectual as well as life trajectories crossed in the nodal points of the Islamic world; by collaborative scholarly and poetic enterprises such as biographical dictionaries, encyclopedias, lexicons, theological treatises, compendiums, anthologies, commentaries, and so forth that gained in circulation through this world via their accumulation of glosses and marginalia; and by translational interactions between Arabic, Persian, and Turkish as linguistic hegemonies and counterhegemonies were imposed according to the shifting lines of imperial power there. The individuals, texts, and languages al-Musawi brings together in this new, mobile constellation of knowledge are—though multifarious and distributed across a massive spatial and temporal terrain—all constituted within and constitute Islam as *episteme*. Hence, a specifically *Islamic* republic of letters.

Al-Musawi's primary target in this work is the discourse of Arab and Muslim modernity that took root in the Middle East during the so-called period of *Nahda*—or cultural renaissance—from the mid-nineteenth to the early twentieth centuries. In his account, "native elites" of this period such as Ahmad Salamah Musa, Taha Hasayn, and Ahmad Hasan al-Zayyat had so thoroughly internalized Enlightenment discourses of modernization and secularization that they could only perceive the voluminous but religiously oriented cultural output of the premodern past in terms of "decadence and stagnation" (al-Musawi 2015, 5, 11). Still widespread at least among nonspecialists in classical Arabic literature, this *mis*perception, he continues, signals a "failure on the part of the architects of modernity to connect effectively with a rich culture of their past" and has contributed to their "failures [in] establish[ing] emotive and cultural links with the Muslim populace" (al-Musawi 2015, 11). As suggested by his title, al-Musawi counteracts this narrative by deploying Casanova's "republic of letters" model and her Bourdieu-infused terminology of "symbolic capital," "cultural capital," "field" and "habitus," "diversion of assets," and so forth. But he does so critically. It is not only Casanova's Euro- and especially Franco-centrism that he seeks to displace via his attention to a literary and cultural "republic" that antedates the European; he also brings into contention her reliance on a core/periphery structure by which the world's literary resources are absorbed into the institutions of the modern imperial metropole, allocated value on the basis of their relative "literarity," and then recirculated back to the world as its own now-distorted image (Casanova 2004, 82–125).¹ Against what he reveals to be these critical and theoretical limitations, al-Musawi's Islamic republic of letters comprises a non-European site of worlded literary and cultural exchange that is anchored not in a single metropolitan center, but rather in Islam for its pervasive mediating impact on such exchange across a range of ever-shifting centers. As such, al-Musawi's model prompts a renewed critical interrogation of current theories and practices of world literature.

In this chapter, I reflect on the implications of al-Musawi's model of a medieval Islamic republic of letters for our understanding of contemporary world literature, especially of the place of Islam within such. I start by tracing the after-history of the Islamic republic of letters to the present, making the argument that the Arabic-Islamic category of *adab* on which it was founded was gradually displaced by a more familiar, European-derived one of "literature" during the period of colonial modernity in the Middle East. Building on the work of Aamir Mufti and Jeffrey Sacks, I continue to argue that premised on this modern and secular notion of "literature," "world literature," from its Enlightenment origins to its current critical, theoretical, and disciplinary institution, almost by definition obscures alternative theories and practices of the literary such as those—in the case of the Middle East—instantiated by *adab*. This observation provides a means to identify and contest problematic practices in the field of British postcolonial studies, as work toward what might be considered a "Muslim world literature" currently taking place there (Rehana Ahmed, Claire Chambers, Lindsey Moore, Peter Morey, Amina Yaqin, etc.) tends to reproduce precisely the unconscious conceptual biases by which the Islamic literary-cultural sphere was overwritten by its worlded counterpart. Against this field's approach to and understanding of Islamic writing in terms of a model of anglophone literary transnationalism, I propose a translational model more properly attentive to the dialectics of Islam, colonial modernity, and secularism as manifest in the worlding of contemporary Middle Eastern literatures. I demonstrate this model through a critical reading of *The Black Book* (1990; trans. 1994 and 2006), a monumental novel by the Turkish Nobel Prize–winning author Orhan Pamuk. While in its translation and reception this novel has been taken to exemplify a worldly and secular postmodernist aesthetic, I show, through a critical emphasis on his treatment of the Islamic sects of Sufism and Hurufism, Pamuk's more nuanced engagement with questions of modernity, religion, and secularism in Turkey. Embodying in its form what I call a cultural neo-Ottoman revivalist aesthetic, this novel, I conclude, both brings to light and negotiates the dialectical logic by which Islam is repressed in the theory and practice of world literature.

Articulations and Disarticulations of *Adab* in World Literature

To initiate this inquiry, it is important to ask what vestige of al-Musawi's world literary system remains in the present, or whether we can conceive of a contemporary Islamic republic of letters along the same lines as his medieval rendition. Strictly speaking, such a thing cannot exist in the sense that he describes—it would be a literary historical anachronism. This is because the medieval republic of letters was constituted in and through the Arabic-Islamic category of *adab* (أدب). To offer a broad generic definition, this Arabic term referred in the postclassical period to a code of practical ethics that guided appropriate customs, manners, etiquette, civility, and refinement in social and political life, and that was undergirded by Islamic precepts and by Arab sociocultural traditions. It was expressed across the range of oral and textual genres then in circulation, from the instructional ("Mirrors for Princes," courtly etiquette manuals, etc.) to the scholarly (theological treatises, biographical dictionaries, encyclopedias, commentaries, compilations, monographs on a vast array of topics, etc.), including what we might now take to be the more specifically "literary": poetry, the *maqāmah*, didactic fables, allegories, anecdotes, satires, (fictional) travelogues, or (auto)biographies. In its early usage (near-)synonymous with the term *sunna*—literally, the way or path of the Prophet—

adab expanded in sense through the Umayyad Caliphate (661–750), and came to designate the sum of knowledge required for cultured and urbane as well as ethical conduct in civilized society. In this period, it thus incorporated a number of humanistic pursuits such as the religious sciences, ancient poetry, tribal lore, history, geography, statecraft, philology, rhetoric, oratory, music, fashion, and so forth. During the subsequent Abbasid Caliphate (750–1258), this intellectual and humanistic sense of *adab* was further consolidated via the (translational) assimilation of Hellenic, Indian, and Persian influences, notably the genre of the didactic fable featuring animals and mythological creatures and designed to educate fledgling elites in eloquence as well as ethics (Allen 1998, 218–78).[2] By the time of al-Musawi's medieval world, which might loosely be signposted by the fall of Baghdad in 1258, it was then possible for the known Cairo-based scholar Ibn al-Akfani to define *adab* as "the ornament of both tongue and fingertips," as an oral and written practice that encompasses the totality of the Arabic-Islamic cultural heritage with the aim of guiding the Muslim subject toward what he calls "the Most Supreme Principles" (al-Musawi 2015, 181, 180). It is in precisely this sense that *adab* acted as the foundation of the medieval Islamic republic of letters.

A contemporary Islamic republic of letters cannot exist because *adab*—in this sense—no longer exists. Indeed, this term was among the foremost objects of modernization and secularization in the Arab cultural sphere during the *Nahda*. *Adab*, al-Musawi summarizes, "became institutionalized as a term referring specifically to literary writing" as European imperial, economic, and cultural influences began to inscribe the Arab world and the Middle East more generally into the narrative of global colonial modernity (al-Musawi 2015, 182). Jeffrey Sacks provides a more detailed account of this process in his recent, Harry Levin Prize–winning book *Iterations of Loss: Mutilation and Aesthetic Form, Al-Shidyaq to Darwish* (2015). There, he foregrounds philology in particular for its role in "the installation of a series of colonial, Orientalist categories" in nineteenth-century Arabic, and thereby in what he calls "the destruction of the terms of language in an older, Arabic-Islamic logocentrism" (Sacks 2015, 78, 77). Through readings of modernizers such as those listed above, Sacks traces sequentially how in a text of 1855 Ahmad Faris al-Shidyaq appropriated the imported Enlightenment category of "man" as a new ground for the Arabic language; how in his lexicon of 1867–1870 Butrus al-Bustani built on this grounding to define "*adab*" as a "communicable, formally monadic, temporally coherent, and legible" event of language; and how in early-twentieth-century Cairo Taha Husayn formalized this understanding of *adab* in terms of literary writing narrowly conceived (Sacks 2015, 78). Hence the institution not just of "*adab*" as "literature," but also of the fields of reading, writing, and literary criticism in the modern Arab world. The institution of modern Arabic literature might therefore be regarded as coterminous with the wider project of modernization and secularization there—it had the effect of severing literature from the wider Arabic-Islamic practice of *adab*, religion from culture, and premodern oral genres from contemporary textual genres. In other words, the Islamic republic of letters is *inherently* medieval.

The trajectory of *adab*'s articulations and disarticulations from Arabic-Islamic antiquity to Middle Eastern colonial modernity I have briefly sketched here makes for a local and specific variation of Aamir Mufti's genealogy critique of the category of "world literature" in general. In his recent article "Orientalism and the Institution of World Literatures" (2010) and book *Forget English!: Orientalisms and World Literatures* (2016), Mufti argues that from its very inception, the Goethean concept of *Weltliteratur* was both derived from and obscured an Orientalist system of knowledge deeply imbricated with the project of colonial modernity. Originating in the period of European colonial expansion, "world literature," he continues, was forged in the crucible of a "philological Orientalism" that, as ideological complement to "the far-reaching refashioning of the cultures and societies of the world," played a key role in "producing and establishing a method and a system for classifying and evaluating diverse forms of textuality, now all processed and codified uniformly as literature" (Mufti 2010, 461, 464–65).[3] Heirs to this codification of "the literary," current theories thus unconsciously reproduce the imperial power dynamic at the heart of nineteenth-century philology—"Whether we view," Mufti concludes, "world literature (with Franco Moretti) as a conceptual organization rather than a body of literary texts or (with David Damrosch) as a special kind of literature, that which circulates beyond its 'culture of origin,' [. . .] we cannot ignore the global relations of force that the concept simultaneously puts in play and hides from view" (Mufti 2016, 3–35, 56–145).[4]

Mufti's primary case study in this work is South Asia, where he reads the philologically induced division between Hindi and Urdu as an enactment on the terrain of language and literature of the national, ethnic, and religious divisions of India and Pakistan during partition. It should be clear, however, that his argument might fruitfully be extended to the Middle East, as long as local variations are taken into account. In this case, the adoption among local elites such as al-Shidyaq, al-Bustani, and Husayn of the categories of colonial philology had the effect of instituting "*adab*" as "literature," and of thereby dissociating "literature" from its specifically Arabic-Islamic manifestation in the region across a millennium. From the vantage point Mufti's work provides, we might say that this process of institutionalization had the further effect of internally rendering Arabic and Middle Eastern literatures amenable to (their export as) world literature in terms of both *form*—in that this process involved the displacement of premodern oral forms by modern textual forms, most importantly the novel—and *ideology*—in that it extricated "literature" from Islam as its hitherto axiomatic *episteme*, and thus ensured "literature's" a priori conformity to modernity's secular resolve. This vantage point therefore provides an entry into my framing question about the implications of al-Musawi's model for our understanding of the place of Islam in contemporary world literature. To extrapolate from Mufti vis-à-vis the Middle East, we might say that "world literature" is made possible by a foundational repression of a notion and a practice of "the literary"—namely, *adab*—in which literature and religion are inextricably intertwined. And furthermore that current theories "hide from view" precisely the "global relations of force" that were to effect the overwriting of the Arabic-Islamic literary world, the Islamic republic of letters, brought forth by *adab* by what has emerged as the world republic of letters. This, al-Musawi has already shown to be the case in his critique of Casanova. Following Mufti, the task at hand is then to restore to critical purview the dialectical logic by which "world literature" is constituted in and through its negation of, in short, Islam.

Toward a "Muslim World Literature"?

This task is particularly urgent in the context of British postcolonial studies, as in recent years scholars variously situated within this field have been working toward something like a "Muslim world literature" as a new critical topos. In texts including *Arab, Muslim, Woman: Voice and Vision in Postcolonial Literature and Film* (2008); *British Muslim Fictions* (2011); *Framing Muslims: Stereotyping and Representation after 9/11* (2011); *Culture, Diaspora, and Modernity in Muslim Writing* (2012); and *Writing British Muslims: Religion, Class and Multiculturalism* (2015), scholars like Rehana Ahmed, Claire Chambers, Lindsey Moore, Peter Morey, and Amina Yaqin—all based in British academic institutions—have sought to disrupt prevailing cultural assumptions about the religion in the wake of the events of September 11, 2001, through readings of diasporic and transnational "Muslim" writing. While the category "Muslim world literature" has not, as yet, been forwarded in this scholarship, it seems apt as a means to define the emphasis placed on the worldly production, circulation, and reception of "Muslim" writing among its practitioners. Further testifying to the worldly orientation of this scholarship, its canons are constructed predominantly around familiar anglophone figures—especially novelists—such as Salman Rushdie, Hanif Kureishi, Ahdaf Soueif, Leila Aboulela, Monica Ali, Mohsin Hamid, Nadeem Aslam, and Kamila Shamsie. Through such figures, these and other postcolonialists have envisioned a liberal and reflexive global Islamic sensibility in which the Muslim subject is in fact a valued participant in multicultural society despite prejudices to the contrary.

This scholarship, it should be noted, makes for a potentially valuable contribution to postcolonial studies, in that it freshly showcases the reach and flexibility of this field's critical resources for probing issues of the upmost sociopolitical consequence in today's world. Up to this point, though, it has fallen short of this promise due to a number of problems inherent to its literary critical, conceptual, and historical framing, two of which require special mention in the context of my inquiry. First, its presentist scope. Apart from neglecting questions of literary history in the Arabic-Islamic world, this scholarship—in its critically determined and thus structural privileging of the contemporary novel as a site of engagement with Islam—presupposes the identification of literarity with global (novelistic) textuality that al-Musawi, Sacks, and Mufti have historicized as a product of colonial modernity, one that has had the effect of repressing or negating Islam as a grounds of literature in the Arab world and the Middle East. Undermining its own impetus toward something like a "Muslim world literature," it thereby perpetuates the very system of classification, evaluation, and codification that was instrumental in uprooting Islam as the basis of an actually existing world literary system. It is no coincidence that the majority of writers on whom these scholars focus evince strong secular-liberal or, at the furthest end of the spectrum, liberal Islamic inclinations.[5] And second, its anglophone canon. In conformity to one of the most disabling and widely criticized facets of British postcolonial studies since its establishment as a field and a practice, this scholarship structures its approach to and understanding of Islamic writing in terms of a model of anglophone literary transnationalism. In so doing, it occludes the majority of literatures actually produced within and engaged with issues pertinent to what is commonly referred to as the "Islamic world," and moreover reproduces in the world of language the core/periphery paradigm al-Musawi, for one, has contended is inapplicable to the history of such writing. Filtered through the anglophone—its linguistic limitations, its philological heritage, its associations with imperialism and neo-imperialism, its global cultural dominance, its publishing industries, and its markets and audiences—Islamic writing can only manifest in a certain way, one which falsifies rather than enhances any critical consideration of Islam in the theory and practice of world literature.

Against the model of anglophone literary transnationalism prevalent in this scholarship, I propose a translational model more properly attentive to the dialectics of modernity, religion, and secularism as manifest in the worlding of contemporary Middle Eastern literatures. Before elaborating on this, though, I would first like to note other possible approaches to this inquiry. One might readily conceive of such along the lines of "minor transnationalism" (Françoise Lionnet and Shu-mei Shih), "south-south comparatism" (Waïl Hassan), "the other global city" (Andreas Huyssen), "global/local" (Rob Wilson and Wimal Dissanayake), and so forth.[6] Approximating al-Musawi's Islamic republic of letters for the present, such approaches—one can imagine—might productively be redeployed for exploring the circulation of Islam as discourse across a network of mutually informing contemporary Arab, Iranian, Turkish, and other Middle Eastern writers and literatures. While attractive, these would need to be cautious not to duplicate the presentism of British postcolonial approaches, as mapping contemporary networks of influence and cross-fertilization does not in itself appear to necessitate deep historical or genealogical analysis in relation to colonial modernity. One might also conceive of an approach based on the organic Muslim intellectual in the Middle East. Writers with strong religious affiliations and attachments such as Ali Garmarudi and Tahereh Safarzadeh in Iran and Ahmet Günbay Yildiz in Turkey might be placed in constellation for their comparable literary-revivalist projects of *adab* in national milieus where modernity, religion, and secularism have played out distinctly. This approach would be apposite if one wished to devise a literary critical correlate to Islamic revivalism, perhaps a contemporary Islamic *state* of letters.

It seems to me that a carefully honed translational model avoids the pitfalls of actual and potential approaches to the question of Islam in world literature, and that it can foreground rather than deflect the dialectics of Islam's negation by the "literature" of colonial modernity. Derived from the work of Lawrence Venuti, David Damrosch, and Emily Apter in particular, the model I propose is focalized around the politics of cross-cultural exchange as embodied in the act of translation; attuned to the negotiation of comparative literary and cultural histories as well as languages therein; attentive to questions of transnational literary production, circulation, and reception; and vigilant of symbolic as well as material incommensurables in global literary and cultural exchange, which Apter defines in terms of "the Untranslatable."[7] Such aims are best encapsulated in Damrosch's well-known metaphor of "elliptical" or "double refraction" as developed in *What is World Literature?* (Damrosch 2003, 283). Against readings that cite it as evidence for what Apter calls world literature's "reflexive endorsement of cultural equivalence and substitutability," I understand the intent of this image to be one of critically pinpointing the political, material, and cultural conditions by which a text in translational circulation "*manifests* differently," as Damrosch puts it, "abroad than it does at home" (Apter 2013, 2; Damrosch 2003, 6). Crystallized in and as what, Damrosch continues, is the "elliptical space" between its "source and host cultures," the text-in-translation is a prism that refracts rather than obscures the distinct light of both (Damrosch 2003, 283).

Along these lines, a translational approach to Islam in world literature would therefore *necessarily* address the politics of East/West literary and cultural exchange; the (Orientalist) logic by which Islam as discourse, as culture, and as politics is mediated in and for the world; comparative literary histories; production, circulation, and reception; and questions of language, philology, modernity, and so forth. These definitive issues are in themselves illuminated by such an analysis of texts from, broadly, the Islamic world in their translation and circulation. As an illustration of this model, I now turn to a critical reading of Orhan Pamuk's *The Black Book*, paying special attention to its translation, its worldly reception, and its treatment of modernity, religion, and secularism in Turkey.

The Black Book (I): Modernity, Religion, and Secularism in Translation

Turkish "literature" might be said to inscribe a distinct iteration of *adab*'s historical trajectory in the Middle East. A product of this history, the modern Turkish word for "literature"—*yazın*—demands closer scrutiny. This term was coined by one Nurullah Ataç, an architect of the process of reformation and reconstitution to which the Turkish language was subjected after the collapse of the Ottoman Empire and the founding of the Republic of Turkey in 1923. Most spectacularly embodied by the replacement of the Ottoman Arabic script by the Latinate in 1928, this process also involved the replacement of the Arabic and Persian loanwords widespread in Ottoman Turkish with native Turkish counterparts. The many state initiatives of this period included the abolition of the Sultanate and the Caliphate (1922–1924); the abolition of religious schools/*medreses* and the Ministry of Religious Affairs (1924); the prohibition of religious shrines, dervish orders, the fez, and other religious attire (1925); the adoption of the European clock and calendar, the Swiss civil code, and the Italian penal code (1926); the adoption of Western numerals (1928); and the introduction of the "law of last names" (1932). Alongside such initiatives, language reform was regarded as an essential component of the Kemalist project of national modernization and secularization during the early years of the Republic.[8] Indeed, Mustafa Kemal Atatürk, the founder and first president of the Republic, himself saw to the establishment in 1932 of the Turkish Language Association (*Türk Dil Kurumu*), an official regulatory body charged with modernizing the language via such means as mentioned above. Under these circumstances, it is understandable that the Ottoman Turkish word for "literature"—*edebiyat*—derived from the Arabic *adab*—should have received special attention.

In his authoritative *A Turkish and English Lexicon* of 1884, the English diplomat and lexicographer Sir James William Redhouse provides contemporaneous Ottoman definitions of both *adab* and *edebiyat*. As is evident from the passages cited below, both words in Ottoman Turkish signify much as they had in classical and postclassical Arabic for centuries.

> A. أدب edeb, *s., pl.* 1. آداب. Discipline of the mind, training, education, learning, accomplishments. 2. Breeding, manners, politeness; respectfulness, modesty. 3. Philological science, especially as applied to the Arabic language and vast literature, prose and verse, sacred and profane. 4. A usually observed mode of action, a rule or custom. (Redhouse 1884, 49)
>
> A. ادبيات edebiyat, *s., pl.* The matters pertaining to Arabian philology, the details of grammar, prosody, rhetoric, and logic. (Redhouse 1884, 49)

Rooted in Arab literary, cultural, and social traditions, and in itself referring "especially" to "Arabic language and [. . .] literature," *edebiyat* was considered by Ataç—a poet, a man-of-letters, and a zealous advocate, even ideologue of Öztürkçe ("pure Turkish")—as incompatible with the objectives of linguistic and literary modernization in the new national(ist) milieu of the Turkish Republic. Among his many notable contributions to the language reform, mainly consisting of the innovation of new, Turkish-derived words to replace foreign loanwords, he thus sought an alternative for *edebiyat*. Finding what he needed in *yazı*, Turkish for "writing," he (arbitrarily) derived the word *yazın*. As with the *Nahda*-era Arab intellectuals discussed above, this act of linguistic substitution had the effect of instituting the Turkish word for and, by extension, concept of "literature"—*yazın*—as functionally equivalent to its European correlates in its reference to literary writing, and of thereby distancing "literature" and, by extension, its practice from its Arabic and Islamic heritage—from the "sacred"—as borne by the Ottoman *edebiyat*.

Of course, Ataç's efforts here did not gain the traction that he desired. *Edebiyat* remains the primary word used in Turkish to refer to literature, and *yazın*—when deployed—is more often than not used alongside the former (as in the phrase "*edebiyat ve yazın*"), as something akin to a supplementary "belles-lettres" rather than as the out-and-out replacement he envisioned. This, though, is almost beside the point. For by the time Ataç set his sights on *edebiyat* in the 1940s–1950s, its meaning and its practice had already so completely deviated from what they had been during the heyday of the Ottoman Empire that it was no longer necessary for anyone but the most hardened linguistic nationalist to worry about the word itself. The fact that he honed in on the Turkish "*yazı*" in particular as a means to express what literature meant in modern Turkey seems to corroborate this. What we see, then, in the passage from *edebiyat* to *yazın* is not only an instance of Turkish modernization and secularization in the domain of language, but also an overarching allegory of the project of Turkish secular modernity per se.[9]

Grounded in a modern and secular concept of the literary, it is no surprise that much of Turkish literary production from the early years of the Republic should manifest as an expression and a continuation of this project. The Turkish novel is a key site for exploring such processes of literary modernization further. During this period, the predominant force in the evolution of the novel was what is known as the National Literature (*millî edebiyyât*) movement. Taking root in the declining years of the Empire, this movement turned to native Turkish sources as a means to define a new national identity against an Ottoman culture saturated with Arab and Persian influences. From the onset of the Republican era, European political, social, and cultural models were increasingly adopted to further the ongoing Kemalist program of state formation. National literature was thus inflected by trends in the European novel, with realism and naturalism coming to particular prominence among the early Republican writers (Yakup Kadri Karaosmanoğlu's *Yaban* [*The Wilds*, 1932] is perhaps the best known of these early novels). By the

1940s and 1950s, realism and naturalism had modulated into particularly Turkish versions of social realism and what came to be called the "village novel." This period saw the emergence of, among other notable novelists, Yaşar Kemal, whose village novel İnce Memed (*Memed, My Hawk*, 1955) brought international renown to Turkish literature, and whose standing in the canon of twentieth-century Turkish literature is second only to Pamuk's. Although cursory, this overview of the Turkish novel in the early to-mid-twentieth century is intended to suggest its formal and ideological constitution within parameters defined by the project of Turkish secular modernity, its thorough mediation by history.[10] It is within this literary historical context that Pamuk's unique contributions to the development of the Turkish novel must be understood.

As a novelist, Pamuk is naturally and inescapably heir to the heritage of the Turkish novel. Nevertheless, he—following in the footsteps of his great literary and spiritual predecessor Ahmet Hamdi Tanpınar—posits the dialectic of past and present, tradition and modernity, religion and secularism that defines the Turkish state and Turkish literature alike as the reflexive critical object of all his work.[11] This imaginative locus is the source and inspiration of every aspect of his writing—from his storylines, modes of characterization, and thematic emphases to his structuring devices, formal innovations, and uses of language to his geographical and historical settings—and it imbues all with the distinct and often melancholy light of deep historical consciousness. In the novels *The White Castle* (1985; trans. 1990) and *My Name Is Red* (1998; trans. 2001), Pamuk re-creates sixteenth- and seventeenth-century Ottoman Istanbul in all its civilizational grandeur, and traverses the discourses and intrigues of empire, statecraft, religion, art, and desire in this time and place for their inverse revelations of the present. In *The Black Book* (1990; trans. 1994, 2006) and *The New Life* (1994; trans. 1998), he charts urban topographies of a self-divided and self-alienated contemporary Istanbul, a city whose inhabitants have become lost to themselves in the labyrinth of modernity and must therefore seek new meaning by excavating their and their city's past. In *Snow* (2002; trans. 2004), he examines Islam in contemporary Turkey more explicitly than ever before, bringing his historical awareness to bear on questions of Islamic revivalism as this has impacted Turkish politics, society, and culture in recent years. And in *The Museum of Innocence* (2008; trans. 2009)—both a novel and an actual museum Pamuk established in Beyoğlu, Istanbul in 2012—he constructs what is in effect an antimuseum of the 1970s–1980s Istanbul occupied not by monuments of national history, but rather by throwaway personal artifacts as indicative of a social and cultural life in transition. This is a rich literary landscape indeed, not yet exhausted by the foregoing thematic survey.[12] Within it, I focus on *The Black Book*. This is because this novel comprises a reflexive literary engagement with the history of modernity, religion, and secularism in Turkey, and thus offers special insight into the scope and essence of Pamuk's project as a whole.

The Black Book, Pamuk's opus of 1990, is a novel ostensibly about Galip, a Westernized lawyer living in Istanbul, and his search for his mysteriously disappeared wife and first cousin Rüya through the backstreets and alleyways of the city. Galip soon realizes that Rüya has likely taken up with his cousin and her half-brother Celâl, a columnist for the daily newspaper *Milliyet*. His search for his wife thus also becomes a search for Celâl. So Galip reads through the thirty-year archive of Celâl's columns, which are reproduced verbatim in chapters alternating with Galip's narrative, seeking clues as to their whereabouts. These have a pronounced impact. They touch in highly literate, self-conscious, and almost Benjaminian ways on Istanbul's and Turkey's cultural history, including their archaeologies, architectures, arts, fashions, people, politics, philosophies, and religions. They initially have the effect of forcing Galip to question his (constructed) Westernized identity, leading to a profound psychological break. Then, through the mystical Sufi doctrine of Hurufism to which they expose him, they prompt him to develop a new interpretive paradigm that allows him, for the first time, fully to read the signs of his city as well as his own historically mediated place within it, his identity. This discovery is simultaneous with that of his vocation as a writer very much in the mode of his (absent) mentor Celâl—indeed, he becomes Celâl's, and Pamuk's, double. It turns out, then, that the novel's apparently simple thematic premise was all along a device for exploring Turkish cultural identity, the traumas resultant from the Kemalist repression of the Ottoman, Islamic heritage during the republican era of modernization and secularization in the 1920–1930s, and the formation of new identity positions that revive or memorialize that past culturally rather than politically.

The Black Book has been translated into English twice, by Güneli Gün in 1994 and by Maureen Freely in 2006. Although my emphasis here will be on the Anglo-American critical reception of *The Black Book* as a work of world literature, it is important to briefly mention the logic behind the respectively foreignizing and domesticating strategies these translations have employed. This is because as Galip digs deeper into his and his city's cultural history, Pamuk—in one of many formal correlatives to Galip's identity quest—increasingly turns in his use of language to the very Arabic and Persian loanwords that had been supplanted by modern Turkish equivalents during the period of language reform. Exhuming such forgotten remnants of the past, he thus layers his text with a subtle commentary on and intervention into the linguistic dimensions of Turkish secular modernity via his use of language. Clearly, it is not possible to articulate either the word-for-word analogue or the wider cultural-historical significance of Pamuk's usage in translation, no matter the strategy attempted—such usage is "Untranslatable" in more senses than one. Gün's foreignizing resolution consists of her unusual sentence constructs, her literal replication of idioms, and, most relevant here, her appeal to synonyms rooted in Greek, Latin, and German rather than in Anglo-Saxon to mirror in English Pamuk's reference to Arabic and Persian loanwords in Turkish.[13] Freely, however, abandons in her domesticating approach any semblance of an English rendering of Pamuk's usage, opting instead for a clean and fluent contemporary English directed more toward his thematic and narrative content (as complex as this is in itself) than on his impossible-to-translate use of language.[14] I will reserve judgment on these strategies at this time, and rather note *The Black Book* as a particularly vivid case study of the loss of the significations that accumulate around language when a text enters the world through translation.

Since its appearance in translation, the Anglo-American critical establishment has nigh-universally understood and presented *The Black Book* in terms of its purportedly "postmodernist" aesthetic. From the *London Review of Books* to *World Literature Today*, reviewers have branded Pamuk's text a "metaphysical thriller," a "Borgesian labyrinth," a "Post-Modern detective novel," a "postmodern metanarrative," an "'Eastern' and 'Western' intertext," a "Borgesian Encyclopedia," and so forth.[15] It should be noted that there has been a little more variety in approach among the scholarly readings, especially those of Turkish critics, and that a degree of critical emphasis has indeed been placed there on the novel's urban setting and Sufi themes in addition to its postmodernism.[16] These readings have, though, mostly proceeding in the same vein, implicitly or explicitly brought the ideological implications of Pamuk's categorization as a "postmodernist" to the fore. For Walter Andrews, *The Black Book* projects a generic (Western) "postmodern condition" as elaborated by the likes of Jean-François Lyotard, Fredric Jameson, and Linda Hutcheon, and—characteristic of its type—"leaves one suspended over the abyss of undecidability" by the end (Andrews 2000, 108, 109–10).[17] For Ian Almond, the novel delves more substantially into Islamic themes than elsewhere assumed, yet nevertheless closes on familiar postmodernist grounds where the myths of personal, national, and religious identity are conclusively deconstructed, where—as Galip is supposed to have discovered by the climax of his narrative—"the secret of our identity is precisely that we have none" (Almond 2003, 81).[18] One would be hard-pressed to locate a serious scholarly reading that disputes or offers a substantial alternative to such accounts of *The Black Book*'s postmodernism.

What we see in the critical reception of Pamuk's text-in-translation is, then, one of the mechanisms-in-action by which world literature assimilates its non-European other according to formal and ideological parameters predefined by world literature's self-constitution in modernity. In this case, *The Black Book* can and must only be read through the lens of postmodernism, as otherwise it might disrupt our dominant narrative of the novel's modern aesthetic evolution. This formal imperative of world literary reception ties neatly in here with one of its key ideological imperatives, in that postmodernist readings compel secular interpretations. Pamuk can and must only be read as a secularist who deconstructs the religious myths in which his compatriots are mired not only for political reasons—though these are of course important—but moreover because the worlding of Middle Eastern literature is, as we have seen, premised on and made possible by the separation of literature and religion. The translational approach to *The Black Book* I have proposed does not stop short at this point, though, where world literature is shown to consolidate and reproduce itself via, again, the negation of Islam, or at least via the critical neglect of Pamuk's nuanced and reflexive engagement with Islam in the context of Turkish modernity. Through its doubly refractive vocation, the approach proposed here also allows for a counterreading of such world literary reception.

The Black Book (II): A Translational Counterreading

Pamuk has himself invited the sort of counterreading I will now pursue. In contrast to those who frame him as an unquestioning advocate of Turkish secular modernity, he, in his famous *Paris Review* interview of 2005, has made clear his qualms with this project and with the generation of Kemalist statesmen who enacted it. As he explains,

> I'm not mourning the Ottoman Empire. I'm a Westernizer. I'm pleased that the Westernization process took place. I'm just criticizing the limited way in which the ruling elite—meaning both the bureaucracy and the new rich—had conceived of Westernization. They lacked the confidence necessary to

create a national culture rich in its own symbols and rituals. They did not strive to create an Istanbul culture that would be an organic combination of East and West; they just put Western and Eastern things together. There was, of course, a strong local Ottoman culture, but that was fading away little by little. What they had to do, and could not possibly do enough, was invent a strong local culture, which would be a *combination*—not an imitation—of the Eastern past and the Western present. (Pamuk, "Interview: Orhan Pamuk," 132)[19]

"I try," he tellingly concludes this passage, "to do the same kind of thing in my books" ("Interview: Orhan Pamuk," 132).[20] How he does so in *The Black Book*, how he brings about a "combination" of "the Eastern past and the Western present," hinges on his treatment of the Sufi and Hurufi sects of Shi'a Islam, their history in Turkey and their afterlives after the founding of the modern and secular Turkish Republic in 1923 ("Interview: Orhan Pamuk," 132). For this, I turn to part two of the novel, the first part of which is largely dedicated to the collapse of Galip's Westernized identity after the disappearance of his wife.

Early on in part two, bringing to culmination a discussion of the varied historical figures that have scattered his columns, Celâl quizzically asks his readers, "Have you seen all these faces? Have you noticed that, in some strange way, they all look alike?" (Pamuk 2006, 269).[21] He then announces a new focus for his investigations into Turkish cultural history, a project for which the reader of *The Black Book* has been prepared by Celâl's previous columns, and which is consequently taken up by Galip and by the novel itself: "From now on I shall devote myself utterly to the hidden poetry of our faces, the terrifying secret that lurks inside our human gaze. So be prepared" (Pamuk 2006, 269). In the immediately following chapter, number 24 ("Riddles in Faces"), Galip, now living in Celâl's abandoned apartment in Nişantaşi seeking clues to his cousin's whereabouts, takes this cue and starts attempting to decipher the faces in Celâl's vast, thirty-year collection of yearbooks, photograph albums, and newspaper clippings. Although Galip vaguely senses in the faces "a melancholy that Celâl had expressed so often in his columns," "a story heavy with terror and memory," they quickly close up to him, becoming "as anonymous as the physical descriptions on identity cards: random arrangements of noses, eyes, and mouths" (Pamuk 2006, 281, 280, 282–83). At this dark moment when, feeling "the indifference of a man who has been divested of his memories, his hopes, his very future," for whom "life had nothing more to offer," Galip turns again to Celâl's archive for guidance, this time to his cousin's "books, treatises, and clippings on Hurufism" (Pamuk 2006, 293, 294). This is because Hurufism, an obscure Sufi sect whose central doctrine of "the mystery of letters" Galip had earlier encountered in passing, promises significant new insight into "the meanings in faces" (Pamuk 2006, 293).

The Hurufi sect, as Galip discovers, was founded by one Fazlallah of Astarabad (or Fażlu l-Lāh Astar-Ābādī), a fourteenth-century Persian mystic who, after a late adolescent spiritual awakening prompted by a nomadic dervish's recitation of Rumi, abandoned his duties as a judge, his family, and his hometown to follow the Sufi path as an itinerant religious seeker. During his travels, which saw him make Haj to Mecca twice before temporarily settling in Isfahan in central Iran, he experienced a series of richly symbolic and prophetic dreams about figures like Solomon, Jesus, and Muhammad. In one such dream, which Pamuk makes sure to mention, he was visited by a dervish who later actually appears, claiming that he had dreamt Fazlallah also. During the actual visit, Fazlallah and the dervish sat together leafing through a book and "saw their faces in the letters," then, on looking up, "saw the letters of the book in each other's faces" (Pamuk 2006, 297). Proclaiming himself a prophet, Fazlallah accumulated a following of seven disciples in Isfahan, and set off to preach that, in Pamuk's words, "the world [. . .] was awash with secrets and that the only way to penetrate these secrets was to penetrate the mystery of the letters" (Pamuk 2006, 298).[22]

For Fazlallah, as H. T. Norris explains in *The Heritage of Sufism* (1999), "the key to open the seven[th] sealed book, the Quran, is a cabalistic system of letters that is expounded, by him, or by others, in the *Hidāyat-nāma*, the *Jāwidān*, and in the *Mahram-nāma*"—the key texts of the Hurufi tradition (Norris 1999, 92). The face of God—immutable, imperishable—is, Norris continues, manifest in man, "the best of forms—*zuhūr kibriyā*," and is exactly replicated in the face of Adam (1999, 92). Further, the twenty-eight letters of the Arabic alphabet—the language revealed to Muhammad—and the thirty-two letters of the Persian alphabet—that revealed to Fazlallah (thus requiring him to account for four extra letters in the face)—are hidden in the face of man. Our two brow lines, four eyelash lines, and one hairline account for seven letters which, at the onset of puberty when, in Pamuk's gloss, our "late-arriving" nose divides the face in two, are then doubled (Pamuk 2006, 297). Taking into account several "real and imaginary lines," this number is doubled again, providing for twenty-eight letters in the face, a number corresponding exactly and not coincidentally to Muhammad's twenty-eight Arabic letters and to the number of God's attributes as revealed in the Quran (2006, 297). Thus divine truth—or God—can, in a sort of hyperliteralization of Emmanuel Levinas, be witnessed through the proper, esoteric interpretation of the letters in the face. For Fazlallah, the divine light shines through the face of man in the form of letters, and this comprises their mystery.

As one might expect given his worship of "letters, people, and idols instead of God," as well as his self-identification as the new Messiah, Fazlallah was imprisoned, sentenced, and executed for heresy at the behest of the Miran Shah in Alinja, a town in what is now Azerbaijan, circa 1394/1395 (Pamuk 2006, 298). Under the new leadership of the poet Nesimi (or Alī 'Imādu d-Dīn Nasīmī), his followers, feeling increasingly persecuted in Iran, emigrated to the momentarily less hostile climate of Anatolia, where their ideas took root and began to spread throughout the villages and towns of the Ottoman heartland. Their most significant influence was on the Bektaşi Order, a Shi'a Alevi Sufi order that, founded in the thirteenth century, was already widespread in Anatolia and the Balkans and continued to prosper among the Ottoman elites and peasantry alike until it was banned by Sultan Mahmud II in 1826 due to the objections of Sunni and more orthodox Sufi religious leaders. Although the Bektaşis enjoyed a brief public and popular resurgence during the Tanzimat, or reformation, period of the Ottoman Empire in the mid-nineteenth century, they, like the Hurufis and the larger and more prestigious Nakşibendi and Mevlevi orders, were dealt a final blow soon after the founding of the Republic of Turkey in 1923. After an initial attempt to incorporate the Sufi orders into the Republic by placing them under the administration of the newly established Ministry of Religious Affairs (which ensured their continued social and legal life while stripping them of genuine political participation—a form of laicism), the Kemalists, taken aback by the Sheikh Said rebellion of February 1925, were forced to take more drastic measures and formally abolished the orders later in the same year. The Sufi orders were thus driven underground, where many maintained a sizable following and continued to function in what Turkish cultural historian Esra Özyürek calls a "public secret" fashion for much of the twentieth century (Özyürek 2007). Only recently have they begun to experience something of a resurgence of public presence under the revivalist or accommodationist policies of former Prime Minister and now President Recep Tayyip Erdoğan and his *Adalet ve Kalkınma Partisi*.[23]

To round off his readings of Celâl's materials on the Hurufis, Galip stumbles upon a treatise, published in 1962, by the unknown (and fictional) author F. M.

Üçüncü, titled *The Mystery of the Letters and the Loss of Mystery*. In this treatise, Üçüncü, after providing an account of Fazlallah, goes on to describe how "the world was divided into two opposing halves" and that "the East and the West were as different from each other as good and evil, white and black, the angels and the devils" (Pamuk 2006, 303–4). Drawing on the evidence of great historical events such as Alexander cutting the Gordian knot, the Crusades, Hannibal's passage across the Alps, the Islamic victories in Andalucía, and Mehmet the Conqueror's triumphant entry into Constantinople, "the winning side" in any historical period, Üçüncü argues, "was the one that succeeded in seeing the world as a mysterious place awash with secret and double meanings" (2006, 304). Given that Hurufism—which provided the means to see mystery—had "vanished from the earth" at the onset of Turkey's Republican era, "the world," he continues, "had lost its mystery, just as our faces had lost their letters" (2006, 305). Üçüncü is thus revealed as the actual identity of Mehmet, an Islamic Revivalist who harangues Galip masquerading as Celâl in a series of increasingly frenetic and threatening phone calls throughout part two. He calls for a revival of Hurufism in Turkey to redress the woeful historical defeat of the East: "it was on Turkish soil that the Messiah who would become the saviour of all the East would make His appearance, and it therefore followed that, in preparation for that day, if they were to recover the lost mystery, His future followers should begin by establishing correspondences between faces and the new Latin alphabet that Turkey adopted in 1928" (Pamuk 2006, 317). Pamuk's stance on such an endeavor is well-indicated by the manipulation of the "mystery of the letters." A Turkish Hurufism would imply further modification, since the Latin alphabet has only twenty-six letters, after the twenty-eight Arabic letters of the Quran had been modified by Fazlallah into thirty-two to suit the needs of his native Persian. This extra twist seems a reductio ad absurdum on the author's part.

It has been important to dwell momentarily on Üçüncü's treatise in order to highlight a key polarity Pamuk devotes much of part two to delineating—that between Mehmet/Üçüncü and Celâl/Galip. On the one hand, Üçüncü's reading of Turkey's modernity leads him to demand, in effect, an Islamic revolution founded on a revival of Hurufi mystery—a form of *political* neo-Ottoman revivalism. On the other, Galip's reading of the history and theories of Hurufism provides him the means of entry into his own hitherto repressed cultural identity, the key to interpreting "the letters in his face," a development simultaneous with and foundational to his discovery of writing as vocation (2006, 321). Realizing at this precise moment in the narrative that *Milliyet* had already reprinted all of Celâl's previously published columns during his absence, Galip, having seen that "his face was a sheet of paper covered in writing, an inscription riddled with secret signs," "wrote" (Pamuk 2006, 322, 325). Channelling Celâl, he writes the first of a series of columns which, reproduced verbatim in the following chapter, is then published under his cousin's name and which continues and extends Celâl's project. He opens this first column with the words, "*I gazed into the mirror and read my face*" (2006, 326, 344). This opening signifies Galip's adoption of Hurufism not just as a means of reading his identity, but also, as with Pamuk, as a content to be inscribed in the form of writing (as opposed to that of direct political engagement), and thus revived or memorialized culturally under the amnesiac conditions of Turkish modernity. In other words, the content of Galip's column, thus overlapping with that of *The Black Book* itself, signifies what I call an aesthetic of *cultural* neo-Ottoman revivalism. As Galip puts it in the novel's closing chapter (chapter thirty-six, "But I Who Write"), when he finally becomes the first person and narrator of his own narrative, "writing," "writing," "writing" is "the only consolation" for the losses of Rüya and Celâl, for those wrought by history (Pamuk 2006, 461).

Conclusion

As I hope to have shown, *The Black Book* traces in its narrative and its form, not the deconstruction of coherent identity positions, but rather the *bildung* of a new identity based on the cultural memorialization of a heritage otherwise lost to the inexorable drive of Turkish secular modernity. This specifically Islamic heritage is lost also on critical readings that seek to frame Pamuk for world literature. Through the translational counterreading I have pursued, *The Black Book* might thus be said to dramatize and expose the dialectical logic by which Islam is negated in world literature. In the process, this reading has opened up a new understanding of the novel's form in terms of cultural neo-Ottoman revivalism, an understanding that more faithfully encompasses Pamuk's reflexive literary negotiation of modernity, religion, and secularism in Turkey. If we are to continue inquiring into Islam in the theory and practice of world literature, then we would be well served to follow a translational model that instills the critical interrogation of categories like "modernity," "religion," "secularism," "world," and even "literature" in its very remit.

Notes

1. For her discussion of the allocation of literary value in the centers of the world literary system, see especially Casanova, *The World Republic of Letters*, 82–125.

2. For a useful overview of the definition and evolution of "*adab*" in early Arabic-Islamic culture, see Roger Allen, *The Arabic Literary Heritage: The Development of Its Genres and Criticism* (Cambridge: Cambridge University Press, 1998), 218–78.

3. Aamir Mufti, "Orientalism and the Institution of World Literatures," *Critical Inquiry* 36, no. 3 (2010): 461, 464–65.

4. As readers familiar with his work will note, I have relied here on Mufti's article of 2010 rather than his more recent book to elucidate his argument about the role of philological orientalism in the formation of world literature. This is because the article provides a condensed (and quotable) summation of arguments and themes pursued across the length of *Forget English!* For further detail on his understanding of the relationship between philology, Orientalism, and the history of world literature, see especially Aamir Mufti, *Forget English!: Orientalisms and World Literatures* (Cambridge, MA: Harvard University Press, 2016), 3–35, 56–145.

5. For a canonical critique of Rushdie's cosmopolitan and dehistoricizing approach to Islam, see Timothy Brennen, *Salman Rushdie and the Third World: Myths of the Nation* (London: Palgrave Macmillan, 1989).

6. See, for example, Françoise Lionnet and Shu-mei Shih, eds., *Minor Transnationalism* (Durham, NC: Duke University Press, 2005); Waïl Hassan, "Arabic and the Paradigms of Comparison," in *ACLA Report on the State of the Discipline 2014–2015*, Ursula Heise, et al., eds.; Andreas Huyssen, ed., *Other Cities, Other Worlds: Urban Imaginaries in a Globalizing Age* (Durham, NC: Duke University Press, 2008); and Rob Wilson and Wimal Dissanayake, eds., *Global/Local: Cultural Production and the Transnational Imaginary* (Durham, NC: Duke University Press, 1996).

7. See Lawrence Venuti, *The Translator's Invisibility: A History of Translation* (London: Routledge: 1995); Lawrence Venuti, *The Scandals of Translation: Towards an Ethics of Difference* (London: Routledge, 1998); David Damrosch, *What is World Literature?* (Princeton, NJ: Princeton University Press, 2003); and Emily Apter, *Against World Literature: On the Politics of Untranslatability* (London and New York: Verso, 2013).

8. For a historical overview of Kemalist policies of modernization and secularization during the early years of the Republic of Turkey, see Erik Zürcher, *Turkey: A Modern History* (London: I. B. Tauris, 2004).

9. For a detailed discussion of the politics, practices, and institutions of language reform in the early years of the Republic of Turkey, see Geoffrey Lewis, *The Turkish Language Reform: A Catastrophic Success* (Oxford: Oxford University Press, 1999).

10. For a more detailed discussion of the development of the Turkish novel in relation to the policies, practices, and ideologies of Turkish state-formation in the twentieth century, see Azade Seyhan, *Tales of Crossed Destinies: The Modern Turkish Novel in a Comparative Context* (New York: The Modern Language Association of America, 2008).

11. Ahmet Hamdi Tanpınar is a mid-twentieth-century Turkish novelist whose literary reflections on the cultural losses wrought by enforced modernization and secularization in Turkey were a pivotal influence on Pamuk and his writing. See especially Ahmet Hamdi Tanpınar, *A Mind at Peace*, trans. Erdag Göknar (New York: Archipelago Books, 2011) and Ahmet Hamdi Tanpınar, *The Time Regulation Institute*, trans. Maureen Freely and Alexander Dawe (New York: Penguin Books, 2013). For Pamuk on Tanpınar's influence, see Orhan Pamuk, *Istanbul: Memories and the City*, trans. Maureen Freely (London: Faber and Faber, 2005), 97–104, 221–38.

12. Pamuk's other novels include *Cevdet Bey and His Sons* (1982), *The Silent House* (1983), *A Strangeness in My Mind* (2014), and *The Red-Haired Woman* (2016).

13. For detailed discussions of Gün's foreignizing translation, see Klaus Gommlich and Esim Erdim, "Evolving Imagery in the Translation of Orhan Pamuk's *Kara Kitap*," *Across Languages and Cultures* 2, no. 2 (2001) and Sevinc Turkkan, "Orhan Pamuk's *Kara Kitap*: (British) Reception vs. (American) Translation," *Making Connections* (Spring 2010).

14. For a detailed discussion of Freely's domesticating translation, see Karim Mattar, "Orhan Pamuk and the Limits of Translation: Foreignizing *The Black Book* for World Literature," *Translation and Literature* 23, no. 1 (2014).

15. See Bill Marx, "Two Worlds: Turkey's East-West Tensions Spin Out Narrative Arabesques," *Boston Phoenix* March 20, 1994; Charlotte Innes, "Istanbul Expressed," *The Nation* 260, no. 12 (1995); Patrick Parrinder, "Mannequin-Maker: *The Black Book* by Orhan Pamuk," *London Review of Books* 17, no. 19 (1995); Walter Andrews, "The Black Book and Black Boxes: Orhan Pamuk's *Kara Kitap*," *Edebiyât: The Journal of Middle Eastern Literatures* 11, no. 1 (2000); Erdağ Göknar, "Orhan Pamuk and the 'Ottoman' Theme," *World Literature Today* 80, no. 6 (2006); and Seyhan, *Tales of Crossed Destinies*.

16. For readings of *The Black Book*'s urban setting, see Enis Batur, "Orhan Pamuk'un Dükkâni," in Nüket Esen, ed., *Kara Kitap Üzerine Yazılar* (Istanbul: Can Yayınlari, 1992) and Seyhan, *Tales of Crossed Destinies*. For readings of the novel's Sufi themes, see Sooyong Kim, "Mürşid ile Mürid: *Kara Kitap*'i Bir Yorumlama Çerçevesi Olarak Tasavvuf," in Nüket Esen, ed., *Kara Kitap Üzerine Yazılar* (Istanbul: Can Yayınlari, 1996); Ian Almond, "Islam, Melancholy, and Sad, Concrete Minarets: The Futility of Narratives in Orhan Pamuk's *The Black Book*," *New Literary History* 34, no. 1 2003); and Brent Brendemoen, "Orhan Pamuk and His 'Black Book'" (2007), http://www.orhanpamuk.net/popuppage.aspx?id=75&lng=eng.

17. Andrews, "*The Black Book* and Black Boxes," 108, 109–10.

18. For a more detailed discussion of Andrews's and Almond's readings, see Mattar, "Orhan Pamuk and the Limits of Translation."

19. Italics mine.

20. Pamuk, "Interview: Orhan Pamuk," 132.

21. Pamuk, *The Black Book* (2006), 269. I rely on Freely's translation for citations from *The Black Book* throughout the following analysis, given what I describe above as her translatorial deployment of a fluent and accessible English.

22. Pamuk, *The Black Book* (2006), 298. For more detail on the life of Fazlallah, see Shahzad Bashir, *Fazlallah Astarabadi and the Hurufis* (London: Oneworld Publications, 2005).

23. For an introduction to the fate of the various Sufi orders in Turkey in the twentieth century, see Ahmet Yükleyen, "Sufism and Islamic groups in Contemporary Turkey," in Reşat Kasaba, ed., *The Cambridge History of Turkey: Volume 4, Turkey in the Modern World* (Cambridge: Cambridge University Press, 2008). For a more detailed anthropological analysis of the practices of the Sufi orders, especially the Nakşibendi order, across the Ottoman, Republican, and contemporary eras, see Brian Silverstein, "Sufism and Modernity in Turkey: From the Authenticity of Experience to the Practice of Discipline," in Martin van Bruinessen and Julia Day Howell, eds., *Sufism and the 'Modern' in Islam* (London: I. B. Tauris, 2007). For discussions of the circulation of Sufi themes, practices, and poetics in, respectively, the post/classical Islamic world and the contemporary Middle Eastern novel, see Al-Musawi, *The Medieval Islamic Republic of Letters*, 245–304 and Ziad Elmarsafy, *Sufism in the Contemporary Arabic Novel* (Edinburgh: Edinburgh University Press, 2014).

Works Cited

Ahmed, Rehana. 2012. *Culture, Diaspora, and Modernity in Muslim Writing*, edited by P. Morey and A. Yaqin. London and New York: Routledge.

———. 2015. *Writing British Muslims: Religion, Class and Multiculturalism*. Manchester, UK: Manchester University Press.

Allen, Roger. 1998. *The Arabic Literary Heritage: The Development of its Genres and Criticism*. Cambridge, UK: Cambridge University Press.

Almond, Ian. 2003. "Islam, Melancholy, and Sad, Concrete Minarets: The Futility of Narratives in Orhan Pamuks *The Black Book*." *New Literary History* 34, no. 1: 75–90.

Andrews, Walter. 2000. "The Black Book and Black Boxes: Orhan Pamuk's *Kara Kitap*." *Edebiyât: The Journal of Middle Eastern Literatures* 11, no. 1: 105–29.

Apter, Emily. 2013. *Against World Literature: On the Politics of Untranslatability*. London and New York: Verso.

Bashir Shahzad. 2005. *Fazlallah Astarabadi and the Hurufis*. London: Oneworld Publications.

Batur, Enis. 1992. "Orhan Pamuk'Un Dükkâni." In *Kara Kitap Üzerine Yazilar*, edited by Nüket Esen. Istanbul, Turkey: Can Yayinlari.

Brendemoen, Brent. 2007. "Orhan Pamuk and His 'Black Book.'" *Orhan Pamuk Site*.
Brennan, Timothy. 1989. *Salman Rushdie and the Third World: Myths of the Nation*. London: Palgrave Macmillan.
Casanova, Pascale. 2004. *The World Republic of Letters*, translated by M. B. DeBevoise. Cambridge., MA: Harvard University Press.
Chambers, Claire. 2011. *British Muslim Fictions: Interviews with Contemporary Writers*. London: Palgrave Macmillan.
Damrosch, David. 2003. *What Is World Literature?* Princeton, NJ: Princeton University Press.
Elmarsafy, Ziad. 2014. *Sufism in the Contemporary Arabic Novel*. Edinburgh, Scotland: Edinburgh University Press.
Göknar, Erdağ. 2006. "Orhan Pamuk and the 'Ottoman' Theme." *World Literature Today* 80, no. 6: 34–38.
Gommlich, Klaus, and Esim Erdim. 2001. "Evolving Imagery in the Translation of Orhan Pamuk's *Kara Kitap*." *Across Languages and Cultures* 2, no. 2: 237–49.
Hassan, Waïl. "Arabic and the Paradigms of Comparison," edited by Ursula Heise, Dudley Andrew, Alexander Beecroft, Jessica Berman, David Damrosch, Guillermina De Ferrari, César Domínguez, Barbara Harlow, and Eric Hayot. *ACLA Report on the State of the Discipline 2014–2015*.
Huyssen, Andreas, ed. 2008. *Other Cities, Other Worlds: Urban Imaginaries in a Globalizing Age*. Durham, NC: Duke University Press.
Innes, Charlotte. 1995. "Istanbul Expressed." *The Nation* 260, no. 12: 245–48.
Kim, Sooyong. 1996. "Mürşid ile Mürid: *Kara Kitap*'i Bir Yorumlama Çerçevesi Olarak Tasavvuf," edited by Nüket Esen. *Kara Kitap Üzerine Yazilar*. Istanbul, Turkey: Can Yayinlari.
Lewis, Geoffrey. 1999. *The Turkish Language Reform: A Catastrophic Success*. Oxford, UK: Oxford University Press.
Lionnet, Françoise, and Shu-mei Shih, eds. 2005. *Minor Transnationalism*. Durham, NC: Duke University Press.
Marx, Bill. "Two Worlds: Turkey's East-West Tensions Spin Out Narrative Arabesques." *Boston Phoenix*. March 20, 1994.
Mattar, Karim. 2014. "Orhan Pamuk and the Limits of Translation: Foreignizing *The Black Book* for World Literature." *Translation and Literature* 23, no. 1: 42–67.
Moore, Lindsey. 2008. *Arab, Muslim, Woman: Voice and Vision in Postcolonial Literature and Film*. London: Routledge.
Morey, Peter, and Amina Yaqin. 2011. *Framing Muslims Stereotyping and Representation after 9/11*. Cambridge, MA: Harvard University Press.
Mufti, Aamir. 2016. *Forget English!: Orientalisms and World Literatures*. Cambridge, MA: Harvard University Press.

———. 2010. "Orientalism and the Institution of World Literatures." *Critical Inquiry* 36, no. 3: 458–93.

Mūsawī Muḥsin Ǧāsim ʿAlī al-. 2015. *Medieval Islamic Republic of Letters: Arabic Knowledge Construction*. Notre Dame, IN: University of Notre Dame Press.

Norris, H. T. 1999. "The Ḥurūfī Legacy of Faḍlullāh of Astarābad." In *The Heritage of Sufism: Legacy of Medieval Persian Sufism (1150–1500)*. Vol. 2, edited by L. Lewisohn. London: Oneworld Publications.

Özyürek Esra. 2007. *The Politics of Public Memory in Turkey*. Syracuse, NY: Syracuse University Press.

Orhan Pamuk. 1994. *The Black Book*, translated by Güneli Gün. San Diego, CA: Harcourt.

———. 2005. *The Black Book*, translated by Maureen Freely. London: Vintage.

———. 2005. "Interview: Orhan Pamuk, The Art of Fiction No. 187." *Paris Review* 47, no. 175: 115–41.

———. 2005. *Istanbul: Memories and the City*, translated by Maureen Freely. London: Faber & Faber.

———. 2010. *The Museum of Innocence*, translated by Maureen Freely. London: Vintage.

———. 2002. *My Name is Red*, translated by Erdağ Göknar. London: Vintage.

———. 1998. *The New Life*, translated by Güneli Gün. London: Vintage.

———. 2005. *Snow*, translated by Maureen Freely. London: Vintage.

———. 1998. *The White Castle*, translated by Victoria Holbrook. London: Vintage.

Parrinder, Patrick. 1995 "Mannequin-Maker: *The Black Book* by Orhan Pamuk." *London Review of Books* 17, no. 19: 22.

Redhouse, J. W. 1884. *A Turkish and English Lexicon: Shewing in English the Significations of the Turkish Terms*, part I. Constantinople, Turkey: A. H. Boyajian.

Sacks, Jeffrey. 2015. *Iterations of Loss: Mutilation and Aesthetic Form, al-Shidyaq to Darwish*. New York: Fordham University Press.

Seyhan, Azade. 2008. *Tales of Crossed Destinies: The Modern Turkish Novel in a Comparative Context*. New York: Modern Language Association of America.

Silverstein, Brian. 2007. "Sufism and Modernity in Turkey: From the Authenticity of Experience to the Practice of Discipline." In *Sufism and the 'Modern' in Islam*, edited by Martin van Bruinessen and Julia Day Howell. London: I. B. Tauris.

Tanpınar, Ahmet Hamdi. 2011. *A Mind at Peace*, translated by Erdağ Göknar. New York: Archipelago Books.

———. 2013. *The Time Regulation Institute*, translated by Maureen Freely and Alexander Dawe. New York: Penguin Books.

Turkkan, Sevinc. 2010. "Orhan Pamuk's *Kara Kitap*: (British) Reception vs. (American) Translation." *Making Connections* (Spring): 39–58.

Venuti, Lawrence. 1998. *The Scandals of Translation: Towards an Ethics of Difference*. London: Routledge.

———. 1995. *The Translator's Invisibility: A History of Translation*. London: Routledge.
Wilson, Rob, and Wimal Dissanayake, eds. 1996. *Global/Local: Cultural Production and the Transnational Imaginary.* Durham, NC: Duke University Press.
Yükleyen, Ahmet. 2008. "Sufism and Islamic groups in Contemporary Turkey." In *The Cambridge History of Turkey: Volume 4, Turkey in the Modern World*, edited by Reşat Kasaba. Cambridge, MA: Cambridge University Press.
Zürcher, Erik. 2004. *Turkey: A Modern History.* London: I. B. Tauris.

Chapter 5

Selective Invisibility

Elizabeth Bishop, Carlos Drummond de Andrade, and World Literature

Luiza Franco Moreira

> [A]nd though I had sold my Estate in the *Brasils*, yet I could not keep the Country out of my Head.
>
> —*Robinson Crusoe*

Elizabeth Bishop's "Crusoe in England" provides a useful vantage point for exploring the perspectives opened up by the category of world literature, together with the difficulties that the category exposes. "Crusoe in England" has been widely interpreted as Bishop's reflection on the fifteen years or more that she lived in Brazil (Millier 1993, 447; Hicok 2016, 1–3; Martins 2006, 35). During this period Bishop successfully pursued her career as an American poet: she published two collections of poetry, *Poems: North and South: A Cold Spring* (1955) and *Questions of Travel* (1965), and received the 1956 Pulitzer prize for the first one. But "Crusoe in England" is a poem from a later stage in her career. It is included in her last collection, *Geography III*, which appeared in 1976, a few years before her death in 1979, and after she had again settled back in the United States. (For a chronology of the composition of the poem, see Millier 1993, 446.) In this dramatic monologue, an old Robinson Crusoe looks back on his travels. The focus falls on the years he spent on a desert island and on his attraction to and affection for Friday. The parallels between the poem's speaker and Bishop's situation in the 1970s are evident. Like the Crusoe of her poem, Bishop had sold her house in Ouro Preto—her "Estate in the *Brasils*"—and had returned to the United States. By laying some stress on the erotic side of Crusoe's love for Friday—the speaker remarks that "he had a pretty body"—Bishop indirectly refers to her own lesbian sexuality, and perhaps even, as many critics have suggested, to her Brazilian lover, Lota de Macedo Soares, with whom she lived for most of her time in the country (Millier 1993, 449; Martins 2006, 35).

World literature—taken here as a perspective concerned with the literary relationship between writers who work in languages or traditions that seem widely separated—brings to light further layers of complexity in "Crusoe in England." This angle of vision directs our attention to Bishop's enduring engagement with Brazilian Modernism. It enables us to recover not only her dialogue with the poet Carlos Drummond de Andrade (1902–1987) but, more interestingly, the importance of this literary relationship for the composition of "Crusoe in England." Bishop translated an early and influential poem by Drummond, "Infância" (Childhood), which likewise relies on an allusion to *Robinson Crusoe*. By reading her "Crusoe in England" together with Drummond's "Infância" and one of the later prose pieces by the Brazilian writer, this chapter explores the complex irony of Bishop's poem, but also the divergent ways in which the two writers rework Defoe's novel. The discussion of Bishop's relationship to Drummond raises the problem of the ways in which current conceptualizations of world literature may both help and hinder its apprehension.

This chapter regards world literature as a *perspective*, instead of seeking to grasp it positively and systematically. It argues that the point of view of world literature is especially productive when it makes us aware of how much we don't know, so as to bring to light new problems for comparative literary scholarship. Drummond's work remains, even now, largely unfamiliar to an English-language audience; as a result, Bishop's nuanced, complex, and fruitful engagement with his poetry easily escapes notice. Yet all the information needed to establish the links between the two poets is widely available in Bishop's *Complete Poems*. Such a pattern of selective invisibility is all too familiar to scholars who work in the American academy with literary languages that appear to be of lesser prestige, or that are, in any case, less commonly taught.

The overall shape of the argument in this chapter is inferential. It begins by exploring the relationship that Bishop establishes to Drummond (which includes at least one thought-provoking omission), and proceeds to examine some of the systematic accounts of world literature that have been proposed in recent years. Pascale Casanova has stressed the constitutive role that inequalities of prestige play in the modern literary world; David Damrosch has proposed that we understand world literature as a detached and active mode of reading across diverse languages and cultures; Alexander Beecroft has identified six complex systems of literary circulation, relying on ecology as a metaphor, while Walter Cohen has offered a broad historical narrative grounded on the varying relationship between literary language and spoken languages. The hidden-in-plain-sight character of Bishop's relationship to Drummond provides the starting point for the discussion of these critical constructions. As we will see, these accounts all prove helpful in exploring Bishop's relationship to Drummond, but only up to a point. More often than not, they also work to obscure the relationship between the two poets, either through an explicit emphasis on the structuring power of the major literary languages, or through a tacit bias for translations into English.

The shift in approach that I am suggesting—to take world literature as a perspective for inquiry rather than to propose a model for world literature—is inspired by the work of historical social scientists concerned with world systems studies. Immanuel Wallerstein has consistently argued that world-systems analysis is a perspective rather than a theory (Wallerstein 1976, 345). In a tightly argued methodological essay, Terence Hopkins has examined the implications of the "angle of vision" of the modern world-system for the ways that social scientists select problems and construct explanations. It seems pertinent to specify here that for Wallerstein and Hopkins the world system is the singular, historically specific "complex of spatio-temporal processes" encompassing the social relations of capitalism (Hopkins 1978, 212).

In contrast to the approach of the historical social scientists mentioned above, my argument does not go as far as to suggest a shape, however provisional, for the literary relations that constitute world literature. Rather, this approach at once recognizes the structuring power of the major literary languages and works punctually against it. It looks for the points of convergence that allow us to see through the prestige of the major languages in order to explore their relationship to traditions and texts that at first seem quite remote. In our example, "Crusoe in England" serves as one such vantage point, by affording a perspective that enables us to retrace Bishop's relationship to Drummond, and to Brazilian Modernism more generally.

The inferential structure of my argument is indebted to an essay on historical method by Carlo Ginzburg, "Clues: Roots of an Evidential Paradigm." Ginzburg argues for the importance of the "conjectural or semiotic paradigm," contrasting it to the ambitions of "systematic thought." Although a complex structure "such as fully developed capitalism" is obscured by "ideological clouds" and may seem inaccessible, Ginzburg maintains that "there are privileged zones—signs, clues—which allow us to penetrate" its apparent opacity (Ginzburg 1992, 123). Bishop's "Crusoe in England" serves here as one such clue, helping dissolve some of the clouds that obscure the reach of world literary relationships.

This chapter will consider a variety of texts to explore Bishop's engagement with Carlos Drummond de Andrade. It will start with a discussion of her interviews, and proceed to consider texts that are increasingly closer to Bishop's poetic practice: her translations and, finally, the poem "Crusoe in England." Bishop's interviews in the period when she was working on her translations betray significant gaps in her knowledge of the material; beyond that, her comments at times betray an impatient tone, somewhere between defensiveness and condescension, which has long proved disconcerting to readers familiar with Brazilian poetry. However, we will see that the closer the focus of discussion moves to Bishop's practice as a poet, the more the relationship that she establishes to Drummond's work appears characterized by complexity, insight, and acceptance.

I

Bishop's interviews from the mid-sixties are revealing about the poet herself, her background, standards, and preferences, but they do not offer much insight into the Brazilian poets that she was the translating at the time. Bishop betrays, instead, a surprising lack of familiarity with Brazilian *Modernismo*, an innovative vanguard movement that began in the 1920 and succeeded in changing the literary norms in the country.[1] Her interview with Ashley Brown for *Shenandoah* in 1966 is a case in point.[2] (Reproduced in Bishop 1996 *Conversations*.) It appeared shortly before *Questions of Travel* was published and ten years before "Crusoe in England" came to be included in *Geography III*.

Brown led Bishop to reflect on her career and its contexts from the 1930s on; he repeatedly asked about the importance that Brazil, Brazilian literature, and the

Portuguese language had for her. The question of whether she could "draw on the social and literary traditions" of Brazil receives a long and meandering answer. But Bishop concludes with a firm denial.

> To summarize: I just happened to come here, and I am influenced by Brazil certainly, but I am a completely American poet, nevertheless. (Bishop 1996 *Conversations*, 19)

The standard against which Bishop measures Brazilian poetry is provided by poetry in English: "Our poetry went off in a different direction much earlier." This claim elicits a follow-up question from Ashley Brown.

> **Interviewer:** When you say our poetry went in a different direction, what do you mean?
>
> **Miss Bishop:** What happened to Eliot and Pound as early as 1910—modernism. The Brazilians' poetry is still more formal than ours—it's farther from the demotic. It's true, of course, that they had a *modernismo* movement in 1922, led by Mario de Andrade and others. But they still don't write the way they speak. And I suppose that they have still never escaped from romanticism. (Bishop 1996 *Conversations*, 19)

This answer apparently assumes a normal course for the development of poetry. Bishop's insistent repetition of the adverb "still"—three times in a short answer—suggests that Brazilian poetry had not quite reached the same level of development as American poetry. The reference to Brazilian Modernism is cursory and offered nearly like a concession. It is difficult to tell if Bishop is familiar with the names of any Modernist writers besides Mário de Andrade, or if she has read them. (It is also disconcerting to note that Bishop implies that Eliot and Pound "write the way they speak.")

Bishop's denials persist when she is asked about her relationship as a poet to Portuguese: "I don't read it habitually—just newspapers and some books." Bishop's incomprehension is especially clear when she attempts to describe Brazilian Portuguese as a poetic language.

From *our* point of view, it seems cumbersome—you just can't use colloquial speech in that way. Grammatically, it is a very difficult language. Even well educated Brazilians worry about writing their own language; they don't speak their grammar, as it were. I imagine it's easier to write free verse in Portuguese—because it gets you away from the problem. They did take to free verse very quickly here. (Bishop 1996 *Conversations*, 20)

It is difficult to fit these remarks into a single, coherent picture. If Bishop considers the colloquial register "cumbersome"—perhaps ineffective or perhaps inappropriate—then why does she also claim that Brazilian poetry has remained "more formal than ours" and has "never escaped from romanticism"? Her comments sound impatient and nearly dismissive, particularly when the poet remarks that free verse is likely "easier to write in Portuguese." Here, and throughout the interview, Bishop focuses on what she expected to find but didn't; she does not seek to understand, on its own terms, the work of Brazilian poets. Not only are her views consistent with a "completely American" perspective; often enough they appear to shade into uncomprehending judgment.

Bishop's comments about colloquial speech are particularly disconcerting to a reader familiar with Brazilian Modernist poetry. We find this surprise articulated by Paulo Henriques Britto, a critic and poet, but also the authoritative editor and translator of Bishop's poetry and prose for a Brazilian audience. Britto discusses Bishop's interview with Brown in the introductory essay for *Poemas do Brasil*, an anthology of her poetry that he edited and translated. Britto stresses his surprise that Bishop, who is a reader and translator of Carlos Drummond de Andrade and João Cabral de Mello Neto, could form the opinion that colloquial Portuguese is incompatible with formal poetic structures (Bishop *Conversations* 1996, 20; Bishop *O Iceberg* 2001, 42). The writers that Britto mentions, Drummond and Cabral, are recognized as some of the most important poets of the twentieth century, indebted both to Brazilian Modernism. As Britto suggests, they are admired for their use of the colloquial register in texts that quite often—though by no means always—adhere to the verse conventions of the Portuguese tradition.

Historians of Brazilian literature have long called attention to the interest of Modernist writers in the colloquial register. In their influential anthology *Presença da literatura brasileira*, Antonio Candido and J. Aderaldo Castello discuss the Modernists' experimentation with the colloquial and its importance for their ambitious project to change what was acceptable in literary language.

From a stylistic point of view, [the Modernists] advocated the rejection of [European] Portuguese norms, searching for a more colloquial form of expression, closer to the Brazilian way of speaking. (Candido 1968, 10)

Such experiments were pursued by a number of diverse writers over a fairly long period; the process was not linear, neither were all the attempts successful. Some early Modernist writers sought to draw from the varieties of oral language spoken all through the territory of Brazil and in the event produced work that was, and remains, nearly impenetrable; several writers managed only uneasy compromises between the nineteenth-century norms for cultivated written language and Brazilian idiom. Carlos Drummond de Andrade is one of a small number who succeeded in creating new ways of writing that are clear, articulate, and subtle, yet do not appear artificial or pretentious to a Brazilian readership. As a result of these efforts, which started nearly 100 years ago, Brazilians can now work with a written language that is closer to the speech and syntactical patterns of the Portuguese spoken in their country. Probably because Bishop was never quite comfortable with Portuguese, and specifically not with everyday spoken Brazilian Portuguese, in this interview she appears unable to grasp or do justice to the achievements of her contemporaries in Brazil, the Modernist writers who reshaped literary language through their work, among other things, with the colloquial register.

II

Neither Bishop's opinions nor her tone suggest that she worked tirelessly, and for years to make Brazilian poetry and literature better known in the United States, or that the conversation with Brown is itself a part of the effort. Bishop approaches her work as translator above all as a poet: she translates texts that have some affinity with her own poetic concerns, while the diction and voice of the translations are recognizably her own. She effectively reinterprets Brazilian Modernism in the terms of her own poetry. The poems and translations that result from this effort are remarkable and quite rewarding in their own right; they have no doubt achieved the goal of making Brazilian poetry better known to a more international audience.

However, if we expand the focus of our attention beyond Bishop's achievement in order to consider the relation of her translations to Brazilian Modernist poetry, a different picture takes shape. The language of Bishop's translations is more standard in syntax and diction than that of Brazilian poets. Her translations draw attention away from the more polemical and vanguardist side of their work. Only readers who know the material will see the way that Bishop's translations modulate Brazilian Modernism; those who count simply on Bishop's translations to approach this body poetry will be unable to appreciate either the risks that the writers took with literary language or their achievement in innovating it. Bishop's translations of Drummond fall into a further, thought-provoking pattern. Drummond's poetry of the 1940s and 1950s, and his prose as well, consistently reflect on the poet's sympathy for the Soviet Union and his subsequent disillusionment. Bishop steers clear from the poems devoted to political themes. Such a choice cannot help but seem frustratingly partial to those who are familiar with Drummond's overall trajectory. This section will focus on Bishop's modulation of Drummond's poetry as a translator, while the topic of what she failed to translate will come to the foreground later, in the discussion of Drummond's treatment of the Crusoe motif in a later prose text.

Bishop's earliest translations of Brazilian poetry were published in 1963, a few years before the 1966 interview with Ashley Brown. The interview follows the publication in the spring 1965 issue of the same journal, *Shenandoah*, of selections of Brazilian poetry and prose translated by Bishop, Brown, and Helen Cauldwell. Bishop contributed to this issue translations of two poems by Carlos Drummond de Andrade, "Seven-Sided Poem" and "Don't Kill Yourself." Nearly ten years later, in 1972, she succeeded in publishing through Wesleyan University Press a bilingual anthology of twentieth-century Brazilian poetry, which included many of her own translations together with translations by other well-known poets. In the intervening years, Bishop steadily published translations of Brazilian poetry, in journals such as *Shenandoah* and *The Kenyon Review*, but very often also in mass circulation periodicals like the *New Yorker*, *The New Republic*, the *New York Review of Books*, and even the *New York Times Magazine* (MacMahon 1980). These translations, along with translations from several other languages, are included in the edition of her *Complete Poems*, a sign that Bishop considers her work as a literary translator integral to her own poetry.

The context of Bishop's *Complete Poems* brings to light suggestive affinities between her poetry and the translations from the Portuguese. Themes that concern Bishop recur in the translations. Drummond's "The Table," "Family Portrait," and "Infancy" are explorations of family and loss, as are the two poems by Joaquim Cardozo, "Cemetery of Childhood" and "Elegy for Maria Alves," while the certainty of loss lies in the background of Manuel Bandeira's "My Last Poem." There is an evident affinity between Bishop's "The Burglar of Babylon" and "The Death and Life of a Severino," an excerpt from João Cabral de Melo Neto's verse narrative of rural migration during a severe drought. Cabral's poem is composed in a meter that is at once very old and characteristic of popular poetry, the *redondilha maior* (or the seven-syllable line). This prosodic choice seems analogous to Bishop's use of the ballad form in "Burglar." Her cruelly descriptive poems about poverty in Brazil find echoes both in Cabral's work and in Manuel Bandeira's prose poem, "Brazilian Tragedy." The irreverent, often unsettling humor of the Brazilian Modernists seems continuous at times with Bishop's own sense of the absurd. A case in point is "In the Middle of the Road," her translation of Drummond's sarcastic avant-garde improvisation on the opening line of Dante's *Inferno*, which the Brazilian poet unceremoniously combines with language from a Parnassian, quite formal sonnet by the Brazilian Olavo Bilac, "Nel mezzo del camin." Rendered in Bishop's precise diction and spare, elegant language, these translations of Brazilian Modernist poets read very well in English.

Nevertheless, scholars of Brazilian literature have fairly often expressed reservations about Bishop's translations. Paulo Henriques Britto, for instance, notes that the quality of her translations "is in general not what we would expect from such a remarkable poet" (Bishop 1999, 39). In part—but only in part—such reservations are the inevitable result of the movement of the texts from one context to another—from Brazilian Modernism to Bishop's "completely American" poetry. Her translation of Drummond's "Infância," a poem directly relevant for the discussion of "Crusoe in England," helps illustrate this point. Drummond's "Infância" holds considerable authority in Brazil. It is the second poem of his earliest collection, *Alguma poesia* (Some Poetry, 1930), which is a landmark of the Brazilian Modernist movement. The poem announces themes that were to occupy him all through his career, such as his family and their past as traditional, wealthy landowners in the rural region of Minas Gerais. Beyond that, the poem has been discussed by numerous influential critics since it was first published. Bishop's translation cannot help but extract this text from a dense literary, critical, and broadly cultural network, where it occupies a central position, in order to introduce it into a wholly new context, where it will be largely unknown. Itamar Ben-Zohar's discussion of the hierarchical relations in the literary polysystem sheds light on the varying levels of prestige held by Drummond's poem and its translation by Bishop: while "Infância" is "central" to Brazilian Modernism, Bishop's "Infancy" remains "peripheral" to American poetry (Even-Zohar 2012, 193). In such circumstances, any discrepancy between Bishop's translation and the source text will likely be taken as a disproportionate loss by those who are familiar with Drummond's poetry and have long admired it.

Yet Bishop's translation of "Infância" has been criticized quite pointedly, in ways that go beyond such general uneasiness (Burns 2002). Tom Burns notes two significant discrepancies, one lexical and the other syntactical, between "Infância" and its translation by Bishop. The first discrepancy lies in the title. A more recent translation by Richard Zenith renders it more accurately as "Childhood," instead of "Infancy"[3] (Andrade 2015, 7). The second, syntactical discrepancy deserves to be examined closely, since it calls attention to some ways in which the translation softens the most experimental aspects of the poem.

The speaker of Drummond's "Infância" recalls the experience of reading *Robinson Crusoe* as a boy, in his family home, not far from his mother and infant brother. The simplicity of the style imitates a child's language and helps establish the boy's perspective. A series of simple sentences and a few nominal ones, joined together by parataxis, suffice to describe the domestic scene. Drummond's reliance on parataxis also exemplifies the Modernists' experimentation with literary language: It is a fair illustration of their effort to move away from nineteenth-century rhetorical conventions, which relied heavily on hypotaxis. Bishop's translation takes away some of the edge of the poem by moving it away from parataxis.

This claim may be illustrated by considering Drummond's poem together with Bishop's and Zenith's translations.

Infancia

by Carlos Drummond de Andrade

Meu pai montava a cavalo, ia para o campo.
Minha mãe ficava sentada cosendo.
Meu irmão pequeno dormia.
Eu sozinho menino entre mangueiras
lia a história de Robinson Crusoé,   5
comprida história que não acaba mais.

No meio-dia branco de luz uma voz que aprendeu
a ninar nos longes da senzala—e nunca se esqueceu
chamava para o café.
Café preto que nem a preta velha   10

café gostoso
café bom.

Minha mãe ficava sentada cosendo
olhando para mim:
—Psiu . . . não acorde o menino.
Para o berço onde pousou um mosquito.
E dava um suspiro . . . que fundo!

Lá longe meu pai campeava
no mato sem fim da fazenda.

E eu não sabia que minha história
era mais bonita que a de Robinson Crusoe.

Infancy

translated by Elizabeth Bishop

My father got on his horse and went to the field.
My mother stayed sitting and sewing.
My little brother slept.
A small boy alone under the mango trees,
I read the story of Robinson Crusoe,
the long story that never comes to an end.

At noon, white with light, a voice that had learned
lullabies long ago in the slave quarters—and never forgot—
called us for coffee.
Coffee blacker than the black old woman
delicious coffee
good coffee.

My mother stayed sitting and sewing
watching me:
Sh—don't wake the boy.
She stopped the cradle when a mosquito had lit
and gave a sigh . . . how deep!

Away off there my father went riding
through the farm's endless wastes.

And I didn't know that my story   20
was prettier than that of Robinson Crusoe.

(Bishop 1974, 86)

CHILDHOOD

translation by Richard Zenith

My father rode off on his horse to the fields.
My mother sat in a chair and sewed.
My little brother slept.
And I, on my own among mango trees,
read the story of Robinson Crusoe.   5
A long story that never ends.

In the white light of noon, a voice that learned lullabies
in shanties from the slave days and never forgot them
called us for coffee.
Coffee as black as the old black maid,   10
pungent coffee,
good coffee.

My mother, still sitting there sewing,
looked at me:
"Shhh . . . don't wake the baby."   15
Then at the cradle where a mosquito had landed.
She uttered a sigh . . . how deep!

Far away my father was riding
in the ranch's endless pastures.

And I didn't know that my story   20
was more beautiful than Robinson Crusoe's.

(Andrade 2015, 7)

It is worth remarking on the poem's diction at the start, however briefly. For a reader familiar with idiomatic Brazilian Portuguese, the preference of the Modernists for colloquial language is evident on line 10: "Café preto que nem a preta velha" (Coffee as black as the old black maid). The poet uses the informal and familiar phrase *que nem* ("as," in Zenith's translation). This phrase has the same meaning as the standard conjunction *como*, yet it is not, even now, acceptable in Brazil's standard written language; it does work well in this poem, however, because the expression is characteristic of a child's speech and helps characterize Drummond's speaker.

The syntactical discrepancy that Burns notes occurs on line 16, when Bishop's translation transforms a nominal sentence into a complete one. She translates *para*, a preposition equivalent to "to," as if it were a verb form, the past tense of the verb *parar* (to stop). A literal translation of line 16, "Para o berço onde pousou o mosquito," reads, "To the cradle where the mosquito has touched down," yet Bishop translates, "She stopped the cradle where a mosquito has lit." The translator silently normalizes Drummond's syntax, by introducing a verb that is absent from the source text. We cannot rule out that Bishop simply decided to correct a line that seemed too much like a sentence fragment. At the same time, perhaps a translation that remained closer to Drummond's text would not work well in a poem in English. Zenith finds a roundabout solution to the problem. By relying on parallelism, his translation calls attention to an implicit verb, *look at*, without directly using it: "Then [looked] at the cradle where a mosquito had landed."

The implications of Bishop's normalizing translation deserve to be explored. Bishop's text does not afford English readers an insight into Drummond's linguistic experimentation, or into his achievements either—for instance, when the poet brings an extremely colloquial phrase such as *que nem* into the poem without a distracting effect. On the other hand, Bishop's translation reads well. It is fluent. Lawrence Venuti has questioned the value placed on fluency in translation, arguing that this linguistic effect is implicated in concealing the work of the translator, rendering her invisible. In the terms of Venutti's argument, Bishop may be seen as a domesticating translator, who chooses to smooth out Drummond's poetry in order to make it more accessible to an audience in the United States.

However, although Bishop may seem invisible as a translator, she is remarkably visible as a poet. Her translation is consistent, above all, with the more standard and neutral register of Bishop's own poetry. As Justin Read has suggested, translation, or mistranslation, serves "as the means through which Bishop asserts her own personality" (Read 2003, 318). At this point of the discussion, her translation of "Infância" affords a retrospective insight into the opinions Bishop voiced in her 1966 interview with Ashley Brown. The comment that Brazilian critics have found so objectionable—"you just can't use colloquial speech in that way"—may be understood more as an expression of the translator's frustration than as a clear-cut judgment on Brazilian poetry. Her remark points to a significant problem that Bishop must have encountered as a translator. It must have been a considerable challenge to translate the use of the colloquial register by Brazilian Modernists and at the same time write poems that would read well in the context of Bishop's own poetry or, more generally, in the context of the work of an American poet of her generation and background.

In her translation of Drummond's "Infância," Bishop at once explores a theme that is important to her own work and confronts the challenge that the distinctive traits of Brazilian Modernism pose to her style. Although "Infancy" is a resonant text in the context of her poetry, when we consider the relation between the translation and Drummond's poem, it becomes clear that Bishop modulates his text by bringing it closer to the standard register that prevails in her own work. Even if this process of reelaboration seems characteristic of the way a poet would approach the work of translating another, Bishop effectively softens the vanguardist edge that Drummond's poem has in Portuguese.[4]

This discussion has followed a double pattern: at the same time as it recognizes Bishop's achievement as a translator, it calls attention to the nuanced, not altogether accepting relationship that her translation establishes to Drummond's source poem in Portuguese. The category of world literature is especially helpful, I suggest, when it leads us to search for perspectives that bring into focus the complexity of literary relationships such as the one Bishop sustains with Drummond. As we will see, although the two poets seem widely separated in terms of language and literary tradition, Bishop's approach to Drummond's poetry proved especially fruitful for the composition of "Crusoe in England."

III

In this farewell poem to Brazil, Bishop again engages with Drummond's work and adapts it to her own purposes. "Crusoe in England" evokes an image of Brazil by taking up a motif that has a similar resonance in Drummond's work—Defoe's *Robinson Crusoe*—yet develops the allusion in a different direction. Drummond sidesteps the novel's colonial outlook. Bishop meanwhile voices the prejudice and violence of colonialism through the speaker, even as her dramatic monologue draws attention, through irony, to the limits of Crusoe's perspective. Bishop further relies on this poetic form to integrate the colloquial register into the poem: she takes up a distinctive poetic strategy of Brazilian Modernism and contains it at the same time, treating the colloquial as no more than an element in the characterization of the speaker. Here, Bishop enacts a dialogue that recognizes the originality of Brazilian poets and at the same time marks the distance between her work and theirs. This chapter argues that, from the point of view of a discussion of "Crusoe in England," the perspective of world literature again helps bring into focus the complex ways in which Bishop's poetry engages with Drummond's.

This argument builds on Maria Lúcia Milléo Martins's discussion of "Infância" and "Crusoe in England," in her groundbreaking comparative work, *Duas Artes*. Martins has argued that both Drummond and Bishop rely on the figure of the island to establish lyric subjectivity and at the same time explore the poet's relationship to a wider world. In the background of her analysis lies an influential reading of Drummond's "Infância" by Silviano Santiago, who sees in this early poem a key moment in the constitution of the poet's subjectivity.

We see Bishop's relationship to Drummond from a new angle, I suggest, if we consider the ways that each of the two poets reworks *Robinson Crusoe*. Crusoe's adventures unfold in the historically recognizable world of European expansion. Through their allusions, the two poets evoke the area and period in which the novel develops, together with its outlook and morals, but also its characters, with their motivations and beliefs. More specifically, Drummond's and Bishop's references betray a parallel concern with a space that plays an important role in the novel, even though it is less in evidence than the desert island—"the Brasils."

The allusion to Brazil is more evident in Bishop's poem. Her dramatic monologue is set in the period when Crusoe, his travels and adventures over, is back in England, living in comfort. A reader of the novel will recall that the character's affluence is the direct result of his long-term business dealings in Brazil. Although neither Bishop nor Drummond mentions it directly, all the while that Crusoe had been living in his desert island, he had been the owner of a profitable "Plantation in *the Brasils*." However, he finds himself penniless when he returns to England: there is "nothing to relieve, or assist" him, because Robinson had been "long given over for dead," and his family had made "no Provision" for him (Defoe 1994, 201). The closing pages of the novel are devoted to his efforts to remedy the unhappy situation. These passages give a detailed account of the voyages, transactions, and legal measures that allowed Crusoe not only to recover the profit that his sugar plantation had made while he was away, but also eventually to sell the entire property in land and, that goes without saying, slaves. By focusing on this final moment of Crusoe's trajectory, Bishop ironically places her speaker in the position of the colonizer who has made his fortune from the commercial exploitation, specifically, of a slave plantation in Brazil. As Bishop once stressed in an interview, Crusoe was "really awful" (Bishop 1996, 88).

In Drummond's "Infância" the allusion to *Robinson Crusoe* likewise evokes the background image of a large rural estate in Brazil, but from a contrasting perspective. It will be clear to a Brazilian reader that the quiet domestic scene that the poet describes takes place in a country property. Short though the poem is, it paints a vivid picture of the social, gender, and racial hierarchies in the young reader's family. The father owns the horse that he rides out on and implicitly the land as well; it is a workday routine for him to visit his property on horseback. The mother is tied to the space of the home in a way that the father is not, and something must be weighing on her, or she wouldn't be sighing so deeply. The picture of a family from the traditional Brazilian elite is completed by the affectionate and markedly racialized language describing the old black woman, the *preta velha*, who had once lived *nos longes da senzala*, or in the faraway slave quarters.

In contrast to Bishop, Drummond strives to depict Brazilian landowners in the perspective of family intimacy, exploring conflicts and bonds from the inside. Not only do the closing lines of "Infância" affirm his claim to poetic voice; they announce a theme that will prove of central importance to Drummond's poetry as a whole. Those who are familiar with his work will recognize the theme of the patriarchal family of the traditional Brazilian elite, which will concern Drummond throughout his career: "I didn't know that my story / was more beautiful than Crusoe's." A seminal essay by Antonio Candido has explored in detail the poet's conflicted treatment of "the extraordinary power of the family group," and in particular his depiction of the "devouring patriarch" (Candido 1995, 144; see also Coelho 1973).

Neither *Crusoe*'s colonial outlook nor the prejudices of its protagonist are relevant to the way "Infância" reworks the intertext. Drummond establishes, instead, a competitive relationship directly with the author, Defoe, by asserting that the *história* he has to tell is *mais bonita* than Crusoe's, literally "more beautiful," but with a wider positive connotation—more attractive, more interesting, better. The poet neatly sets aside here the exoticism that is so prevalent in the novel. Yet the line resonates further still, since the *história* that the poet claims as his own is at once a "story" and "history." Drummond implicitly calls here for a history constructed from a different, *mais bonita*, and perhaps better perspective than Defoe's.[5]

Elizabeth Bishop, in contrast, has the protagonist of Defoe's novel serve the crucial function of speaker in her dramatic monologue. Unlike Drummond, whose speaker is firmly rooted in traditional Brazilian society, Bishop imagines a traveler who belongs neither in the island nor in the estates he owned, and implicitly not even in England. By focusing attention on Crusoe's prejudices and colonial background, this approach opens the way for much of the poem's irony.

Helen Vendler's comments on a recurrent structure in Bishop's poetry offers a productive perspective for retracing the irony of "Crusoe in England." Vendler notes that a "compelled dark triad" repeatedly brings together the exotic, the fantastic, and death in Bishop's poetry. In "Crusoe in England," this complex is given "full imaginative play" twice. The first instance is an actual death scene. "Crusoe's hands fantastically 'dye' a baby goat bright red" with the result that his mother no longer recognizes him and, Vendler infers, the "undernourished" baby goat dies. The other death scene is a dream in which Crusoe kills a human baby, after mistaking it for a baby goat (Vendler 2002, 31). Defoe's novel, for its part, insistently pairs two out of the three elements in Bishop's triad, the exotic and death. By bringing the fantastic in as a third element, Bishop alters the relationship between the other two terms, opening up a wide and unsettling perspective on the intertext.

The close relationship between the exotic and death is very evident in the passages of *Robinson Crusoe* that describe the protagonist's obsessive dreams of killing "Canibals" and "Savages." Before Friday appears, Crusoe has a series of near and increasingly closer encounters with indigenous people: he sees a footprint in the sand, then he finds the remains of a fire, together with "Skulls, Hands, Feet, and other Bones of humane Bodies"; finally, he observes cannibalism from a distance, through a looking glass (Defoe 1994, 112–34). Each episode is followed by a long period of overwhelming fear—"Apprehension," "Frights and Terror"—in which Crusoe finds himself in "the Murthering humor" and ceaselessly makes plans to "destroy some of these Monsters." At night he dreams about it.

> [A]nd then [I] propos'd, that I would place myself in Ambush, in some convenient Place, with my three Guns, all double loaded; and in the middle of their bloody Ceremony, let fly at them, when I should be sure to kill or

wound perhaps two or three at ever shoot; and then following upon them with my three Pistols, and my Sword, I made no doubt, but that if there was twenty I should kill them all: This Fancy pleas'd my Thoughts for some Weeks, and I was so full of it, that I often dream'd of it; and sometimes that I was just going to let fly at them in my Sleep. (Defoe 1994, 122)

The exotic indigenous people appear here as "Canibals," at the same time as the European, alone in the exotic island, responds to their presence with fantasies of murder. In this passage as in many others in the novel, murdering violence defines the characters of the stranded Englishman and the native inhabitants alike, and further frames their relationship.

The figure of the cannibal, nearly a commonplace of the discourse of European expansion into the Americas, takes shape in Defoe's novel as a modulation of the exotic as murderous. Bishop's retelling of Crusoe's dream of murder is obscenely violent, yet very funny at the same time.

But then I'd dream of things
like slitting a baby's throat, mistaking it
for a baby goat. I'd have
nightmares of other islands (ll. 131–34)

The internal rhyme "throat/goat" is at once unexpected and obvious. It is hard not to laugh. Bishop brings to the foreground and undermines, all at the same time, the exoticism, violence, and colonial outlook of the Defoe intertext. My comments here find a parallel in Kim Fortuny's argument about Bishop's use of the techniques of comedy to mock "the colonial enterprise" in this poem (Fortuny 2003, 85).

Bishop's ironic treatment of the character she borrows from Defoe is especially evident in the detailed descriptions of the island's "flora," "fauna," and "geography" seen from his perspective. This lengthy passage takes up most of the eight initial stanzas of the poem; it reads like a parodic, nightmarish inventory of the motifs of tropical exoticism. The turtles and goats borrowed from Defoe's novel recur insistently, and together with them an accumulation of motifs evoking the nature of the tropics: volcanoes, waves, clouds, rain, folds of lava, tree snails, gulls, water spouts. Fantastically, "sometimes the whole place hissed," with large, heavy, grotesque turtles that sound "like teakettles." By the end of this descriptive passage, immediately after Robinson recounts his murderous dream, the islands themselves appear multiplied and distorted, absurdly proliferating into infinity.

> [. . .] I'd have
> nightmares of other islands
> stretching away from mine, infinities
> of islands, islands spawning islands,
> like frog eggs turning into polliwogs
> of islands [. . .] (ll. 134–38)

Although Crusoe stresses the strangeness of the scene from the beginning, his tone becomes increasingly impatient as the poem develops, until the lines just quoted, when he reaches the high point of a crescendo of exasperation. (The new stanza that begins after this passage breaks the pattern of multiplicative description and takes the poem into a different direction: "Just when I thought I couldn't stand it / another minute longer, Friday came.")

The absurdist tenor of Bishop's portrayal of Crusoe's island brings to mind a memorable passage on the strangeness of nature in Albert Camus' "The Myth of Sisyphus." At the start of his essay on the difficulty and joy of living in a world lacking the illusion of transcendent meaning, Camus explores "the feeling of absurdity." One of his examples is the sudden, unexpected awareness that nature is dense and foreign to us—in a passage that reads nearly as if Bishop had glossed it in this poem: "these hills, the softness of the sky, the outline of these trees at this very minute lose the illusory meaning with which we had clothed them, henceforth more remote than a lost paradise" (Camus 1975, 14).

The reference to "The Myth of Sisyphus" is useful in calling attention to a theme that remains half-hidden in "Crusoe in England" but that offers, nonetheless, one of the keys to the construction of the poem: that of the meaning of Crusoe's experience on the tropical island. Although the treatment of the exotic as absurd occupies the foreground and takes up most of the space, a few passages of Crusoe's speech suggest that there was more to the time he spent on the island. In the first stanza, introducing his "un-rediscovered, unrenamable island," Crusoe stresses that "none of the books has ever got it right." The motif reappears later, when Crusoe moves beyond the description of the strange island to the recollection of his joyful life with Friday: "Accounts of that have everything all wrong."

Through the contrast between these brief asides and the lengthy descriptions of the island, the poem adds depth to Crusoe's story, suggesting that something about the experience goes beyond what he is able to put into words, and further beyond the stories that the "books" and "accounts" have been able to tell.

The suggestion that all along there was more to what Crusoe could say reappears in the coda of the last two stanzas, in a passage that directly brings up the topic of the meaning of his experience. After an abrupt shift from Crusoe's recollections to his present, the poem develops an image from Defoe's novel, the knife that had been essential to the survival of the protagonist.

> [. . .] I'm old.
> I'm bored too, sipping my real tea,
> surrounded by uninteresting lumber.
> The knife there on the shelf—
> it reeked of meaning, like a crucifix.
> It lived. How many years did I
> beg it, implore it not to break?
> I knew each nick and scratch by heart,
> the bluish blade, the broken tip,
> the lines of wood-grain on the handle . . .
> Now it won't look at me at all.
> The living soul has dribbled away.
> My eyes rest on it and pass on. (ll. 159–70)

The poem establishes here a series of overlapping contrasts: past and present; England and tropical island; old age and youth; on the one hand, uninteresting lumber, tea, and a knife "there on the shelf," while on the other, a knife that had "reeked of meaning" and had had "a living soul." The existential implications of Bishop's enduring interest in travel come to the fore. Camus' Sisyphus lets go of hope for the future and passionately struggles to live in "the present and the succession of presents" of the world (Camus 1975, 63). In contrast, Bishop's Crusoe is quite bored by his static and uninteresting present in England, but has found meaning in the past, even if he and all others remain unable to articulate it.

The creation of this inarticulate speaker is key to the construction of "Crusoe in England": this formal element enables the full play of the poem's irony. By creating a Crusoe who is at once loquacious and massively uncomprehending, Bishop opens up new perspectives on the Defoe intertext. At the same time, the poem makes it clear that Crusoe's perspective does not define him entirely. Bishop suggests the overwhelming depth of the speaker's experience on the island and with Friday by contrasting his lengthy speech to some quiet, mostly brief asides that hint at what he cannot quite put into words. The overall effect of the poem hinges on a Crusoe whose speech betrays more than he realizes, but who at the same time remains unable to express or maybe even grasp the meaning of his time on the island.

Accordingly, the voice of the speaker is informal throughout the poem, and often quite rough: Crusoe's island is "a sort of cloud-dump"; the noise of goats, seagulls, and turtles, he remembers, "got on my nerves," while "dreams were the worst." Even as the informal language is consistent with Defoe's character, in the light of Bishop's engagement with Drummond another aspect of the speaker comes to the fore: the voice of the old Crusoe integrates the colloquial register into this poem. We may discern in Bishop's adoption of this composition technique a poet's homage to Drummond, perhaps even more generally to Brazilian Modernism as a whole. Nevertheless, despite her reliance on colloquial diction, "Crusoe in England" is a reserved and elegant poem; it is precise and polished, and all the more unsettling for that. The form of the dramatic monologue allows Bishop to take some distance from Drummond and keep the colloquial register contained thereby. Again in this instance, the poet reinterprets Drummond's work in the terms of her own poetry.

A fundamental contrast in the relationship that Drummond and Bishop establish to Defoe's novel becomes clear as a result of this discussion. In "Crusoe in England," Bishop retains the perspective of the colonizer even as she makes it the focus of the poem's irony. In contrast, Drummond's "Infância" is lightly and thoroughly dismissive of both Defoe's story and the outlook of his protagonist.

This reading of "Crusoe in England" in the light of Bishop's relationship to Drummond's poetry offers, finally, some insights into the limits of the category of world literature. Bishop's enduring and thoughtful engagement with Drummond's work has largely escaped the attention of critics working in English. It is not difficult to grasp what motivates such a blank in scholarship. There is a language barrier to consider, first of all. Drummond writes in a language that is unfamiliar to students of Bishop's works; in addition, only a portion of his poetry is available in translation in English or any other major European language. Beyond that, it seems necessary to call attention to the differences in literary prestige between English and Brazilian Portuguese. The significance of Drummond's poetry for Bishop does not appear as self-evident to an English-language audience. In contrast, the same audience will easily identify and explore the links between Bishop's poem and Defoe's novel—even as it fails to see that Drummond mediates Bishop's approach to *Crusoe*. The discussion of Bishop's relationship to Drummond brings to light, at this point, an inequality of literary prestige that is constitutive of the field of world literature. It further shows the profound effect that disparities such as this may have in directing critical approaches to comparative analysis.

IV

In the 1950s, Carlos Drummond de Andrade had a Sunday column in *Correio da Manhã*, one of the most important newspapers in Rio de Janeiro. By then, he had more than established his reputation as a poet; he was also recognized as an influential Left intellectual. Drummond generally published short prose pieces, or *crônicas*, in this Sunday column. This was the context of the initial publication of "Divagações sobre a ilha" (Digressions on the island), a text in which the poet describes himself as a *pequeno Robinson moderno*—a "little modern Robinson"— because of his escapist fantasy of living in an island. This *crônica* was later to become the opening piece of a prose anthology published in 1952; it also suggested the title for the collection, "Passeios na Ilha," or *Walking around the Island* (Andrade 1952). This contextual information is useful to show that Drummond's reworking of motifs from *Robinson Crusoe* circulated widely in Brazil in the 1950s; Bishop, who began living in Rio de Janeiro in 1951, is likely to have been familiar with this aspect of his work, and in particular with this text, which was quite well-known then and remains so even now.

The *crônica* "Divagações sobre a ilha" implicitly reflects on the poet's conflicted relationship to Communism. Brazilians know well that during World War II Drummond was sympathetic to the Soviet Union: he wrote pro-Soviet poetry, publishing it at times in Communist-leaning journals, but at times also in mass circulation newspapers that varied in their political tendency. In 1945, he published a collection of poetry, *A Rosa do Povo* (The People's Rose), in which he included poems on the war and political themes, together with several other topics. This book is widely taken to illustrate Drummond's achievement in writing poetry that at once exemplifies political commitment and questions the project of committed literature (Simon 1978). In addition, the poet served on the editorial board of a Communist newspaper, *Tribuna Popular* (Popular Tribune), and regularly contributed to it

(Segatto 1982, 77). However, Drummond soon stopped sending his work to this newspaper, and he broke with the Brazilian Communist Party in October 1945. Years later, in 1951, Drummond published another major collection of poetry, *Claro Enigma* (Clear Enigma), which has been widely interpreted as a reflection on political disillusionment (Camilo 2001).[6]

The prose collection that cites Defoe's novel, *Passeios na ilha* (Walking around the Island), was published shortly after *Claro enigma* (1951). Brazilian critic Vagner Camilo has carefully reconstructed Drummond's break with Communism and the attacks that the poet suffered from the Party in its aftermath. Camilo has argued that this context sheds light on the transformation in Drummond's between the 1945 and the 1951 collections of poetry. For this critic, the Communist Party is the "evident addressee" of the *crônica* in which Drummond cites *Crusoe*, "Divagações sobre a ilha" (Digressions on the island). Camilo further shows that this prose text is key to understanding Drummond's movement away from the poetics of commitment in the 1945 collection *A rosa do povo* and toward his "new attitude"—pessimistic and disillusioned—in the 1951 collection *Claro enigma* (Camilo 2001, 92–93).

"Divagações sobre a ilha" is a brief, conversational, and digressive journalistic piece; it may be easily enjoyed as a piece of light Sunday reading. Yet the poet's quarrel with the Communist Party is never far from the surface.[7] The *crônica* revolves around the poet's fantasy of one day buying an island. This conceit opens the way for Drummond to examine the claims for commitment made by those who "seek the center of action itself," balancing them against the natural human tendency of appreciating "the grace of unaffected gestures, the cultivation of spontaneous forms, the pleasure of being one with animals, plant species, and atmospheric phenomena." Drummond takes a good-humored distance from Defoe's novel. By stressing that he does not want encounters with animals that challenge men's "strength and fear," he alludes to the mostly tame turtles, goats, and fowl of Crusoe's island. At the same time, pointedly departing from Crusoe's exclusively Christian reading habits, Drummond stresses that he will allow "neither the Bible nor vinyl" in his fantasy. He proceeds to stress that, despite Plato's interdiction, poets are acceptable, but only so long as they "behave as if they were not poets."

The polemic with Communism fully emerges in the closing paragraphs.

> There comes a time when it's best to escape, not so much from man's malice, but from his incandescent kindness. Abstract kindness makes us merciless.

And the thought of saving the world often leads to the most abundant—and needless—carnage. (Andrade 1952, 16)

In the paragraph that follows, the next to last, the poet briefly identifies himself with Robinson. He stresses that the price of an island is "relatively high" because it usually amounts to "disillusion." He proceeds to mention, as if in passing, "the weight of attacks leveled" against the "little modern Robinson," who has chosen to "take his distance from small quarrels" by dreaming of an island. At this point, contextual information is again helpful. Vagner Camilo has shown that Drummond was a "preferred target" of the communists in their attempts to demoralize, "in speech and in print," the non-Stalinist Left (Camilo 2001, 70–73).

Despite Bishop's sustained engagement with Drummond's poetry, the political resonance of his treatment of the Robinson motif, in this *crônica* at least, is remarkably absent from her work. Beyond that, working as a translator, Bishop sets aside a significant body of poetry in which Drummond reflects on commitment and its difficulties, on the War, and eventually on political disillusionment. If we were to judge from what Bishop filters out from Drummond's work, it would be difficult to guess that the Brazilian poet had such a long and conflicted history with communism, that political engagement and the movement away from it play a crucial role in the development of his poetry, or that political themes are of crucial importance to the collections that include many of the pieces Bishop translated.

Bishop's omissions may be understood from more than one point of view. Her choices as a translator make sense when they are considered in the perspective of her own poetry. Most of the poems that she translated rework themes that concern her as well, such as family and loss. At the same time, the overtly pro-Soviet poems that Drummond included in *A rosa do povo* are unlike anything Bishop could write. They are direct and referential; they tend to the prosaic and may seem formless.[8] It is not difficult to see that a poet as understated, elliptical, and controlled as Bishop would not be interested in translating Drummond's lengthy "Carta a Stalingrado" (Letter to Stalingrad), his "Telegrama de Moscou" (Wire from Moscow), or yet his "Mas Viveremos" (We'll Live), an implicit reflection on the end of the Third International as Julio Castañon Guimarães has shown in the critical edition of his poetry he organized (Andrade 2012, 478).

However, the fact that Bishop leaves Drummond's fraught relationship to communism out of the picture deserves to be understood in historical terms as well. It will be helpful to call attention here to some internal evidence that suggests that Bishop was familiar with Drummond's *crônica* on disillusionment: "Crusoe in England" briefly converges with some details of Drummond's prose text. Whereas the Brazilian poet forbids the Bible on his island, Bishop also takes her distance from Defoe's puritanical moralism by mocking the "miserable philosophy" that was "the smallest" of his "island's industries." Like Drummond, Bishop stresses that the animals of the island are tame. Despite such indirect allusions, Bishop sets aside in her poem any reference to the disillusionment with communism that informs Drummond's desire to escape to an island. Bishop's own position vis-à-vis communism must have played a part in this omission.

We find a broad characterization of Bishop's political views at the beginning of Steven Gould Axelrod's essay on the poet's distinctive "textual anticipation of a queer politics." Axelrod notes that Bishop participated in a liberal, "anti-Communist, pro-social justice" consensus, which was characteristic of mainstream American culture in the mid-twentieth century (Axelrod 2014, 36). Harris Feinsod has recently examined Bishop's anticommunism in the context of her years in Brazil. Feinsod argues that Bishop engaged in an effort of "anti-communist cultural diplomacy" while she was in the country; in particular, he shows that Bishop sought and at times obtained support for her literary initiatives from the Congress for Cultural Freedom (Feinsod 2017). It seems disingenuous to claim that Bishop's anticommunism did not play a role in her selective engagement with Drummond's poetry, both as a translator and in the composition of "Crusoe in England." Bishop's omissions are consistent with the broader context of American Cold War anticommunism.

V

The preceding exploration of Bishop's engagement with Drummond's work speaks in a variety of ways to current discussions of world literature. The point that compels attention, first and foremost, is that is very easy *not* to notice Bishop's relationship to Drummond; this connection has remained largely "un-rediscovered, un-renamable," much like the island in Bishop's poem. The hidden-in-plain-sight character of the relationship by itself provides a useful angle of approach to both the perspectives that world literature affords and the thorny difficulties that it exposes as a category of literary scholarship. Bishop's engagement with Drummond's poetry developed over a fairly long period, at least from 1963, when she first published translations of his poetry, until 1976, when "Crusoe in England" appeared in the collection *Geography III*. The interviews in which Bishop discusses Brazilian poetry, her translations, and her own poetry, all help retrace an enduring and many-sided engagement. Yet these diverse texts do not necessarily add up to make a single, unequivocal picture. In her interviews, Bishop seems predominantly concerned with asserting her claim to remaining a "completely American poet." In her translations Bishop mainly explores themes that are central to her own poetry, but at the same time she confronts the challenges posed by the linguistic experimentation of Brazilian Modernists. In "Crusoe in England," finally, we see Bishop hold on to her distinctive style, concerns, and approach—and remain faithful to the character of a "completely American" poet—yet make room for the voice of the Brazilian poet, at least to some extent. Suggestively, in this poem Bishop relies heavily on the colloquial register, a poetic strategy that she had at first criticized. We have seen, then, the poet's attitude to Drummond (and Brazilian Modernism) change from denial and defensiveness, in early interviews, to considered dialogue in "Crusoe in England." Nevertheless, there is a point at which Bishop absolutely keeps her distance from Drummond: she neither engages with the poems that directly explore political themes nor acknowledges his pro-Soviet sympathies and subsequent disillusionment.

A number of topics that are recurrent in systematic attempts to conceptualize world literature have come to the fore in the course of this discussion: the structuring power of the major literary languages, English in this case; the crucial role played by translators, like Bishop, as mediators between literary languages, and the perennial challenge posed by the diversity of the world's languages, so many of which, like Portuguese, have never been fully integrated into a world literary system.

Pascale Casanova has approached these problems from the perspective of the sociology of literature. In her view, the hierarchical structure of modern world literature is defined by systemic imbalances of prestige. The power of literary institutions is highest at the center, while truly innovative writing is created in the periphery. The system remains dynamic thanks to the work of translators, who mediate between center and periphery and thereby open the way for writers of "dominated" languages to receive "consecration" at the center (Casanova 2004, 135). In the terms of Casanova's argument, Bishop has played such a mediating role in relation to Drummond's poetry, not just as a translator but as a poet as well. It seems necessary to stress, however, the extent to which consecration has proved elusive for the Brazilian poet. For all Bishop's efforts, Drummond's poetry has not as yet attained recognition in the circuit of world literature.

Walter Cohen's recent *A History of European Literature* considers the historically changing relationship between powerful literary languages and spoken languages in order to propose a model for the development of world literature. Taking as a model a literary system defined both by cross-cultural influence and by shared themes and forms, Cohen identifies five historical periods altogether, which span from the moment when literacy was invented five millennia ago up until the present. For Cohen, the most recent period, which starts after World War II and is marked by an unprecedented expansion of European literature, has resulted in the creation of a new "global literary system" through a process of "self-abolishing contradiction" (Cohen 2017, 7). The role of global English is not a given in this context. English may "eventually restrict access to other literary languages or even undermine them," but it may also come to "function like earlier cosmopolitan languages, such as Sanskrit and Latin, or even French and Occitan, encouraging vernacular art." Cohen calls for a commitment to work toward bringing about the second alternative (Cohen 2017, 493). The story of Bishop's engagement with Drummond is consistent with the two possibilities Cohen outlines. Because of structural differences in the prestige of English and Brazilian Portuguese as literary languages, it is all too easy to overlook the relationship between the two poets. At the same time, the effort to call attention to Bishop's engagement with Drummond may itself serve as a way to resist the homogenizing power of English. It is nevertheless difficult to be optimistic about the effectiveness of this attempt or others like it, such is the hegemonic power of English.

Alexander Beecroft likewise calls attention to the importance of literary languages in making up the complex systems of circulation of literary texts. However, Beecroft proceeds to identify, in addition, five other operative "patterns of constraint": politics, economics, religion, cultural politics, and technologies of distribution (27). Through their interaction, these six factors shape a series of successive and complex "literary biomes." In Beecroft's account, Bishop's approximation to Drummond develops in the context of a worldwide system of competing national literatures. (Beecroft, unlike Cohen, places a global literary system in the hypothetical future.) This model is helpful, above all, in suggesting some reasons why the literary relationship between Bishop and Drummond has remained mostly invisible: each writer's work circulates within a circumscribed national system; the circulation of Drummond's poetry is certainly more restricted than Bishop's.

David Damrosch's influential account of world literature, in contrast, does not bring linguistic diversity to the foreground as a problem for consideration. Rather than having a hierarchical or complex structure, for Damrosch world literature is constituted through acts of reading, when "several foreign works begin to resonate together in our mind" (298). Translation enables this dynamic process: not only does it make possible the international circulation of literary works; it exemplifies the detached mode of reading that characterizes world literature, independent from a specialist's outlook or nationalist commitments. It seems necessary to note, however, that throughout his argument Damrosch implicitly has in mind translations *into* English. The opening chapter of *What Is World Literature?* clarifies his perspective.

> I will be concentrating predominantly (though not exclusively) on world literature as it has been construed over the past century in a specific cultural space, that of the formerly provincial and now metropolitan United States. (Damrosch 2003, 27)

These remarks follow closely on paragraphs that stress that "world literature itself is constituted very differently in different cultures" and illustrate this point with brief discussions of India and Brazil (Damrosch 2003, 26–27). Nevertheless, our discussion of Bishop and Drummond has shown that it is quite easy to lose sight of a major Brazilian poet. It does not seem likely that world literature, when constituted from the perspective of Brazil, should gain much traction internationally.

Although most accounts of world literature stress the importance of translation, scholars committed to translation studies have expressed significant reservations about this category. Gayatri Spivak discerns in "U.S. style world literature" a project of disciplining, or reining in the languages of the Global South; she calls instead for an opening up to other languages, so that comparative literary scholarship may also flourish in other, different contexts as well (Spivak 2003, 39). This critique rests on Spivak's understanding of translation as an ethical practice that requires the patient, always incomplete effort to learn more languages in order to establish a relationship at once responsible and intimate to cultural others. Nevertheless, Spivak's philological commitments undercut such a utopian vision. Spivak stresses that she never teaches "anything whose original [she] cannot read" (Spivak 2000, 23). The necessary conclusion to this line of thought is that Spivak would teach Elizabeth Bishop but not Carlos Drummond de Andrade—with the inevitable result that the relationship between the two poets would escape consideration.

Emily Apter, for her part, criticizes world literature as a liberal, "agglomerative rubric" that blunts "political critique." These reservations are grounded in her understanding of translation as negotiation (Apter 2013, 40). Apter proposes that a focus on translation and its thorny difficulties—untranslatability, mistranslation, language conflict—will open the way for comparisons on a planetary scale that do not reproduce the logic of empire. In part, this approach sheds light on Bishop's engagement with Drummond: the challenges that Bishop found in translating his poetry bring to light a sharp contrast between her project and that of the Brazilian Modernists. Nevertheless, the specifically political aspect of their relationship becomes clear only when we consider all that Bishop chose *not* to translate. The significant body of poetry in which Drummond explores his conflicted relationship to Communism—his approximation, his enduring reservations, and his eventual disillusionment—escapes consideration for as long as we keep our focus on what Bishop has in effect translated. Bishop's omissions refer us, rather, to the historical context of the 1960s. They are best understood through ever-expanding circles of historical interpretation: her selections are consistent with Bishop's anticommunist opinions; they make Drummond's poetry more accessible to an American reading public that generally shares such an outlook; finally, they are consistent with the cultural policy, and more generally with the foreign policy of the United States toward Brazil, and Latin America as a whole.

By looking into Bishop's approach to the poetry of Carlos Drummond de Andrade, this chapter has shown that the American poet engaged in a sustained, generous effort to establish an effective relationship to a tradition that must have been entirely unfamiliar to her—an enduring "effort of affection," to borrow the title of her essay on Marianne Moore, but also that of Paulo Henriques Britto's Portuguese translation of her selected prose (Bishop 1996). However, current accounts of world literature shed light on this relationship only in part; they partly obscure it as well, and at times work to exclude it from consideration altogether. The same is also true of current critiques of the category.

In order to bring Bishop's relationship to Drummond into better focus, it has been necessary to move back and forth between English and Portuguese and the traditions of these languages. Such oscillations allow us to appreciate the way Bishop modulates Drummond's poetry while she translates it, develops motifs shared with the Brazilian poet, and even brings his diction to some extent into her own work; at the same time they enable us to catch Bishop's consequential omissions. This discussion has called attention to further literary connections. Each poet has established a distinctive relationship to a shared early modern intertext: while Bishop re-creates Robinson's colonial outlook and ironically points out its limitations, Drummond dismisses the discourse of colonialism, laying claim to a historical perspective different from Defoe's, and *mais bonita*.

The kind of triangulation pursued by this argument is akin to binocular vision: without it we are left only with flat images of the poets and lose sight of the depth and complexity of literary relationships. I'd like to suggest that the category of world literature is at its most productive when it leads us to search for such double, perhaps even multiple perspectives. This approach helps recover some of the information that, as Beecroft points out, is inevitably reduced out of the system. I hope that I have been able to show that the noise in the system is interesting, and may reward the effort to pay attention with new insights.

Notes

1. In Brazil, the word *Modernismo* refers to a movement of artistic renewal inspired by the European avant-garde. It is taken to begin in the 1922 *Semana de Arte Moderna*, but its influence is felt well into the 1940s. In the body of this chapter, I simply use the English word *Modernism* to refer to the Brazilian movement. For a discussion of vanguardism in Latin America that considers Brazilian *Modernismo* as well, see Unruh 1994.

2. See also Paulo Henriques Britto's discussion of this interview in Bishop 1999, 38.

3. Compare to Hicock 2016, 95. Bishop's slip as a translator does matter here, because it alters the poem. The title of Bishop's translation suggests that the figure of an "infant" plays a significant role in the poem; on the contrary, in Drummond's text the perspective of an older "child" serves as the focus for the speaker.

4. The softening effect of Bishop's translations may be further illustrated with a line from Drummond's "A Mesa" ("The Table"). This poem explores the poet's conflicted relationship to his father. When the poet recollects the way that the father treated his sons, he writes: *e com ira amaldiçoava*. A literal translation of this line would read "and cursed us in rage," but Bishop renders it as, "and fiercely swore at us" (Bishop 1994, 249).

5. I wish to thank Fabio Cesar Alves for this observation.

6. See also Miceli 1978, for a sociological discussion of Drummond's function as a high-ranking functionary in the cultural apparatus of Brazil's federal government during the period that Getúlio Vargas was president.

7. When this *crônica* was published, the Communist Party had been made illegal in Brazil. It seems helpful to specify that it would not be possible to mention the Party directly in print in a major newspaper.

8. Murilo Marcondes de Moura has shown, for instance, that the collection *A rosa do povo* organizes the poems that focus on World War II in a sequence that reproduces the chronology of the war (Moura 2016, 125).

Works Cited

Almeida, Sandra Regina Goulart, Glaucia Renate Gonçalves, and Eliana Lourenço de Lima Reis, eds. 2002. *The Art of Elizabeth Bishop*. Belo Horizonte, Brazil: Editora UFMG.

Andrade, Carlos Drummond de. 1952. *Passeios na ilha: Divagações sobre a vida literária e outras matérias*. Rio de Janeiro, Brazil: Organizações Simões.

———. 1981. *The Minus Sign: A Selection from the Poetic Anthology*, translation and introduction by Virginia de Araujo. Manchester, UK: Carcanet Press.

———. 1986. *Traveling in the Family: Selected Poems by Carlos Drummond de Andrade*, edited by Thomas Colchie and Mark Strand, with additional translations by Elizabeth Bishop and Gregory Rabassa. New York: Random House.

———. 1992. *Poesia e prosa*. Rio de Janeiro, Brazil: Aguilar.

———. 2012. *Poesia 1930–62*. São Paulo, Brazil: Cosac Naify, edited by Júlio Castañon Guimarães.

———. 2015. *Multitudinous Heart: Selected Poems*, edited and translated by Richard Zenith. New York: Farrar Straus Giroux.

Apter, Emily. 2013. *Against World Literature: On the Politics of Untranslatability*. London: Verso.

Axelrod, Steven Gould. 2014. "Bishop, History, Politics." In *The Cambridge Companion to Elizabeth Bishop*, edited by Angus Cleghorn and Jonathan Ellis. Cambridge, UK: Cambridge University Press.

Bishop, Elizabeth, and Emanuel Brasil. 1974. *An Anthology of Twentieth-Century Brazilian Poetry*. Middletown, CT: Wesleyan University Press.

———. 1994. *The Complete Poems 1927–1979*. New York: Farrar, Straus and Giroux.

———. 1996. *Conversations with Elizabeth Bishop*, edited by George Monteiro. Jackson: University of Mississippi Press.

———. 1996. *Esforços do afeto e outras histórias: Prosa reunida*, edited and introduction by Robert Giroux; translated by Paulo Henriques Britto. São Paulo, Brazil: Companhia das Letras.

———. 1999. *Poemas do Brasil*, edited, introduction, and translation by Paulo Henriques Britto. São Paulo, Brazil: Companhia das Letras.

———. 2001. *O Iceberg imaginário e outros poemas*, edited, critical introduction, and translation by Paulo Henriques Britto. São Paulo, Brazil: Companhia das Letras.

Burns, Tom. 2002. "Bishop, Translator of Drummond." *The Art of Elizabeth Bishop*, edited by Sandra Regina Goulart Almeida, Gláucia Renate Gonçalves, and Eliana Lourenço de Lima Reis. Belo Horizonte, Brazil: Editora UFMG.

Camilo, Vagner. 2001. *Drummond: Da Rosa do povo à rosa das trevas*. São Paulo, Brazil: Ateliê Editorial.

Camus, Albert. 1975. *The Myth of Sisyphus and Other Essays*, translated by Justin O'Brien. New York: Alfred A. Knopf.

———. 1968. *Le mythe de Sisyphe: Essai sur l'absurde*. Paris: Gallimard.

Candido, Antonio, and José Aderaldo Castello. 1968. *Presença da literatura brasileira, III*. São Paulo, Brazil: Difusão Europeia do Livro.

———. 1995. "Inquietudes na poesia de Drummond." *Vários escritos*. São Paulo, Brazil: Livraria Duas Cidades, 111–45.

Casanova, Pascale. 2004. *The World Republic of Letters*. Cambridge, MA: Harvard University Press.

Coelho, Joaquim-Francisco. 1973. *Terra e família na poesia de Carlos Drummond de Andrade*. Belém, Brazil: Universidade Federal do Pará.

Cohen, Walter. 2017. *A History of European Literature: The West and the World from Antiquity to the Present*. Oxford, UK: Oxford University Press.

Damrosch, David. 2003. *What Is World Literature?* Princeton, NJ: Princeton University Press.

———. 2018. *How to Read World Literature*. Hoboken, NJ: Wiley Blackwell.

Defoe, Daniel. 1994. *Robinson Crusoe: An Authoritative Text Contexts Criticism*, edited by Michael Shinagel. New York: W. W. Norton.

Even-Zohar, Itamar. 2002. "The Position of Translated Literature within the Literary Polysystem." *The Translation Studies Reader*, edited by Lawrence Venuti. London: Routledge.

Feinsod, Harris. 2017. "Questions of Anticommunism." In *The Poetry of the Americas: From Good Neighbors to Countercultures*. Oxford Scholarship Online. DOI 10.1093/050/ 978019068202.003.006. Accessed March 3, 2019.

Fortuny, Kim. 2003. *Elizabeth Bishop: The Art of Travel*. Boulder: University of Colorado Press.

Ginzburg, Carlo. 1992. *Clues, Myth, and the Historical Method*. Baltimore: Johns Hopkins University Press.

Hicok, Bethany. 2016. *Elizabeth Bishop's Brazil*. Charlottesville: University of Virginia Press.

Hopkins, Terence K. 1978. "World Systems Analysis: Methodological Issues." In *Social Change in the Capitalist World Economy*. Beverly Hills, CA: Sage Publications, 199–217.

———. 1982. "The Study of the Capitalist World Economy: Some Introductory Considerations." In *World Systems Analysis: Theory and Methodology*, edited by Terence K. Hopkins and Immanuel Wallerstein. Beverly Hills, CA: Sage Publications.

Martins, Maria Lúcia Milléo. 2006. *Duas Artes: Elizabeth Bishop e Carlos Drummond de Andrade*. Belo Horizonte, Brazil: Editora UFMG.

MacMahon, Candace W. 1980. *Elizabeth Bishop: A Bibliography 1927–1979*. Charlottesville: University of Virginia Press.

Miceli, Sérgio. 1978. *Intelectuais e classe dirigente no Brasil*. São Paulo, Brazil: Difusão Europeia do Livro.

Millier, Brett. 1993. *Elizabeth Bishop: Life and the Memory of It*. Berkeley: University of California Press.

Monteiro, George. 2012. *Elizabeth Bishop in Brazil and After: A Poetic Career Transformed*. Jefferson, North Carolina: McFarland.

Moura, Murilo Marcondes de. 2016. *O Mundo sitiado: A poesia brasileira e a Segunda Guerra Mundial*. São Paulo, Brazil: Editora 34.
Read, Justin. 2003. "Manners of Mistranslation: The Antropofagismo of Elizabeth Bishop's Prose and Poetry." *New Centennial Review* 3, no. 1: 297–327.
Santiago, Silviano. 2002. "Introdução." *Poesia completa de Carlos Drummond de Andrade*. Rio de Janeiro, Brazil: Nova Aguilar.
Segatto, José Antonio, Jose Paulo Netto, José Ramos Néto, Paulo Cesar de Azevedo, and Vladimir Sacchetta. 1982. *PCB: memória fotográfica 1922–1982*. São Paulo, Brazil: Brasiliense.
Simon, Iumna Maria. 1978. *Drummond: uma poética do risco*. São Paulo, Brazil: Ática.
Spivak, Gayatri. 2000. "Translation as Culture." *Parallax* 6, no. 1: 13–24.
———. 2003. *Death of a Discipline*. New York: Columbia University Press.
Sussekind, Flora. 1993. "A Geléia e o engenho: em torno de uma carta-poema de Elizabeth Bishop a Manuel Bandeira." In *Papéis colados*. Rio de Janeiro, Brazil: Editora UFRJ.
Unruh, Vicky. 1994. *Latin America Vanguards: The Art of Contentious Encounters*. Berkeley: University of California Press.
Vendler, Helen. 1987. "The Poems of Elizabeth Bishop." *Critical Inquiry* 13: 825–38.
———. 2002. "Long Pig: The Interconnection of the Exotic, the Dead, and the Fantastic in the Poetry of Elizabeth Bishop." *The Art of Elizabeth Bishop*. Belo Horizonte, Brazil: Editora UFMG, 25–38.
Venuti, Lawrence. 2008. *The Translator's Invisibility:* New York: Routledge.
Wallerstein, Immanuel. 1976. "A World-Systems Perspective on the Social Sciences." *British Journal of Sociology* 27, no. 3 (September 1976): 343–52.

Chapter 6

Latin America and the World

Borges, Bolaño, and the Inconceivable Universal

Patrick Dove

The growing influence of world literature as critical concept coincides with the newest wave of integration of the global capitalist system together with its turbulent impact on local, national, and regional forms of social organization. The proliferation of digital, real-time technologies, an increasingly interconnected global capitalist economy, and new patterns of displacement and migration generate new planetary forces against which the local and regional structures of containment invented by modernity offer little effective resistance. Contemporary literary production, meanwhile, is informed by experiences of spatiotemporal compression that give shape to new networks of publishing, distribution, and translation. World literature, to be sure, does not constitute a single, homogeneous critical perspective. It names a range of practices whose differences are difficult to reconcile, as can be seen when one juxtaposes Franco Moretti's "distant reading," David Damrosch's concerns with circulation, translation, and critical self-distance, and Pascale Casanova's interest in cosmopolitanism and literary autonomy. What these critics share despite their important differences is their rejection of the old paradigm of national literature together with a distrust of boundless globalism or the infinite accumulation of indifferent particularities (cultures, traditions, writers, works, etc.) that obtains once the world system has been freed from the restraining structures

145

of political modernity. If world literature aspires to be more than just an empirical project of documenting differences, if it is to constitute itself as a truly critical endeavor, then it must invent new tools and methods for understanding how the local and the global determine one another reciprocally, and how global capital and its newest forms of production and accumulation produce gaps, fissures, and unevenness instead of uniformity.

The prospects for bringing Latin American literary studies into a world literature critical project remain fraught with obstacles and uncertainties. Some form of inclusion is necessary for the consolidation of world literature as a conceptually consistent and legitimate practice. However, such an incorporation faces resistance from certain Latin Americanist critics who are inclined to view the deployment in Latin American contexts of critical paradigms produced in the developed world as epistemological imperialism.[1] The recent revitalization of world literature as critical concept, rooted principally in French and Anglo-American postcolonial contexts, helps us to see why the global fulfillment of the concept as critical practice cannot avoid its own fundamental contradiction: as soon as one begins to define the self-consistency of the project in terms of how to include those geographical and cultural contexts in which the concept has not emerged more or less organically, one invariably introduces an identitarian criteria whose logic is indistinguishable from that of the market. The boundless globalism of which critics like Damrosch are rightly skeptical has always already cast its shadow over the project as soon as the question of inclusion presents itself as unavoidable. If a world literature without Latin America would be something other than truly worldly—a repackaging of Eurocentrism as Franco and Anglo postcolonialism, for instance—then a world literature that concerns itself with negotiating the inclusion of Latin America will have difficulty distinguishing itself from a mere reproduction of the organizing logic of capital—and thus worldly only if we concede that world and market are now conceptually indistinguishable.

Although there may be no way of completely avoiding one or another of these fates, a partial solution can perhaps be found by insisting on the need for critical reevaluation of the component terms themselves, *world* and *literature*, the status of which are often taken for granted, it seems to me, by those working in the name of world literature. This would require us to address the question of what it means to speak of "the world" and "literature" today. What, for instance, is the relationship between "world" and "globalization"? Are technological and economic globalization something that happens to the world, or does its occurrence coincide with a new world? Or does it in fact inaugurate something incompatible with what we call world—a totality in which all possibility for creation has already been captured by the logic of the market, or a world consumed in the throes of autoimmunitarian violence? And as for literature: to what extent does this term refer to a historical object? If what we call literature does indeed possess a historical specificity, how can we be certain that we can still speak meaningfully of it in a time when the forms of social organization associated with the modern nation-state are no longer dominant? If the task of criticism is no longer tied to the history of national culture and its ideological appropriations, how can we be certain that there will still be something called literature awaiting critical inquiry today? Then again, what aspects of this thing called literature are not historical? If literature names or possesses a nonhistorical component or force, what could it tell us in the historical time of global capital? These are some of the questions that await world literature in its endeavor to constitute itself as a truly critical practice. I believe that we can find in Latin American literature ways of working out these questions, although in some instances the responses may leave us less certain than ever as to whether or not we understand what we are talking about when we speak of literature and world.

No assessment of Latin America's place within critical discussions of world literature would be conceivable without consideration of the work of Jorge Luis Borges, whose prose fiction of the 1940s and 1950s inaugurates a "world-literary" effect *avant la lettre*. Not only is Borges one of the very first Latin American writers to be translated and gain a favorable critical reception in postwar European intellectual circles, his unequivocal rejection of cultural nationalism and anti-Semitism in Argentina during the 1930s and 1940s is accompanied by a vast and broad-ranging knowledge of Western and non-Western literary and intellectual traditions. Borges was an active promoter of transcultural exchange and translation, while his quasi-encyclopedic familiarity with classical and modern archives provides the raw material for his own literary production, which characteristically unfolds as a reading and/or rewriting of texts, images, and ideas borrowed from one or another remote cultural history. Borges's work is an embodiment of the concept of world literature, and no text of his more exemplifies this incarnation of the idea than his 1945 short story "El Aleph," a text that transforms the relation between world and locality into a literary problem. In his recent study of Latin America in the context of world literature, Héctor Hoyos (Hoyos 2015) concurs about the importance of Borges's text for contemporary debates. As will be clear, however, my reading of "El Aleph" differs in subtle but important ways from his.

147

The Universal in the Particular:
On Literature as Revelation in Borges

Once described by Borges's friend and eminent Uruguayan literary critic Emir Rodríguez Monegal as a "tour de force of condensation" (Borges 2003, 455), "El Aleph" offers a reflection on seeming antitheses: love and abandonment; memory and forgetting; the universal and the particular; the One and the many; and eternity and time. It is also concerned with what is historical and what lies beyond all history as its possible horizon: revelation. The eponymous Aleph in Borges's text metonymizes world literature through two distinct registers. First, and most obviously, the point that is the Aleph thematizes the *multum in parvo*; it is a punctual condensation of the world and its history qua totalities within a finite space or a point. At the same time, the narrator reminds us, the name invokes a network of literary circulation and borrowing that includes the first letter of the Hebrew alphabet and a key figure in the mystical Kabbalistic tradition for which the letter represents "the pure and boundless godhead" and is likened to the calligraphic figuration of a man pointing both to heaven and earth, as well as Cantor's theory of transfinite numbers, for which Aleph initiates the naming of those nonfinite numbers "of which any part is as great as the whole" (Borges 1999a, 285).

Ostensibly recounted in 1942, the story is told by a writer, "Borges," who is equally unhappy in love as in literary fortune. A quick summary of the story will help to situate my reading of the text, which will focus on time, space, and the question of revelation. Some thirteen years after the death of Beatriz Viterbo, the woman with whom he was enthralled, we find "Borges" to be immersed in a seemingly interminable mourning. Every year on the anniversary of her death he makes a point of visiting Beatriz's family house, where he gradually insinuates himself into the intimacy of the dinner ritual. He forms a nominal friendship with her cousin, the writer Carlos Argentino Daneri, who will turn out to have been the narrator's rival in two separate spheres: for the literary accolades that unfairly elude the narrator and for Beatriz's romantic interest and affections—when living she seemed scarcely inclined to acknowledge "Borges's" existence. As a romantic rival Daneri is an improper figure who cofounds two forms of being together, kinship and Eros. As a writer he represents everything that Jorge Luis Borges never ceased to satirize and condemn: verbal ostentation, chauvinistic attachment to local color, and the reduction of literary creativity to a reflection of a preexisting world or reality. One day "Borges" receives a frantic phone call from Daneri, who discloses that the family house is slated to be torn down by its owners in order to make room for expansion of their business; in the cellar of that house, Daneri adds, resides something he calls an Aleph, a "place where, without admixture or confusion, all the places of the world, seen from every angle, coexist" (Borges 1999a, 281). A skeptical and wary "Borges" pays a visit and descends to the basement where, after some uncertainty, he beholds the Aleph in its splendor. He describes it as a "small iridescent sphere of almost unbearable brightness," approximately two to three centimeters in diameter (Borges 1999a, 283). At first glance the disc appears to be spinning, but the perceived movement is an optical illusion generated by the spatiotemporal plenitude it contains: the Aleph displays anything and everything that is, that has been, or that will be on earth, and it presents this multiplicity of things and beings in their immediacy, from every conceivable angle and without effacing the particularity proper to each.

The ensuing description of the Aleph constitutes what the narrator calls the "ineffable center" of the story. This core, which comprises slightly less than one quarter of the entire text, poses a fundamental aesthetic problem: that of representing the infinite, which is necessarily to say representing it within finite bounds. This literary portrait is a variation on what Borges describes as an aesthetic event, defined elsewhere as "the imminence of a revelation that does not take place" (Borges 1999b, 346, translation modified). For "El Aleph" the aesthetic problem is not a temporal contradiction between what occurs and what is deferred but the logical contradiction of a point or place in which all other points or places are contained. The prospect of presenting such a contradiction in literature, "Borges" tells us, forces the writer to confront a profound hopelessness or desperation [*deseperación de escritor*]: it signals an impasse, to be sure, but things only become desperate because one still must write. No paralysis and no silence here, just the impossibility of not proceeding together with the certainty that whatever one says or writes will unavoidably erase or obscure the singularity of what takes place.

> I come now to the ineffable center of my tale; it is here that a writer's hopelessness begins. Every language is an alphabet of symbols the employment of which assumes a past shared by its interlocutors. How can one transmit to others the infinite Aleph, which my timorous memory can scarcely contain? In a similar situation, mystics have employed a wealth of emblems: to signify the deity, a Persian mystic speaks of a bird that somehow is all birds; Alain de Lille speaks of a sphere whose center is everywhere and

circumference nowhere; Ezekiel, of an angel with four faces, facing east and west, north and south at once. (It is not for nothing that I call to mind these inconceivable analogies; they bear a relation to the Aleph.) Perhaps the gods would not deny me the discovery of an equivalent image, but then this report would be contaminated with literature, with falseness. And besides, the central problem—the enumeration, even partial enumeration, of infinity—is irresolvable. In that unbounded moment, I saw millions of delightful and horrible acts; none amazed me so much as the fact that all occupied the same point, without superposition and without transparency. What my eyes saw was *simultaneous*; what I shall write is *successive*, because language is successive. Something of it, though, I will capture. (Borges 1999a, 282–83, translation modified)

It is fitting that in the "ineffable center" of the story we encounter the presentation of what the narrator terms the "central problem" of the text: the impossibility of enumerating the infinite, of presenting a nonfinite totality using finite and sequential means, on the one hand, and the imperative of speaking or writing, on the other. Literature is itself the name of this impasse, as both the maker of images and the realm of fiction that is forever contaminating the true and confounding our efforts to tell true and false from one another.

As David Johnson observes in his impeccable reading of Borges's text, the writer's conundrum is to a certain extent the dilemma faced by all linguistic beings when it comes to speaking or writing about experience (Johnson 2012, 172–73). On the one hand, the text tells us that language presupposes a shared past in which all speakers partake. What linguistic beings have in common is not a lived experience but an implicit recognition of a prior agreement as to how each word stands in relation to all other words—and thus, by extension, how it is that words can be said to designate things. This pact, radically anterior to any and all linguistic activity, nullifies in advance any possibility of an idiolect, a language of one that would be particular to an individual. It is not just communication that finds itself mediated by this shared anteriority: so-called personal or individual experience is likewise informed by a preexisting network of associations and conventions that operates like a language. Personal experience in its uniqueness and immediacy is thus always already mediated. What is mine is already an experience *of the other*; experience of the here and now is already contaminated by the anteriority of the common. Of course, the encounter with the Aleph would seem to entail—it ought to entail—something for which no prior accord could prepare us, an unprecedented occurrence for which all conventional signs and preconceived images would be inadequate. As the narrator observes, the sequential structure of narrative and syntax can only distort the myriad sensory perceptions emanating from the Aleph, which somehow present themselves to him in precisely the same place and time. The apparent contradiction between perceptual simultaneity and immediacy, on the one hand, and linguistic sequentiality and mediation, on the other, illustrates how the Aleph destabilizes the familiar and seemingly self-evident distinction between time and space. Moreover, in trying to draw a distinction between temporality and an experience outside of time, the narrative account of the Aleph in fact shows to us that time constitutes the inescapable horizon of all experience, discourse, and thought. Not even the appeal to "simultaneity" can avoid it, since the concept only makes sense if we presuppose a temporal succession within which more than one thing occur "at the same time." This, in my view, is the real aporia at the heart of Borges's text: that we do not know what we are talking about when we speak of time, yet speak of it—and live in it—we must. As Jacques Derrida puts it in regard to Heidegger's efforts in *Being and Time* to differentiate what he calls metaphysical and authentic conceptions of time, time itself shows us that the distinction between metaphysical or vulgar conceptualizations and authentic, nonideological understandings falls apart: any and all conceptualizations of time are "vulgar" because they ignore this fundamental unknowability, and hence none are (Derrida 1982, 52–53, note 32).

A point in space, the Aleph is also all places (*hic stans*); an "unbounded moment" (*instante gigantesco*), it is also the eternal existence formerly attributed to God (*nunc stans*), understood not as infinite duration but as presence not subject to time. Borges's literary meditation imparts an important insight about the ground or essence of space and time, which are not themselves spatial and temporal in nature. When we speak of time we typically think of a succession of moments or presents. For a given present to constitute itself as present moment, there must be what Derrida calls an "interval" (Derrida 1982, 13) separating it from all other moments, all other presents, those past and those still to come. While the interval is not itself temporal, there could be no such thing as time qua sequentiality without it. But the ontological dependency of the present time on such an interval also separates the present *from itself*. For one, if the interval is not itself temporal then its nature must be spatial, and it thereby introduces a logic of spacing into what ought to be the temporality of time. There can be no such thing as pure temporality; in its "essence" time is always already spacing. The need for an interval exposes the way in which the present cannot be identical to itself; the being of the present relies on a supplement of nonbeing, a being-situated toward what has no being because it is not (yet): the past and the future. The interval qua difference and deferral is also a relation, and it is this relatedness, which *is* not, that constitutes the being of the present and not the other way around.

In the lengthy paragraph that follows after the "ineffable center" we find an enumeration of the myriad images that "Borges" saw as he peered into the Aleph. The lengthy description is structured by anaphoric repetition of the phrase "I saw . . ." [*Vi* . . .], which critics such as Jon Thiem have associated with the presentation of divine revelation in Dante's *Paradiso* (Thiem 1988). What interests me here is not the list itself but its culmination. First, we are presented with an abyssal image: within the Aleph "Borges" tells us that he saw Earth itself, and within this image of Earth he saw the Aleph, and then in this secondary Aleph he again saw (another) Earth. Then, by way of synthesis, the narrator reports that he was overcome by dizziness and tears when it dawned on him that he was viewing "that secret and conjectural object whose name is usurped by men but which no man has truly looked upon—the inconceivable universe" (284, translation modified). I will say more about these two points momentarily. For the moment, suffice it to say that between these two sentences there emerges a subtle but important tension between a representational paradox (the mirror within the mirror) and the limits of knowledge, a conjectural site whose name can only be deployed improperly and which cannot become the object of representation. It is as if, in composing the first statement describing the mise en abyme, the narrative process became aware of the inadequacy of representational paradoxes when it comes to speaking of the Aleph.

The ontological problems discussed earlier in the context of space and time can be located within each of the thematic pairings in the text: truth and falsity, literature and reality, memory and forgetting, permanence and change, and so on. Although it is tempting to read the story as a reminder of the unacknowledged fragility and fictive kernel in everything that we take to be permanent and real, such a reading alone is unable to make its way to the interpretive knot at the center of the story. It is only when we reach the end of the story that we become fully aware of this shortcoming, to which I now turn.

Borges criticism has generated ample discussion of the intertextual resonances in "El Aleph," especially in relation to the work of Dante of which Borges was an enthusiastic reader and commentator. The Dantean connection is theological in nature and rests on the association between the visible and truth, representation and revelation. To be sure, "El Aleph" contains frequent allusions to its object as source or exemplar of Truth: as the permanence of eternal existence and as the self-presence of unlimited perspective. However, critical attention to the classical intertext, in presuming that Dante provides the explanatory ground for what Borges is up to, is obliged to ignore the enigmatic presence of the "Postscript of 1 March 1943," published in 1945, together with the "original" account dated as 1942. In the postscript the narrator unexpectedly offers a refutation of the veracity of the 1942 account, declaring that what he saw on Garay Street three years ago was in fact a "false Aleph," and that the true Aleph is to be located inside one of the stone columns of the mosque of Amr in Cairo. "Borges" supports this surprising claim by referring to another discovery: the alleged uncovering, made by his friend the Dominican literary critic Pedro Henríquez Ureña in a Brazilian archive, of a (fictitious) nineteenth-century manuscript by the British explorer and Orientalist Richard Francis Burton, who suggests that the true Aleph is only accessible to the faithful who attend the mosque of Amr. One might conclude that this negation engages in a form of Platonism, positing the existence of the True based on the evidence that the here and now is imperfect and fleeting (which evidence of course comes with the destruction of the place that housed the Aleph of Garay Street). In my view such a reading is mistaken because too *theoretical*, that is, still too rooted in the Platonic determination of truth as specular relation between appearance and contemplation (Heidegger 1977, 163–64).

The purported Burton text describes an array of Aleph-like objects: mirrors, cups, and spears capable of reflecting the entire world from their own finite space. However, Burton concludes that all of them are false; they all suffer from the defect of being "optical instruments." These images of the universal within the particular are guilty of what Hegel calls picture-thinking: they collapse their concept into the realm of the visible, which has always served as a metaphor for knowledge as dominion of the subject. Because these "optical instruments" presuppose the vantage point of a viewing subject, they foreclose the fact that the universal as such, qua "secret and conjectural object" (*objeto secreto y conjetural*), could never become the object of a representation by and for the subject.

By contrast the Burton text asserts that the faithful who attend the famous mosque of Amr in Cairo know without doubt that the universe resides within one of the stone columns of its central courtyard. While of course no one can see it, those who put their ear to the surface of the stone declare that they can hear its bustling murmur (*rumor*).² The Spanish *rumor* ("buzz," "murmur") can also mean "rumor," and that is how Hurley translates it. I see "murmur" as preferable as it emphasizes the aural register of indeterminate noise in contrast to the determinate realm of visible images, but Hurley's choice of "rumor" has the literary virtue of reintroducing the issue of knowledge and certainty, of different forms of knowledge together with the possibility that the form of knowledge associated with seeing may not be the path through which the experience of the absolute is to be found. After all, how could one be certain—the phrase Borges's text uses is "saben muy bien": the faithful know very well—that the noise one is hearing is that of the universe itself? What sort of noise would the universe make? How would the human ear be capable of discerning that this noise is indeed that of the universe itself? This puzzling assertion, attributed to the authority of a preeminent British Orientalist, poses a question about knowledge and universality: knowledge of the One, on the one hand, and also the one true knowledge versus the possibility of other forms of knowledge, including but not necessarily limited to faith as form of knowing, on the other hand. But if the true Aleph cannot be the object of representation for a subject and if it is instead an object of faith, could the universal still assume phenomenal form in a world of multiple and conflicting faiths? The Postscript does not provide an answer, nor for that matter does it even pose the question. We are left with an enigmatic conclusion that places us in a peculiar interpretive bind: if we accept the narrator's retrospective judgment that the Aleph of Garay Street was a false manifestation because still too visible, and that any and all visible Alephs would therefore be false, then we must also accept a rather conventional temporal structure according to which the truth arrives with the final word and the final perspective determines the truth of that which precedes it.

The portion of the Burton text cited by the narrator concludes by noting that the mosque in question was built in the seventh century and that the material for its columns was taken from pre-Islamic temples, since "in the republics founded by nomads, the assistance of foreigners is essential for those things that bear upon masonry" (286).³ In this casual reference to the heterogeneous architectural history of what is in fact the first mosque built in Egypt and all of Africa, we encounter a topos familiar to readers of Borges: the *arkhé*, which is to say the foundation, the beginning, as well as the first ordering principle of a realm, turns out to be of the other. The ground or base from which it is possible to determine what is proper to this order has itself been taken from another tradition and has been reassembled by outsiders. Thus what takes itself to be imperial command can never fully constitute itself as One and selfsame. It has always already been contaminated by an outside, not unlike the image that "Borges" refrains from seeking because it would contaminate his account with the falsity of "literature."

This eternally entombed Aleph, whose presence is detectable only through the indistinct noise it produces, decisively wrests the question with which Borges's text is preoccupied—that of the infinite or universal in the finite or particular—away from the realm of the visible in which the metaphysical tradition has always situated it since Plato's allegory of the cave. The universal, we are told in this Postscript, cannot become the object of representation for a subject. The secret of which "Borges" speaks does not designate a phenomenal content that remains hidden but which could in principle be revealed. It is of a different, nonphenomenal order, and in this respect "El Aleph" marks a literary departure from the gesture and discourse of revelation itself. It does not free itself entirely from the revelatory tradition, for the simple reason that its fundamental gesture is to remark the inadequacy of revelation qua metaphor for thinking what it is that literature does. In this sense the text can be read as a literary elaboration of Borges's account in "The Wall and the Books" of the aesthetic event as a "revelation that does not take place" (*una revelación que no se produce*) (Borges 1976, 13; Borges 1999b, 346).

As Johnson observes, "El Aleph" confronts the problem of how to narrate plenitude or full presence without contaminating it with mediation and absence, and in a language that inevitably destroys any pure presence insofar as it relies on succession, mediation, metaphor, and other forms of mediation. But the text thereby destroys the very possibility of plenitude or full presence as such, even as it feigns to place such a presence beyond language. As first letter of the Hebrew alphabet the Aleph is the signifier of the One, the beginning. But insofar as it comes first it is not yet a signifier, or it will not have been one until there is a second, a second for which it, the Aleph, will stand as having come first. Already, then, at the origin there is repetition and hence literature, falsity.

The Secret of the World: Global Capital and the Crisis of the Political Reason of Modernity

I have proposed that, as part of any meaningful development of world literature as critical concept, the status of what we continue to call literature not be taken for granted. The work of the Chilean-Mexican-Catalunyan writer Roberto Bolaño provides a step in this direction through its concerns with the history of the present and with the roles of art and literature in a time when modernity's forms of social organization and logics for rationalizing destruction and violence have lost their sway. I discuss elsewhere how Bolaño's prose fiction engages with the dominant aesthetic ideologies of modernity (Dove 2016). Here I focus on two aspects of Bolaño's posthumous novel *2666*: its treatment of the free trade zone on the Mexican-US border as a symptom of what is going badly with the world today; and its experimentation with crime fiction and the detective genre as a site for rethinking the reflexive association of literature with representation. There is in Bolaño's work a debt to Borges, the elucidation of which can help to make clear how a quasi-philosophical meditation on art and literature interacts with historically rooted concerns about the present.

Among all late twentieth- and early twenty-first-century Spanish-language writers, Bolaño's work affords one of the most intriguing case studies for looking at how Latin American literature might fit into contemporary discussions of world literature. No writer today, and perhaps none since Borges, better exemplifies the rejection of national literature than Bolaño. His own coming of age happened at the tail end of the generational tumult of the 1960s and early 1970s, and his autobiographical ties with the revolutionary fervor of that time are less those of a participant-survivor than of a peripheral observer who now finds himself the witness to a shipwreck. His novels offer a sustained meditation on the foundering of the Latin American Left and its revolutionary projects together with the retreat of emancipatory imaginaries following the military dictatorships of the 1970s. Bolaño unapologetically distances himself from a long-standing Latin American tradition of hitching the fortunes of literature to libidinal images of the homeland. But no one would confuse Bolaño's novels with a celebration of the neoliberal hegemony arising in the time of postdictatorship either. His novels offer a starting point for exploring how Latin America might insert itself into critical conversations about world literature without losing sight of how local histories inform uneven integration into global networks of production, distribution, and consumption.

It is not my intention, however, to argue that Bolaño is a good example or case study for the inclusion of Latin America in a world literature critical paradigm, nor do I wish to enter into the debate about the critical merits of positioning his work as representative of contemporary Latin American literature (Pollock 2009; Pollock 2013; Hoyos 2015). To argue for or against the premise that Bolaño's work is representative of an entire region and its literary production is precisely to miss what his literary project is up to, which is nothing more or less than a rejection of any supposed equivalency between literature and representation. Instead, I propose that Bolaño invites us to explore literature as a site for reflecting on the limits of representation understood in a very specific sense: as the loosening of ties—ties of meaning, belonging, legitimacy and authority—in contemporary Mexico, and by extension in Latin America as a whole, in the context of globalization and narco-capitalism.

Bolaño's posthumous novel *2666* reflects on how NAFTA-era globalization has transformed the social topography of northern Mexico while generating what Antonio Gramsci termed the morbid symptoms that arise when the prevailing social order is in decline and its hegemonic procedures no longer generate consensus (Gramsci 1971, 276). In a 2003 interview with Mónica Maristain, and less than a year prior to his death, Bolaño described his vision of Ciudad Juárez, a place he would never see in person, as a contemporary and terrestrial hell. Juárez, he says, is "our perdition and our mirror, the disquieting mirror of our failures and of our vile interpretation of freedom and desire" (*nuestra maldición y nuestro espejo, el espejo desasosegado de nuestras frustraciones y de nuestra infame interpretación de la libertad y de nuestros deseos*) (Maristain 2010, 29–30). In this metaphor one hears the echoes of Plato's famous illustration of mimesis as a mirror held up to the world. Ciudad Juárez would be the part that brings into the view the whole, the place that puts on display the ghastly phenomena unleashed across the planet once global capital has been freed from all of the restraining structures devised by political modernity. Thus, it is the part that makes visible the coming apart of the whole today, the unraveling of the forms and logic that gave order to the world in the time of modernity.

Bolaño's description also invokes Freud's conceptualization of the uncanny: a mirror image or double, the appearance of which unsettles what we think we know about ourselves and the world (Freud 1955). The mirror as uncanny surface returns at various points in *2666*, most notably in the passages describing the mirrors in Liz Norton's Santa Teresa hotel room (Bolaño 2004, 149–55). The uncanny for Freud is an aesthetic experience that coincides with the frightful appearance of a figure that turns out to have been once familiar but long forgotten. Freud notes that not all "returns" or "doubles" are experienced as frightful, but he has difficulty pinpointing exactly what it is that makes some of them uncanny. He considers a variety of hypotheses: the uncanny double as reminder of the archaic time of primary narcissism in which the child projects copies of itself into the world; as echo of the superego's attempt to expel negativity by projecting it onto an Other; or as return of dreams and utopian scenarios that had to be relinquished because they conflicted with the reality principle, and so on. If there is a common thread among these various hypotheses it is that in all of them the appearance of the double reactivates an archaic memory of primordial uncertainty as to what is real and what is not, what is mine and what is other, or what is proper and what is improper: in short, a zone of indistinction that would subsequently have to be eliminated in order for the Ego (or community, etc.) to constitute itself as a self-certain, self-conscious subject. The appearance of the uncanny double is thus a stand-in for a reality that has never possessed phenomenal status: a "difference" or a "doubling" that could never see the light of day because it precedes the distinction between identity and difference, being and non-being. The unexpected appearance of the double will turn out to have been a return. It is this a posteriori structure of recognition, which signals the archaic division or splitting of the subject (Self, community), that distinguishes the uncanny from all other aesthetic experiences. If the unearthly appearance of Ciudad Juárez provokes an experience of the uncanny, this is because it brings us into the proximity of an ontological limit, the return of violent contradictions that can no longer be mapped and mediated using the geometrical procedures of political modernity.

Earlier I mentioned that Bolaño's *2666* engages in a critical reexamination of the detective genre. According to Borges, the invention of the detective story with Edgar Allan Poe produced a new kind of reader or, better, a new way of reading that is transferrable to any work or genre from any place or time (Borges 1982). Borges considers Poe's contribution in this regard to be double: in his wake we come to see literature as an intellectual endeavor rather than a spiritual experience and we learn to think and act like detectives while reading, which is to say that we treat words just as the detective treats a crime scene: as a space in which clues about the truth are hidden amid deceptive appearances. If we take Borges's assertion seriously we can surmise that what Bolaño does with the detective genre in *2666* has something important to say to modern ways of thinking about literature in general. Bolaño's novel implicitly takes up Borges's equation of reader with detective so as to delineate a connection between the unsolved murders of Ciudad Juárez and the new order in which political decision-making has been subjugated to the real and perceived demands of global capital. By the same token, Bolaño appropriates the notion that our experience of literature today bears a fundamental if sometimes unacknowledged debt to the detective genre, in order to cast doubt on the old notion that the truth hides beneath appearances and that literature can be tasked with revealing what lies hidden.

According to Marcela Valdés, Bolaño began working on an early version of the *2666* manuscript in the early to mid1990s, a few years before Ciudad Juárez would acquire international infamy as the murder capital of the world. From the distance of Cataluña he reportedly devoured whatever information he could get his hands on about what was happening to young women in Juárez, and he entertained more than one hypothesis about who might be behind the sinister accumulation of mutilated, violated bodies (Valdés 2008, n.p.). As someone puts it in *2666*, although nobody pays any attention to these crimes, the secret of the world lies hidden in them (Bolaño 2004, 439). It is not difficult to imagine that one of the initial impulses behind Bolaño's last literary project may have been to denounce an epidemic of violence that was receiving scandalously little attention from the international media and the Mexican government. By 1999, meanwhile, Bolaño had reportedly exhausted the limited archive of available information on the murders of Ciudad Juárez. Acting on the advice of friends in Mexico he contacted the journalist Sergio González Rodríguez, who was then working on his own investigative book on the subject, which would be later published as *Huesos en el desierto* (González Rodríguez 2002). It was González Rodríguez who disabused Bolaño of the notion that there was a single diabolical serial killer on the loose in Ciudad Juárez. González described how narcocapitalism was generating a network of violence, corruption, complicity, and impunity that extended far beyond the handiwork of any individual. The conversation would seem to have played a major role in reshaping the literary landscape of the published version of *2666*, pushing Bolaño toward an understanding of violence as systematic in origin. Akin to earlier Bolaño novels such as *Estrella distante* (1966), *2666* is a detective novel in which classical conventions of the genre are interwoven with literary reflection on late-twentieth-century atrocities. Unlike those earlier works, however, Bolaño's posthumous novel does not culminate in a reproduction of the detective convention par excellence: it does not take us from deceitful appearances and mistaken certitude to the unveiling of true criminal identity, motive, and so on. While the novel does feature a series of detective-like figures, literary thematization of crime and evil occurs not at the level of individuals but as something that can be intuited but not perceived, something that we could call the nonpresentable excess of representation and individuation. The question of the secret ("the secret of the world") in Bolaño's *2666* has a way of undermining its own presuppositions just as we seem to be on the verge of reaching the interpretive heart of the matter. The novel offers us a chain of detectives and detective-like figures—Lalo Cura, Juan de Dios Martínez, Kessler, and of course the critics themselves—whose investigations ultimately yield no conclusive results and who sometimes (Kessler) themselves end up disappearing. The novel stages a question—Who is killing the vulnerable women of Ciudad Juárez and why?—that will resonate unanswered through the final pages of the book. Ciudad Juárez would seem to mark a limit where the principle of reason—the principle mandates that for everything that exists there must be a why, for every cause an effect—wavers. The secret to which Bolaño's novel refers turns out to have been purloined by literature with its enigmatic treatment of language and reference.

Bolaño's treatment of detective reason as a literary figuration of the act of reading can be further explored in relation to the problem of literature and referentiality discussed by Jacques Derrida in his essay on Baudelaire's "Counterfeit Money" (Derrida 1992). As Derrida notes, literature is the one mode of linguistic discourse for which a proper referential register can never be definitively determined. Convention and pretense notwithstanding, what we call literature does not and cannot refer to what we call the real world. Although literature may borrow proper names associated with the world and its history, and may construct scenes that resemble familiar places and episodes from history (Santa Teresa in *2666* bears a likeness to Ciudad Juárez), these names in fact do not refer to anything that possesses existence, depth or substance outside of the moment in which they appear on the page. But literature cannot for that matter be purely self-referential either. The experience of reading depends on a referential pact that enables the reader to proceed as if the world of the novel were a substantive, phenomenal world. In *2666* we leave the critics and their pursuit of Archimboldi at the start of the second part, and when we finally encounter Archimboldi in the final part it is as if we were meeting someone of whom we had heard a great deal. Akin to watching a film, to read is to agree to the addition of a specular third dimension of depth and substance to the flat, two-dimensional space of the page or the celluloid. A text whose language abandoned the referential pact in favor of pure self-reference would be simply illegible. Reading would be unable to make headway and would be akin to Kant's dove which, imagining that it could fly more freely in a vacuum, discovers that resistance is in fact a necessary condition for all movement. What literature keeps to itself, its fundamental secret, is the fold whereby its language, pretending to point to a phenomenal order, turns back on itself, albeit without fully suturing this turning-back as another form of reference: self-reference. The turn back or folding generates a nonreferential excess, which in turn assumes the name of the secret.

The literary problem of reference discussed by Derrida has a correlate in Bolaño's allegorical treatment of Ciudad Juárez—through the fictive city of Santa Teresa—as a part or place that has something important to tell us about the totality that is our world. This sprawling city is the part that discloses a truth about which the rest of the world, and in particular the apologists for neoliberal privatization, want to know nothing. The truth of this particular whole is that systematicity and asystematicity have become difficult to tell apart; the world today comprises a whole that is unable to administer to its own contradictions and incapable of constituting itself as a true totality. Ciudad Juárez is the symptom that exposes the violent and rending consequences of the incorporation of the local into a global capitalist system. This system is tendentially unified by real-time digital and mediatic technics, forces that appear to be incapable of providing a totalizing logic. Juárez puts on display the precarity that obtains with new migration patterns arising in response to the diversification of production in the time of post-Fordism. It also discloses the state's inability to regulate the ebbs and flows of capital, populations and contraband or, in many cases, to sustain the distinction between legitimate and illegitimate uses of force.[4] It is the birthplace of what is now called the narco-state, which in the years since Bolaño's death has taken over the entirety of Mexico and Central America as well as much of South America. Juárez attests to how destruction, dissociation, and precarity, once considered the contingent and correctable byproducts of modernization, have become integral elements for capitalist accumulation. In addition to designating a place on the map, the place name "Juárez" stands for how the geopolitical coordinates of modernity, its boundaries, relations and procedures for producing social space are being destabilized and reconfigured today (Galli 2010). If Juárez is the part that stands for the whole by making visible a truth that is indigestible for celebratory accounts of globalization and the neoliberal end of history it is also a signifier that points to how the spatial concepts of political modernity are no longer capable of ordering the conflicts generated by global capital with its attendant forms of production and accumulation. Thus, the synechdochal logic of Bolaño's characterization violently undermines itself, tearing itself asunder, and we are left with a rhetorical gesture that announces the unraveling of the very referential system in which this logic ostensibly acquires its meaning.

Bolaño's novel thematizes not criminal investigation and revelation of forensic truth but the way in which the fundamental rationality of political modernity—the equation of the state with monopolization of the legitimate use of coercion—has come off its rails. Nowhere is the arrest of detective reason more evident than in the scene where the seasoned cop Epifanio advises the young detective Lalo Cura that his cherished handbook, *Modern Methods of Police Investigation*, will prove useless to him in Santa Teresa (Bolaño 2004, 658). The novel both sets up the hermeneutic expectation of uncovering something of a referential order—a truth or the Truth—out there in the Sonoran desert, hidden beneath the illusory surface and its appearances, and simultaneously ruins this expectation. The secret of the world in *2666* may then be that there is no secret, nothing to reveal, nothing left for revelation.

Perhaps the literary reflections on world and universe in Borges and Bolaño, both of whom approach their object as an impasse for presentation, perception and language, has something fundamental to tell us about the question of totality as such. In chapter 3, section 16 of the first division of *Being and Time*, Martin Heidegger thematizes what he calls world as the pre-ontological horizon of understanding that structures our experiences, thoughts, and practices. World in Heidegger's sense is neither a being in the world nor the sum total of such beings, and yet "it determines innerworldly beings to such an extent that they can only be encountered and discovered and show themselves in their being, insofar as 'there is' [*es gibt*] world" (Heidegger 2010, 72). Neither transcendent nor immanent, world names the (always contingent) horizon that conditions the way in which beings disclose themselves to one another. "World" refers not to a sum total of objects and beings but to a structure of interrelatedness that logically precedes the emergence of determinate beings that populate a world. Heidegger's formulation, *es gibt* world, says literally "it gives world" rather than "there *is* a world." The *es gibt* positions the thought of world prior to ontology and its mode of inquiry, which characteristically asks about essences. World is Heidegger's attempt to think an opening for thought and practice that precedes and conditions any determination of being, and it is only from within such an opening that ontology can take on its role of inquiring into the essence or being of beings. "World" is thus a name for a thought of interrelatedness as prior to essence or ipseity. Heidegger's term for this relationality is *Verweisung* (reference); the term refers to forms of usage rather than to language in the narrow sense. Heidegger illustrates the connection between reference and world through the example of a carpenter's workshop, where referentiality takes the form of the practical and mutual implicatedness of instruments: the hammer is a hammer only in relation to nails, the saw in relation to the vise, and by implication the workshop itself in relationship to an entire process of production, distribution, and consumption. Like the carpenter we ordinarily remain unaware of the world we inhabit; we move about in our networks of significant connections while taking them for granted and never stopping to question its structures or reflect on their contingency. It is only when something unexpectedly fails—the hammer breaks, for instance—that we suddenly become aware of the worldliness of our world.

In relation to the philosophical discussion of world that I have just rehearsed, *2666* can be read as a novel in which the totality that is world only becomes perceptible in and as unworlding—not unlike the inconceivable totality that is the object of Borges's "El Aleph." The form that totality takes under neoliberal-administered globalization is that of a bad infinity, an accumulation of particulars that has no unifying principle and no conceivable limit. As Brett Levinson has argued, Bolaño's novel precisely reproduces this illogic of the bad infinity in its own formal composition (Levinson 2009). I have been suggesting, however, that the novel also initiates something that may be irreducible to, if not antithetical to, this mimicking of the logic of global capital. Bolaño's novel is a literary performance of the short-circuiting of referentiality together with the unraveling of one of modern literary criticism's pillars: the detective genre and the association of investigative reason with reading and critical thought. In contrast to many of the experimental novels of the Boom and the neobaroque, *2666* does not engage with linguistic play or otherwise threaten to do away with referentiality altogether. Instead it leaves us in a position of unresolvable indeterminacy with respect to the referential status of narrative discourse. The result, I propose, is a reopening and reorientation of the old Platonic suspicions about literature and its presumed lack of essence or being. Here we find another way of working through the enigmatic formulation about literature and the secret of the world: the literary names an experience of language that brings traditional ontology to a standstill insofar as it leaves hanging the question about essence. Ever since Aristotle the metaphysical tradition has understood its task as that of asking about the essence of beings. Metaphysics takes its orientation from the question, *to ti esti*: "what is it?" or "what is its essence?" It never stops to consider that the question about essence stems from a prior determination of being as that which resides beneath the surface of appearances. Literature, at least as it has been understood since the mid- to late nineteenth century, unleashes a force that causes the ground of metaphysics to tremble. It thereby has a chance of bringing about something analogous to what Heidegger describes as the breakdown of reference that in turn brings us into confrontation with the fact that there is a world.

Although Bolaño may at one point have imagined that he was writing the novelistic denunciation of a problem that neoliberalism cynically refuses to acknowledge, it seems to me that in the end *2666* has something perhaps even more disconcerting to say to us, in that it offers no transformative knowledge of the real and no stable distance from the structures that we as critics and scholars seek to examine. That may be the real secret, the horrifying truth contained in the part about the Crimes, and that is why the descriptions go on and on and on. But the refusal of aesthetic remedies and compensations for social and historical problems in Latin America may in fact constitute a salutary step, not just because of what it renounces and certainly not because it would lead us finally to abandon literature in favor of more practical pursuits, but because it leaves us with a certain unavoidable *desasosiego*, an anxious disquiet, and this in turn may be an incitement to thinking, which is something very different from knowledge. It calls for thinking in the absence of comforting ideas and in the ruins of the history of metaphysics and ontotheology. "The world is alive," Bolaño explains to Mónica Maristain, "and there is no remedy for what is living. Such is our fortune" (*El mundo está vivo y nada vivo tiene remedio y ésa es nuestra suerte*) (Maristain 2010, n.p.).

Notes

1. See, for example, Hugo Achugar's contribution to Sánchez Prado (2006), titled "Apuntes sobre la 'literatura mundial,' o acerca de la imposible universalidad de la 'literatura universal.'"

2. "Los fieles que concurren a la mezquita de Amr, en el Cairo, saben muy bien que el universo está en el interior de una de las columnas de piedra que rodean el patio central . . . Nadie, claro está, puede verlo, pero quienes acercan el oído a la superficie, declaran percibir, al poco tiempo, su atareado rumor" (Borges 1994, 174).

3. In a different version of his translation of "El Aleph," published one year prior with Allen Lane/Penguin Press (1998), Hurley inexplicably translates *albañilería* as "carpentry." The mistake is corrected in the 1999 Penguin edition.

4. The work of Rosanna Reguillo (2010) and Rita Segato (2013) offer important contributions to understanding the specific ways in which the narco wars in Mexico act to destabilize distinctions between legality and illegality while thereby calling into question modern ways

of configuring the legitimacy of the state (i.e., Weber's notion of the monopolization of legitimate uses of coercion).

Works Cited

Bolaño, Roberto. 2004. *2666*. Barcelona, Spain: Anagrama.
Borges, Jorge Luis. 1976. *Otras inquisiciones*. Madrid, Spain: Alianza.
———. 1982. "El cuento policial." Prologue to *Seis problemas para Isidro Parodi*. Barcelona, Spain: Bruguera.
———. 1994. *El Aleph*. Madrid, Spain: Alianza.
———. 1999a. *Collected Fictions*. Translated by Andrew Hurley. New York: Penguin.
———. 1999b. *Selected Non-fictions*. Translated by Eliot Weinberger. New York: Viking.
———. 2003. *Ficcionario*. Edited by Emir Rodríguez Monegal. Mexico City, Mexico: Fondo de Cultura Económica.
Derrida, Jacques. 1982. "*Ousia* and *Grammē*: Note on a Note from *Being and Time*." In *Margins of Philosophy*. Translated by Alan Bass. Chicago, IL: University of Chicago Press.
Dove, Patrick. 2016. *Literature and "Interregnum": Globalization, War, and the Crisis of Sovereignty in Latin America*. Albany: SUNY Press.
Freud, Sigmund. 1955. "The Uncanny." Translated by James Strachey. *The Standard Edition of the Complete Psychological Works* XVII. London: Hogarth.
Galli, Carlo. 2010. *Political Spaces and Global War*. Translated by Elisabeth Fay. Minneapolis: University of Minnesota Press.
González Rodríguez, Sergio. 2002. *Huesos en el desierto*. Barcelona, Spain: Anagrama.
Gramsci, Antonio. 1971. *Selections from the Prison Notebooks*. Translated by Quintin Hoare and Geoffrey Nowell Smith. New York: International.
Heidegger, Martin. 1977. "Science and Reflection." In *The Question Concerning Technology and Other Essays* translated by William Lovitt. New York: Harper & Row.
———. 2010. *Being and Time*. Translated by Joan Stambaugh. Bloomington: Indiana University Press.
Hoyos, Héctor. 2015. *Beyond Bolaño: The Global Latin American Novel*. New York: Columbia University Press.
Johnson, David. 2012. *Kant's Dog: On Borges, Philosophy, and the Time of Translation*. Albany: SUNY Press.
Levinson, Brett. 2009. "Case Closed: Madness and Dissociation in *2666*." *Journal of Latin American Cultural Studies* 18, no. 2–3: 177–91.
Maristain, Mónica. 2010. "Bolaño en México." Interview. *La última entrevista a Roberto Bolaño y otras charlas con grades escritores*. Mexico: Axial.

Pollock, Sarah. 2009. "Latin America Translated (Again): Roberto Bolaño's The Savage Detectives in the United States." *Comparative Literature* 61, no. 3: 346–65.

———. 2013. "After Bolaño: Rethinking the Politics of Latin American Literature in Translation." *PMLA* 128, no. 3: 660–67.

Reguillo, Rosanna. 2010. "La in-visibilidad resguardada: Violencia(s) y gestión de la paralegalidad en la era del colapso." *Diálogos transdisciplinarios en la sociedad de la información II*: n.p. http://www.fundacionredes.org/index.php/descargas/category/8-revistas?download=18%3Arsiduos-electronicos. Accessed June 21, 2017.

Sánchez Prado, Ignacio, ed. 2006. *América Latina en la "literatura mundial."* Pittsburgh, PA: Instituto Internacional de Literatura Iberoamericana.

Segato, Rita. 2013. *La escritura en el cuerpo de las mujeres asesinadas en Ciudad Juárez*. Buenos Aires, Argentina: Tinta Limón.

Thiem, Jon. 1988. "Borges, Dante, and the Poetics of Total Vision." *Comparative Literature* 40, no. 2: 97–121.

Valdés, Marcela. 2008. "Alone Among the Ghosts." *The Nation*. December 8. http://www.theinvestigativefund.org/investigations/international/1015/alone_among_the_ghosts. Accessed June 21, 2017.

Chapter 7

Analysis of the Socio-Culture in the Study of the Modern World-System

Richard E. Lee

Our social world, the modern world-system, came into being during the long sixteenth century as a singular and historically unique set of long-term or *longue durée* structures.[1] An axial division of labor established a world-scale hierarchy of production and distribution activities; unequal remuneration and exchange relations assured the world-scale polarization of the accumulation of capital, its concentration and centralization, over the long term. The interstate system molded coercion and decision-making processes and defined the always partial autonomy of states based on the fluctuating permeability, even existence, of "international borders." These two large-scale structures in the economic and geopolitical arenas worked together to guarantee the availability of labor in the more developed zones of the world-economy during periods of expansion while regulating unwanted migration during contractions, all the while fracturing class solidarity, and thus resistance, at the world level. Relative power relations among the states secured maximum mobility of capital and the pliability of rules for the circulation of goods and services to favor accumulation in the core areas of the world-economy. Today, however, the crisis of historical capitalism is apparent, for instance, in that there are no longer any pools of untapped labor to incorporate at the bottom of the wage hierarchy to pull the world-economy out of periods of contraction and bolster the rate of profit in the system as a whole.

167

Since this has been the schematic form in which world-systems analysis has most often been understood and applied, it is not surprising that the absence of a direct way of addressing questions that fall generally into the domain of culture has been one of the most salient and persistent critiques of the world-systems approach. However, as early as 1958, Fernand Braudel wrote that "Mental frameworks are also prisons of the *longue durée*" (2009, 179). And this was even recognized from within world-systems analysis. In 1982 Terence Hopkins described the first two sets of processes as: "The *processes* of the world-scale division and integration of labor and *processes* of state-formation and deformation . . . that constitute the system's formation and provide an account, at the most general level, for the patterns and features of its development" (Hopkins & Wallerstein, et al. 1982, 12). Nonetheless, in another article in the same collection, Hopkins and Wallerstein et al. also claimed that there was "a third fundamental aspect to the modern world-system . . . the broadly 'cultural' aspect . . . even though little is systematically known about it as an integral aspect of the world-historical development . . . [and] much preliminary work needs to be done" (Hopkins & Wallerstein et al. 1982, 43). This was an explicit recognition of the existence of a third great overarching structure that was just as constitutive of, and fundamental to, historical capitalism. And over the past three decades much of this preliminary work has been done, conceptualizing this third arena in terms analogous to those of the world-economic and the geopolitical as that of cognition and intentionality, or the *longue durée* structures of knowledge.[2] The processes reproducing the structures of knowledge framed over the long term what was to be considered authoritative knowledge—universal, factual, scientific—to take precedence over other knowledges relative to particular sets of values, and therefore what action would be deemed legitimate and could be undertaken with some degree of possible success by social agents.

Indeed, the key word in the first part of the above citation from Hopkins and Wallerstein is "systematically." Most scholars today will admit that present relations of production and distribution display such an attribute, and that over a relatively long period, but not eternally and in all places. Furthermore, many scholars will even admit that decision making and coercion on a world scale may be analyzed in holistic terms. The point is that despite the historicity and attention to detail in recent studies in the third arena, the sociocultural domain, they generally focus on a case, or cases, of the historical construction of a category (in the sense of a classification criterion) or the explanation of some concrete event, state of affairs, or period in terms of such a category or categories. They thus remain rooted in nineteenth-century social science, either constructing, or confirming, or applying "universal" explanatory models through the analysis of variance or recounting "particular," interpretive, local accounts of difficult to gauge large-scale social impact.

The problem here is an obvious one. When attempts are made to articulate cases of categories, obtained in the second, classical approach, with instances of processes, the product of the first, systemic perspective, the methodological incompatibility of the two different logical spaces becomes clear. In fact, the most critical problem to be addressed in the general sociocultural area by world-systems analysts has been its specification in a way that would allow the relationships, interactions, mutual impact and reciprocal constitution with, and of, the axial division of labor and the interstate system to be specified as a unitary whole. In other words, how would it be possible to go beyond a particularist understanding of the cultural arena as either a self-contained realm of the aesthetic, the circumscribed anthropological terrain of multiple "cultures" or symbolic ways of life, or the (now largely discredited) "high culture-non-culture" divide to a conceptualization that stipulates a unique and singular structure recognizable over the long term that frames observable change and diversity as does the axial division of labor and the interstate system.

The structures of knowledge approach has begun to address this issue by identifying and tracing the long-term processes producing and reproducing the constraining relational framework—what has remained the same, the separation of the good from the true—of cognition and intentionality unique to the modern world-system. These processes may be more readily grasped when conceptualized as the initial production and reproduction of a set of hierarchical intellectual and institutional structures constitutive of the system over its entire life span and analogous to the axial division of labor and the interstate system. Once instantiated, the processes reproducing the structures of knowledge, like their analogues, have exhibited two forms of "movement" deriving from their internal contradictions. These may be differentiated by duration: that is, long-term development, a secular trend; and medium-term fluctuations—I have termed these "logistics"—that both assure stability, or the reproduction of regularities, and account for change manifested in the secular trend (see Lee 2003b).

During the European medieval period, knowledge in the Western world was relegated to either of two realms, the earthly or the heavenly. Although each was constituted in different ways, each dealt with both what was true, or not, and what was good, or not. The late medieval period, however, began to experience a shift, a radical epistemological divorce of truth, which came to be identified with facts, from the good, which was associated with values, restructuring the legitimate ground of authoritative knowledge claims. Such a split, recognized in the division between the humanities and (what would come to be known as) the sciences and unknown at any other time or place in the world, came into being along with a large-scale axial division of labor and the interstate system. The deepening of this split as a long-term trend, rationalization, however, has been punctuated by medium-term realignments responding to real-world crises contingent on the material contradictions endogenous to the processes reproducing all the structures of the modern world as a whole.

The first great phase of development, or consolidation, of the structures of knowledge corresponds to the period of long-term inflation and deflation running generally from the emergence of historical capitalism, roughly the fifteenth century, through the first third of the eighteenth century. The Thirty Years' War, the Westphalian solution, and the establishment of world leadership, or hegemony, on the part of the Dutch mark the period. The movement in the direction of secularization, the growing separation of facts from values, the true from the good, becomes increasingly apparent. The synthesis of Baconian induction, Cartesian reductionism and deduction, and a growing emphasis on experimentation and quantification brought forth a mechanistic model. The model, symbolically and substantively manifested in the work of Isaac Newton, was interventionist as well.

The second great period of development in the structures of knowledge takes place from the mid-eighteenth century through the late nineteenth century. It too is marked partway through by a thirty-years-long world war and the reestablishment of a state of hegemony in the interstate system with Great Britain as the leading power. The medium-term consolidation of the basic structure separating knowledge according to two separate epistemologies was confirmed and sealed when "science" became the epitome of authoritative knowledge. Classical science, built on the model of celestial mechanics, held that observable effects were physically determined and the discovery of universal laws would lead to prediction of both future and past. The humanities, at the opposite pole of the structures of knowledge, were concerned with the finitude of the unique and unpredictable rather than the certitude of regularities, but they also had to account for change, including emergence. Individual agency was the solution they offered and imagination served as the connecting link between mind and world.

From the late nineteenth century, this structural antinomy, the oppositional relationship between systematic knowledge and meaning or values, became a subject of vigorous debate in both philosophy and economics; eventually, the objective, value-neutral, problem-solving spirit of science was advanced and institutionalized in a set of intellectual disciplines to resolve questions in the domain of human action. This scientific study of society was what many put forward as a framework for a separate, or third, disciplinary domain, between the sciences and the humanities, the social sciences. If one could uncover the laws governing change—assuring predictability of interventions—in this area (that is, of human action or the social), or complementarily, delineate what could be considered essential features of different human subgroups (that is, as "facts" of nature) and therefore unchangeable, one could make predictions within some reasonable and diminishing margin of error and thus control the future in the name of "progress," without recourse to decisions grounded in the relativity of human values. This third great period in the development of the structures of knowledge begins in the late nineteenth century and although today appears to be in crisis, it does not yet seem to be totally exhausted. This period is also marked by a thirty-years-long world war that resulted in a new state of hegemony in the system, with the United States in the position of world leadership from the end of war in 1945 until the late 1960s/early 1970s.

Thus, the evolving hierarchical structure of the sciences, the social sciences and the humanities privileged, as authoritative, the universalism that was purportedly an attribute of knowledge produced in the sciences, the empirical and positivistic sphere of "truth, "over the particularism characteristic of the humanities, the impressionistic and anarchic realm of "values." This two-cultures conception of knowledge, the sciences and the humanities with the social sciences poised precariously in-between, was at its apogee during the two decades following the end of war in 1945. Its dominance was never total, however, and a number of approaches were developed from multiple disciplinary vantage points (e.g., general system theory, the structuralisms, the nonfiction novel, and the *nouveau roman*) that contested the prevailing model in terms of theoretical frameworks, or methodological practices, or even proprietary subject matters, and sometimes all three. By the end of the 1960s, however, challenges to the liberal order (such as the Vietnam War; the civil rights, feminist, and student movements; and the active engagement of third world scholars and activists) grounded in practice the direct challenge across the disciplines to the dominant two-cultures structure that would eventually be embodied in new fields such as cultural studies and complexity studies. And this was not to be simply the beginning of a medium-term adjustment, but was indeed a secular crisis and part of the transformation of the modern world (-system) as a whole.

For instance, scholars in cultural studies recognized the inadequacies of received categories of analysis; stressed rationality, decentered, and destabilized the naturalized separation of the humanities and the social sciences; and emphasized values and interpretation in social analysis. The emphasis in complexity studies—on contingency, context-dependency, multiple, overlapping temporal and spatial frameworks, and deterministic but unpredictable systems whose development displays an arrow-of-time—suggests, as some scientists are beginning to say, that the natural world as they now see it is beginning to look unstable, complicated, and selforganizing, a world whose present is rooted in its past but whose development is unpredictable and cannot be reversed. In a word, it is beginning to look more like the social world—undermining the purported "scientific grounding" of the social sciences.

One way the structures of knowledge articulate with the economic and political processes is in the area of local struggles of labor (which have always been opposed to capital) to hold on to as much as possible of the surplus that they produce. And indeed, the solidarity that could make class struggle viable at the world level has been consistently broken up across national boundaries (resulting in the medium-term chimera of a better life through the conquest of state power). These struggles have often been openly violent, but violence comes at a cost, to both capital and labor. The resolution to protracted periods of struggle, or often even the possibility of such, is that each gives in to some extent in order not to pay the greater price. Equally important, however, to the material consequences that both capital and labor wish to avoid is the consensus around the possibility of generational progress, a solution much cheaper for capital than conflict. Here the structures of knowledge play a key role in legitimating class inequalities in the present and underpinning the promise of progress in the future.

At this juncture, rather than arguing this point explicitly, which I have done many times before, I would like to propose three examples of the type of research and research conclusions that this view of the world suggests. Each of these projects addresses the question of how we can approach cultural objects, cultural practices, and cultural institutions to understand better how our world works and what alternatives we might imagine for the future. Two are institutional in nature. The first considers the university in general as knowledge producer and as, today, a putative avenue to the good life. The second is a study of the Library of Congress of the United States as an instrument of state formation, identity construction, and ultimately, the legitimacy of geopolitical power, or hegemony. The third example on which I would like to reflect, more in the terms of a question, poses many more difficulties since its status as "representation" is one of the things to be explored; here I am talking about Western musical forms.

The structures of knowledge as we have known them over the past five centuries, I have argued, are in terminal crisis, a crisis that is part of the crisis of historical capitalism. And this may certainly be demonstrated for the university as an institution. Universities have consistently been institutional sites of knowledge production and cultural reproduction in the modern world-system. But today, as a direct consequence of the intellectual crisis of knowledge formation, and the delegitimation of the disciplines of knowledge founded on the hierarchy privileging the sciences over the social sciences and the humanities, universities are faced with the dilemma of a future that will be drastically different, but unpredictably so, from any that could be directly connected to their long-term development. As for the material institutions in which our inherited patterns of knowledge production live, these too seem to have reached a point from which further development is most problematic. And this is coming from the demand side (for instance, more and more students in search of a credential and PhD candidates in search of dissertation projects) and the supply side (politically, can we really see an expansion of resources in the foreseeable future?). From a long-term perspective and in articulation with political and economic realities, there are several clear alternatives, but these alternatives will work themselves out differently given the different historically informed possibilities available on different campuses.

One possibility, to do nothing, is simply inoperable, except for the very largest institutions with the biggest endowments. The Harvards and the Stanfords of the world can perhaps wait without taking the risks that new initiatives comport; that said, it is already clear, however, that large institutions have been at the forefront of experimenting with the virtual classroom and online course work. But for most institutions, not changing is simply not an option. The pressures for efficient curriculum delivery, declining public support, and the competition from the for-profits are several commonly cited reasons this solution is not practicable. Certainly, many institutions around the world will be left behind and many may just cease to exist; in fact, the world has already changed.

For instance, one of the most important concrete developments of the many already underway today, and which will have enormous impact in the years to come, is the way the divide between the scholarly and nonscholarly is now facing challenge. Academics and laypeople alike, we have all been impacted by the advances in information technology and communications. As a result of advances in search engine technology, everything on the internet is equidistant from every other thing in cyberspace, as well as from every single individual user. Every classification criteria too, then, is clickably equal to all others; concomitantly, the scholar no longer inhabits a privileged space in the world of knowledge. No literature can remain proprietary; academics and nonacademics alike can and now do access literature, and intervene directly in debates, without regard for scholarly discipline or institutional status. The disciplines themselves, indeed all institutions and the "status" they enjoy, are thus deprived of much of their gate-keeping function and thereby destabilized. Just as new cultural communities and political constituencies are being created around issues previously segregated in noncommunicating areas of knowledge, the consequences of rethinking the opposition between ideas and action are already having an effect on political practice as well as in an expanded conception of market interactions. What then of the credentialing of faculty, their hiring and tenuring, student evaluation even? These are issues that will have to be faced.

Alternatively, it would certainly be possible to simply do more of what we already do and do it better, sometimes repackaging it. This seems not so much a second way of academics sticking their heads in the sand, but rather a rearguard action that does not address either the intellectual problem of the disciplines or the issues involved with declining institutional resources. Indeed, many campuses may try to take this route, or at least not go too far out on a limb experimenting with really new ways of structuring knowledge and its production. This will be especially true of the medium-sized, relatively high-quality institutions, which must decide where to put their not limitless resources with the least risk. We already see this in the way European national systems have sought to consolidate and streamline. Also, many of these institutions are public and, in the United States, prey to the partisan imperatives of the states that see them as sites where the political necessities of controlling the commodification of brain power and constraining ideological positions are located.

Nonetheless, a huge problem for many institutions as the intellectual grounding of disciplinary structures collapse is and will continue to be how to negotiate the maintenance of traditional, inherited disciplinary/departmental arrangements and at the same time move forward in a world in which the best scholarly work and our most useful ways of understanding the world are impeded by adherence to disciplinary boundaries. Professors teach in the disciplines; are hired in the disciplines; and then expect students to think in ways that collapse purely disciplinary competencies—unlike in the first alternative, here the problems are at least recognized. Some institutions are already trying out a middle ground by instituting projects meant to realize medium-term results or products (say after five years) that combine the particular disciplinary strengths of a campus. The Gulbenkian Commission (1996) made this one of their suggestions; a second was similar: bring scholars together in institutions close to universities or allied with them to pursue a common theme within a limited time frame. This is becoming common practice in the utilitarian fields of the sciences, engineering, and health care. These groups even sell themselves to administrations and funding agencies as interdisciplinary, which they are, narrowly, thereby acknowledging that the future resides somewhere other than in the isolation of the standard disciplines. Such initiatives are also spreading to the humanities and the social sciences in an effort of emulation and a way of effecting economies while leaving everything the same.

But these alternatives do not confront the scope of the actual dilemma head-on. The real choice seems to be the following: do we limit ourselves to reposing the model of the university as it has come down to us, but with various technological upgrades and increased emphasis on work-force development—albeit in well-paid STEM jobs? Or do we consider how twenty-first-century realities call for a new twenty-first-century model. The real winners down the road will likely be those campuses that consider what this last might mean in terms of institutional structure. Several of the things that might have to be considered are the "compulsory joint appointment of professors" and "joint work for graduate students" (Gulbenkian Commission 1996, 104–5)—across disciplines, or even without any departmental affiliation whatsoever. The field of environmental studies is in many ways a harbinger of an emerging model: scholars and students alike must be conversant with the scientific, political, economic, philosophical, ethical, and moral issues involved in order to do their best work. In any case, it seems that institutions will be most pressed in the short term to do something with the social sciences and the humanities. This is where the major contraction in funding is occurring and where the crisis of disciplinary structures is most evident. Of course, the normative argument—what is the "best" route to the future—will have to be made by the actual protagonists on individual campuses with their unique histories and traditions. The long-term analysis is, however, that fundamental change is unavoidable.

The second example I would like to explore concerns the development of the United States Library of Congress (LC) as an institution in the structures of knowledge shaping identities and influencing the relative legitimacy afforded geopolitical action in the interstate system.[3] The roots and traditions of the Library of Congress of the United States are firmly embedded in eighteenth-century European ideals and practices, but specific to what was to become the United States. The original idea for the library was simply to forge another tool for governing, a tool to facilitate the drafting of legislation. Although at the outset perhaps inadvertently, it nonetheless fell into line with the nineteenth-century view that equated a strong state with strong educational and cultural institutions. But as the Union grew, fulfilling its "manifest destiny" underpinned by the myth of "exceptionalism," so did the library grow and change focus to become a great national institution, all the while providing the cultural underpinning for these very components of self-definition in the United States. Eventually, circumstances, and the internal development of the library itself, guided by strong personalities, determined what would become the international scope of the institution.

The United States emerged from the Second World War in 1945 in a position of supremacy in the interstate system. Militarily, it was stronger than any possible coalition that could be assembled against it; economically, it could undersell any competitor any place and had become the financial center of the world-economy; and, liberalism—individualism, incremental progress, self-determination, and the expansion of the role of the state in the well-being of its citizens—became the dominant, but not uncontested, political agenda throughout the world. In this sense, the United States had achieved hegemony within the capitalist world-economy and could dictate the rules of interaction to its own advantage (e.g., the Bretton Woods system). Hegemony is never total, however, and maintenance of superiority is costly and eventually collapses as other states "catch up." In any case, the advantage of such a condition of the system for one state, initially based on force of arms, soon declines, and if hegemony is to be extended, it must be increasingly based on consensual relations. The element in question here is the way in which cultural institutions shape expectations of the effectiveness of action and the legitimacy of outcomes among diverse populations to the benefit of the hegemon.[4]

The Library of Congress was one of those institutions that served as a foundation guaranteeing a purported cultural superiority of the United States—and therefore the legitimacy of the rules it sought to impose. Certainly, hegemony would be even more short-lived if it were not for the groundworks of consensus afforded by cultural institutions like LC, whose multiple functions and services served as tacit reminders of preeminence and active interventions of hierarchical ascendency.

From its inception, the Library of Congress collected the best in Americana, and indeed continues to do so today. When the United States came out of the Second

World War not only were its archives intact, but within the walls of its national library, it could document its short history as "exceptional." It could picture its own superiority to itself and abroad in terms of democracy, private property, and a free market, equality and individual liberty, scientific progress, and social mobility and cultural achievement, represented in the collections as a series of successes. Of course, there were other great national collections and they documented much longer histories. LC, however, also made it its business to collect great national collections from all over the world, making it not just a "world library" but a "library of the world"—where many local populations in peripheral zones of the world-economy had to go to find their own pasts documented—and thus a central node in world cultural production and political legitimation.

Coincident with the international projection of its power by the United States, the turn of the twentieth century was marked at the Library of Congress by the decision to introduce a new classification system so that all its material would be retrievable. The new Library of Congress Classification (LCC) system became very popular very quickly, but among the consequences of any classification scheme is the stealth imposition of a specific vision of the world. In the international arena, thanks to the acceptance of foreign materials for copyright and the specific programs for the collection and classification of foreign materials, suddenly decisions regarding the relative merits—value—of local histories and cultural production wherever, and especially how they interrelated (reflected in descriptive classification and subject cataloging), were being made by cataloging specialists in Washington and reexported as cards for library card catalog files around the world. Once institutionalized in this way, matters such as social identities, cultural, ethnic, and racial attributes, and the political divisions that they supposedly undergirded, or even scientific information so often presented shorn of the history of its dissemination and diverse impact, can lose the dynamic quality of their interconnectedness. Historically contingent relationships may thus become "naturalized." Their human constructedness obscured, it becomes more difficult to justify arguments for their change. The lowly, but ubiquitous three-by-five-inch LC catalog card, hole-punched at the bottom for the guard rod rigidly assuring its location vis-à-vis all the other cards in the file, was the tangible representation of the superiority, and authority, of Western knowledge forms, the legitimacy of the power of the United States, and the seemingly unchanging quality of received hierarchies—all backed by the prestige of the institution the Library of Congress had become.

But in the core zones of the world-economy, the relative concentration of wealth and power, and their relative distribution, began to decline in the late 1960s. About the same time in the world of knowledge, so too did the essentialist, ahistorical foundations and unquestioned assumptions of the scaffolding of cultural superiority that legitimated that polarization become seriously contested by women, minorities, and third world scholars. Internationally, the value of indigenous cultural forms was reassessed and deployed to underpin the political agendas of national liberation movements. At the Library of Congress received relationships had already been baked into the system; what changed, what could and did change, was not the system as a whole or even individual cataloging decisions, but how knowledge would be accessed and managed in the future. The pivotal element has been the progress of automation, specifically, the application of digital computers to library operations.

Technological innovation to facilitate library operations has been of serious concern to librarians since the mid-nineteenth century, although the Library of Congress avoided computerization as long as possible and never envisioned the possibility of any "ideal" system. Nonetheless, in 1966 initial tape distributions of the pilot project MARC (Machine Readable Cataloging, the heart of the data base by which individual catalog records are computerized to be retrieved, read, searched, and used for the production of a variety of printed documents) to participating libraries for testing and evaluation began, with full-scale delivery of the refined MARC II format launched in 1969. As distribution of the system proceeded, and especially today with the progress of digitization, so too has the most common mode of access to print material of all kinds changed and the status of libraries in general been transformed.

Two events are notable in characterizing in a concrete way the dilemma of the future for the Library of Congress. The restored Main Reading Room—that glittering monument to emerging supremacy that opened in 1897—has been reopened after extensive renovation. It is splendid, as are the collections and services provided for over a century. But, forced to face a future of uncontrollable vandalism and theft (and shelving difficulties of such a huge collection), LC closed its stacks to the public in 1992. This could be seen as the first real shot fired in the face-off between the printed book on shelves organized by complex classification schemes and electronic access through information processing available from the CRT screen of any personal computer connected to the internet.

In fact, democratization of access and sophisticated search capabilities imply the decline of centralized gate-keeping, an increase in the ease of implementation of the social aspects of knowledge where "truth" and "values" may be seen in combination, and the waning of the divide between the scholarly and nonscholarly (see Lee

2010, ch. 4). The implications range from placing expanded powers of observation, dissemination, and persuasion under the fingers of bloggers and pundits, or the public at large, to the difficulty of establishing the defensibility of claims (e.g., "fake news"). Certainly, the ways we interact with knowledge stores and the actions we deem appropriate and effective as a result of the multiplying relationships we may discern among them are changing. These developments, of course, do nothing to diminish the cumulative value of the magnificent collections housed at the Library of Congress or the cultural productions the institution sponsors, to the benefit of the whole world. Clearly, however, in an unpredictable future of fundamental social transformation the sub-rosa institutional justification of received hierarchies of all kinds is becoming a thing of the past (see Lee 1996, 2005).

In the first instance examined, the university as an institution of knowledge production, reproduction, and dissemination, it is clear that the long-term perspective available through the structures of knowledge approach makes it possible to say several important things about the future. First, the institution as we know it will have to change in fundamental ways, indeed is already changing; and second, there is a limited range of possible alternatives that the change may take. In the second instance, the Library of Congress of the United States, the structures of knowledge approach suggests how the function of such institutions, which would include museums for instance, will be fundamentally altered. Their collections will maintain their historical value, but must be reinterpreted and redeployed in light of the ways in which they have functioned to date, but can no longer. My third instance presents, however, particular difficulties, and here I will limit the exposition to a statement of the problem.

In the following discussion of my third instance, it must be acknowledged that serious work has been done in the humanities analyzing the way identities and political/economic ideas shaping social action (the "legitimacy" of inequalities for instance) have been formed through "cultural production." Of course, the methodological problem linking the "fictions" of literature or much in the fields of visual and plastic arts to the real word subsists; however, these often score high on the scale of representation. But what of music, where representation is not so obvious (and roughly analogous to abstract or nonrepresentational arts)? The intellectual question is as follows. How could one approach a long-term project with the goal of understanding the development of Western musical forms over the past five centuries as fundamentally implicated in the material processes reproducing the politics and economics of the modern world? Quite simply, how is meaning made in music (apart from any lyrics that might give a clue); what is the relationship between the development of the internal structures of tonal music and the social formation in which it is embedded?

The emphasis on Western forms here is dependent on the observation that the processes of historical capitalism have expanded from its Western European center to dominate, but not without resistance, the entire globe. With this expansion have spread properties of the structures of knowledge propagated through music, some examples of which are gendered identities (e.g., the masculine and feminine cadence); predictability or at least inevitability; closure, goal orientedness, and the fiction of autonomy (e.g., the leading tone, the governance of the tonic); individuality coexisting with cooperation and the collective will; the compatibility of progress and order (e.g., the concerto form), and the depiction of Oriental exoticism, of the "other" (e.g., chromaticism, descending minor seconds, the pentatonic scale).

The overarching argument of such a project is that music is neither trivial (only accessible by way of aesthetic ideals or analytic deconstructions) nor simply a reflection or superstructural effect of the material world. In a word, the undertaking confronts directly the primarily "internalist" history of Western music that is and has been the most common musicological approach to analysis, rather than how musical conventions developed and functioned socially, and in fact became entrenched as social relations.[5] Certainly, composers are "agents" in the sense that they must bring their own individual experience and expertise to solving the particular problems of composition with which they are presented. Not only is this an existential necessity inherent in the choice of practicing one life activity instead of another, but for the practicing musician who makes a living composing, it is also a matter of professional reputation and material survival. These agents, however, act within time- and place-specific extra-musical circumstances not of their own choosing. Paradoxically, though, the music they compose takes on a life of its own, independent of, but nonetheless the product of, the conditions of its making: "Music adds something to other things by adding itself, but loses nothing when it takes itself away" (Kramer 2002, 4). Thus, no matter the impact that music may have at any particular time and place—not always just that of its composition—it retains the capacity for making meaning, of structuring cognition and intentionality, even when it is experienced in completely different social situations.

This project acknowledges how we often realize that cultural objects and cultural practices are not simply there for sensual enjoyment; they can have a shaping effect or constraint on the development of peoples' lives, on the social relations from which they spring and of which they are constitutive. In this instance, what does music, just the music, mean? And how does it achieve an impact?

As these three examples show, world-systems analysts now have the tools to understand how processes in the sociocultural realm function and to make some defensible statements about the future. It is now up to us to produce the same high level of fine-grained analysis that has been forthcoming in the areas of the world-economy and geopolitics.

Notes

1. The literature is extensive. See especially: the three volumes of Immanuel Wallerstein's *The Modern-World System* (1974, 1980, and 1989) and his seminal articles collected in *The Essential Wallerstein* (2000); for a schematic overview, Wallerstein (1983); for an introduction including origins and development, Wallerstein (2004).

2. See Lee 1996, 2003a, 2003b 2004, 2010; Lee and Wallerstein 2000, 2004.

3. For a detailed exposition, see Lee (2015).

4. There have been three such instances of hegemony, or maximum relative polarization of power in the modern world-system: centered on the United Provinces in the mid-seventeenth century, on the United Kingdom in the mid-nineteenth century and on the United States in the mid-twentieth century (see Wallerstein 1983). On liberalism as a political agenda, see Wallerstein (1995).

5. See, for instance, Wolff (1987), Kramer (2002), McClary (1992, 2000, 2007).

Works Cited

Braudel, Fernand. 2009. "History and the Social Sciences: The *longue durée*," translated by Immanuel Wallerstein. *Review of the Fernand Braudel Center* 32, no. 2: 171–203.

Gulbenkian Commission on the Restructuring of the Social Sciences. 1996. *Open the Social Sciences: Report of the Gulbenkian Commission on the Restructuring of the Social Sciences.* Stanford, CA: Stanford University Press.

Hopkins, Terence K., Immanuel Wallerstein, and Associates. 1982. *World-Systems Analysis: Theory and Methodology.* Beverly Hills, CA: Sage.

Kramer, Lawrence. 2002. *Musical Meanings: Toward a Critical History.* Berkeley: University of California Press.

Lee, Richard E. 1996. "Structures of Knowledge." In *The Age of Transition: Trajectory of the World-System 1945–2025,* coordinated by Terence K. Hopkins and Immanuel

Wallerstein, with John Casparis, Georgi M. Derlugian, Satoshi Ikeda, Richard Lee, Sheila Pelizzon, Thomas Reifer, Jamie Sudler, and Faruk Tabak, 178–206. London: Zed Books.

———. 2003a. *Life and Times of Cultural Studies: The Politics and Transformation of the Structures of Knowledge*. Durham, NC: Duke University Press.

———. 2003b. "The 'Third' Arena: Trends and Logistics in the Geoculture of the Modern World-System." In *Emerging Issues in the 2st Century World-System*, edited by Wilma A. Dunaway, 120–27. Westport, CT: Greenwood.

———. 2004. "Complexity Studies." In *Overcoming the Two Cultures: The Sciences versus the Humanities in the Modern World-System*, co-coordinated by Lee Richard E. and Immanuel Wallerstein, 107–17. New York: Paradigm.

———. 2010. *Knowledge Matters: The Structures of Knowledge and the Crisis of the Modern World-System*. St. Lucia, AU: Queensland University Press.

———. 2015. "The Library of Congress of the United States: An Institutional Trajectory in the Geopolitics of Culture." *Review of the Fernand Braudel Center* 38, no. 3: 177–203.

Lee, Richard E., and Immanuel Wallerstein. 2000. "Structures of Knowledge." In *The Blackwell Companion to Sociology*, edited by Judith Blau, 227–35. Cambridge, MA: Blackwell.

Lee, Richard E., and Immanuel Wallerstein, coordinators. 2004. *Overcoming the Two Cultures: The Sciences versus the Humanities in the Modern World-System*. New York: Paradigm.

McClary, Susan. 1992. *Georges Bizet: Carmen*. New York: Cambridge University Press.

———. 2000. *Conventional Wisdom: The Content of Musical form*. Berkeley: University of California Press.

———. 2007. "Towards a History of Harmonic Tonality." In *Towards Tonality: Aspects of Baroque Music Theory*, 91–117. Leuven, Belgium: Leuven University Press.

Wallerstein, Immanuel. 1974. *The Modern World-System I: Capitalist Agriculture and the Origins of the European World-Economy in the Sixteenth Century*. New York: Academic Press.

———. 1980. *The Modern World-System II: Mercantilism and the Consolidation of the European World-Economy, 1600–1750*. New York: Academic Press.

———. 1983. *Historical Capitalism*. London: Verso.

———. 1989. *The Modern World-System III: The Second Era of Great Expansion of the Capitalist World-Economy, 1730–1840s*. New York: Academic Press.

———. 1995. *After Liberalism*. New York: New Press.

———. 2000. *The Essential Wallerstein*. New York: New Press.

———. 2004. *World-Systems Analysis: An Introduction*. Durham, NC: Duke University Press.

Wolff, Janet. 1987. "Forward: The Ideology of Autonomous Art," In *Music and Society: The Politics of Composition, Performance and Reception*, edited by Richard Leppert and Susan McClary, 1–12. Cambridge, UK: Cambridge University Press.

Chapter 8

Ethics of Skepticism

A Case Study in Contemporary World Cinema

Jeroen Gerrits

Introduction

As a medium, film has a privileged relationship to what Kant, in a note in the preface to the second edition of *The Critique of Pure Reason*, called the "scandal of philosophy and of universal human reason," namely the apparently offensive fact that "the existence of the things outside us should have to be assumed merely on faith" to the effect that, "if it occurs to anyone to doubt it, we should be unable to answer him with a satisfactory proof" (Kant 1998, B:xxxix). Ever since his first attempt at drawing out this connection between film and skepticism in *The World Viewed* (1972), Stanley Cavell has kept exploring ways in which film expresses the possibilities for and limitations of our human capacities for knowing the world, other minds, and ourselves. His explorations, which specifically focus on the ethical ramifications of the problem of skepticism, have recently regained new valence, up to the point that Cavell has become a central figure in the emerging field of film-philosophy.[1] In this case study, I will discuss the pertinence of Cavell's concerns through a comparative analysis of Lucrecia Martel's *The Headless Woman* (*La mujer sin cabeza*) (Argentina/France/Italy/Spain, 2008) and Nuri Bilge Ceylan's *Three Monkeys* (Üç Maymun) (Turkey/France/Italy, 2008), two examples of contemporary global art cinema that showcase what I call the *virtual point of view*. Before providing detailed discussions of the opening scenes of these films, I shall first outline an ethics of skepticism based on Stanley Cavell's philosophical work and draw out its relation to cinema. I will then situate the films in the larger context of cinema history, which should help to call attention to their specificity.

Cavell's Film Philosophy

Ethics of Skepticism

Within the field of philosophy, Stanley Cavell is best known for his magnus opum *The Claim of Reason* (1979), in which he argues that skepticism of other minds is not merely a subcategory of epistemological skepticism generally. Cavell argues over the span of 500 dense pages, that inquiring whether we can know that another being is human (rather than a machine, an angel, a demon), requires a different set of criteria than asking whether we can know whether the world exists (as we think it does) outside of our minds. From this basic distinction Cavell developed this "moral perfectionism" that relies on a fundamental difference between moral and epistemological arguments. Cavell did explore cinematic expressions of moral perfectionism—most notably in his books *Pursuits of Happiness* (1984) and *Contesting Tears* (1997). Here, however, I will focus primarily on the relevance of epistemological skepticism in contemporary world cinema.[2]

Cavell distinguishes three positions regarding this mind-world skepticism: the skeptical impetus, the skeptical conclusion, and the defeat of skepticism. The first of these is the one that the great modern philosophers were struggling with. Centering on Descartes and Kant, Cavell argues that they formulated truth (or "impetus") of skepticism precisely in their attempts to counter its threat: They acknowledge that human subjectivity is not merely quantitatively or empirically limited, but finite in nature and in qualitative terms. Kant's concept of a fundamentally inaccessible noumenal world, for example, stands for the fact that our human capacities for knowing are conditioned, have insurmountable boundaries, and are by that same token bound to acknowledge the fact that the world is not simply given to us.

However, Cavell crucially argues that an acknowledgment of this skeptical impetus does not necessarily lead one to draw the skeptical conclusion. To arrive at the latter, one would need to infer from the limitations of human subjectivity that the world is fundamentally unknowable, that it, in fact, may just as well not exist at all. That the world may be a mere simulation, a dream, a trick played on us by some evil genius—represented in films such *The Matrix* (1999) or *Inception* (2010)—is the kind of hard-boiled skeptical position that Descartes and Kant were hoping to avoid.

Under pressure of this disturbing skeptical conclusion, one may indeed aspire to the third position regarding skepticism: its total defeat. Yet Cavell warns that this third position has its suspicious aspects, especially since it implies that the conditions of human subjectivity are shortcomings to be overcome. From an ethical point of view, that sounds as dangerous to Cavell as the skeptical conclusion itself. The skeptical conclusion is likely to spark cynicism and may well desensitize us by rendering our separation from the world an absolute form of isolation, thus abandoning any serious form of responsibility. But in order to be done with the threat of skepticism once and for all, one would have to overcome the human condition as such, or improve the species. Finding a balance between accepting the skeptic's truth while avoiding the snare of his or her conclusion requires a continuous acknowledgment of our human distance from the world without ever giving up on the effort to establish connections with it. For this much the Romantics knew well: the world *will* withdraw once we turn away from it.

Cinematic Skepticism

In his self-proclaimed "little book on film"—the 1972 work *The World Viewed* (a title that alludes to Heidegger's concept of *Weltanschauung*)—Cavell relates these three skeptical positions to the medium of film.[3] The desire to defeat the skeptic is ingrained within the material condition of cinema as a photographic medium. Expanding Bazin's famous account of the "myth of film," according to which analog photography automatically reproduces the world in its own image, Cavell writes that film "promises a miraculous neutralizing of the need to connect with reality" (Cavell 1979, 195).[4] This is not to say that we mistake a diegetic world for the real one in a temporary suspension of disbelief, but that the fictive world of film is made up of what Cavell dubs *automatic world projections*. After all, the moment one pushes the camera's recording button, the mechanical processes of photography (and film) bypass the mediation of human subjectivity, no matter how much control may be asserted before and after this crucial moment. Put this way, the quality of cinematic indexicality takes on mythical proportions (Cavell called it film's *promise*, not its actual achievement), but even as a myth it manages to place a remarkable ontological pressure on the viewer.[5]

At the very moment film taps into a desire to defeat the skeptic by promising to connect us to the world automatically, it moves the viewer into the opposite position. As Cavell eloquently puts it with a pun on the word *screen*: "In screening reality, film screens its givenness from us, it holds reality before us, i.e., withholds reality before us" (Cavell 1979, 189). In other words: in the very act of bypassing human subjectivity in the act of recording, film, once projected, reduces the spectator's relation to that world to one of viewing it from a distance. Indeed, it renders the viewer's isolation absolute: the world, or its successive projections on screen, is not one the viewer has access to. Without the need to arrive at it logically (or even consciously), as viewers we "draw" the skeptical conclusion automatically.

While these two positions—the skeptical conclusion and the promise of its defeat—are intrinsic to the medium of analog film, what I call cinematic skepticism proper is the continuous negotiation between these positions as it is played out on the level of the film's narrative and in the use of specific cinematic techniques. Cinematic skepticism is not necessarily at play or at stake in *every* film, yet it does pervade the history of cinema and continues to do so today. It remains the task of the film critic to interpret its significance and its specific application in each film and in response to changes intrinsic to cinema, if not to the world at large.

The Changing World of Cinema

Since Cavell's writings in the early 1970s the world of film has undergone dramatic changes. On a technological level, the digital turn ushered an alleged break from what D. N. Rodowick dubbed "automatic analogical causation" (Rodowick 2007). In terms of production, distribution, and exhibition, cinema has undergone another turn: a global one. While the two turns mutually reinforced one another, I will here limit my focus to the global turn.

Emerging in the mid-1990s, numerous "new cinemas" have given rise to a revival of independent filmmaking on a global level. The films associated with this tendency counterbalance the spectacular blockbusters exploiting the possibilities of digital animation with a minimalist realism—another possibility offered by the digital turn, which has made filmmaking technology relatively affordable and manageable. These new cinemas can in some way be seen as revivals of the (now "old") national cinemas. But unlike the latter, they are not based on state sponsorship and they do not tend to engage in the creation of a national(istic) identity—New Argentine Cinema and New Turkish Cinema being no exceptions to this. It makes more sense, therefore, to approach them as instantiations of a global art cinema, not least because, despite relative affordability, the overwhelming majority of these films rely on transnational forms of financing, production, distribution, and exhibition. Martel's production team includes members from Argentina, of course, but from Spain, France, and Italy as well, while companies from the latter two countries (along with Turkey) also invested in Ceylan's film. Neither *The Headless Woman* nor *Three Monkeys* could rely on their home audiences to bring in the necessary revenues, and depended on the international festival scene for survival. The two films actually competed with one another for the Palme d'or at the 2008 Cannes Film Festival. Neither ended up winning, though Ceylan received Best Director award for his film and would win the Golden Palm a couple of years later. In fact, both directors have long been favorites at Cannes.

I take these conditions as a warning against reading global art films by default as though they were national allegories—as has happened with both films I am about to discuss. Indeed, the task of the critic and theorist of world cinema today is one of discerning the global tendencies and concerns, while staying attuned to the local specificities through which they are expressed. There is nothing specifically new about cinematic skepticism, which continues to preoccupy the new cinemas. What I do see as new, however, is a number of themes and forms through which cinematic skepticism is expressed. We can distinguish several subgenres of global art film in this regard, each of which captures something that seems emblematic of contemporary experience.

A well-known example of such a subgenre that emerged in the mid-1990s and still thrives today is the home-invasion film. In films of this kind, not necessarily hostile looking strangers invade a household and gradually pervade it with an uncanny, if not unholy presence. As such, home-invasion films have often been interpreted as commenting on the questionable relations between the inside and the outside, or, by extension, between the private and the public, which are put under pressure in a networked world. Think of Haneke's *Funny Games* (Austria 1997; USA remake 2007) and *Caché* (France/Austria/Germany/Italy 2005); Kim

Ki-duk's *3 Iron* (South-Korea, Japan, 2004); Lynch's *Lost Highway* (France/USA 1997); Morales's *Uninvited Guest* (Spain, 2004), or Van Warmerdam's *Borgman* (Netherlands/Belgium/Denmark, 2013).[6]

The two films I am about to discuss belong to a subgenre I suggest may be called the *collision film*. Traffic collisions are, of course, a standard staple in chase scenes and action films. Yet for all their spectacular effects, most of these barely impact the lives of the people involved, least of all when interchangeable, numerical entities such as "cops" turn their death-proof cars into heaps of scrap metal by the dozens (*The Blues Brothers* [USA 1980] and its sequence *Blues Brothers 2000* [USA 2000], both directed by John Landis, offer well-known illustrations of such chases.

The opposite is the case in the collision film proper. Just as the phenomenon of home-invasion as such has long been a staple in horror and thriller genres, but was reinvented beyond the trope of the murderer in the basement in the 1990s, the collision film has all but entirely stripped the crash of its potentially spectacular value. At times the crash is even withheld from view altogether in order to focus instead on the—often indirect—effects on its survivors. Again, like the home-invasion genre, films of this kind emerged in the 1990s. Notable examples include Kieślowski's *Three Colors: Blue* (Poland/France, 1993), Cronenberg's *Crash* (Canada/UK, 1996), Egoyan's *The Sweet Hereafter* (Canada, 1997), and Alejandro Amenábar's *Open Your Eyes* (Spain/France/Italy, 1997) and its Hollywood remake *Vanilla Sky* (2001). The subgenre has expanded exponentially since the turn of the century, with films like *A Separation* (dir. Asghar Farhadi, Iran, 2011), *Adaptation* (dir. Spike Jonze, USA, 2002), *Amores Perros* (dir. Alejandro Gonzalez Iñárritu, Mexico, 2000), *Child's Pose* (dir. Calin Peter Netzer, Romania, 2013), *The Headless Woman* (dir. Lucrecia Martel, Argentina/France/Italy/Spain, 2008), *Louder than Bombs* (dir. Joachim Trier, Norway/France/Denmark, 2015), *Premonition* (dir. Norio Tsuruta, Japan, 2004), *Reservation Road* (dir. Terry George, USA/Germany 2007), *Three Monkeys* (dir. Nuri Bilge Ceylan, Turkey/France/Italy 2008), *The Watchtower* (dir. Pelin Esmer, Turkey/France/Germany, 2012), and *Whiplash* (dir. Damien Chazelle, USA, 2014).[7]

The accidents in these films are emblematic for contemporary experience. Collisions raise the questions about individual agents and their personal responsibility within complex networks of traffic systems. In collision films, crashes are not a consequence of a heroic escape from the law; rather, their significance lies in the radical unpredictability and high degree of chance and randomness involved in the accident, combined with the sudden loss of control, not only over the car, but—survival permitting—over one's life. The point of the films is not to occasion a reconstruction of the truth of what happened at the specific occasion of the collision. Instead, the accidents occasion discoveries of interwoven networks: even a minor accident in a traffic system can open up deeper fissures in family ties and often touch on profound sociopolitical pressure points. The accidents thus reach beyond the significance of their own (literal and figurative) impact: they all-but-instantaneously reshuffle the premises and promises of one's quotidian existence against the daunting scale of a global politics, calling for a reevaluation of the moral conditions under which it had been lived day-to-day.[8]

Case Study

The Headless Woman and *Three Monkeys*

Martel's *The Headless Woman* (*La mujer sin cabeza*) and Ceylan's *Three Monkeys* (Üç Maymun) have so much in common that it is all but uncanny to think they were indeed competing with one another for the Palme d'or, as pointed out above. Both films start with a hit-and-run accident shown (or, rather, withheld from view) in the prologue. The main body of each film deals with damage control, and concludes with definite shedding of responsibility. Meanwhile, however, the main characters are subject to serious crises and revelations that challenge them to rethink the nature of their relation to the world in general. The films further include an important adulterous relationship and the mysterious presence of a drowned boy. The similarities trickle down all the way to the details. Both films share the pervading audible presence of ringing cell phones, for example, and insist on the allegorical significance of water, with the respective protagonists having bottled water poured over the backs of their heads. Yet it is the way in which both Martel and Ceylan give specific significance to what I will call *the virtual point of view* that stands out most significantly, especially as the use of this technique sheds a distinct light on cinematic skepticism and its ethical ramifications. I will describe each of the three-minute-long scenes of the accidents as shown in the respective prologues in order to explicate this.

The Accidents

The scene of the accident in Martel's film opens with a blonde middle-aged woman—her nickname is Vero, Italian for *true*—driving in broad daylight on a deserted country road alongside an empty canal.⁹ After a short, near-subjective through-a-windshield shot that shows nothing of interest, the camera, ostensibly placed on the passenger seat, laterally frames Vero for the entire duration of the scene, with the exception of a brief but remarkable interruption that I shall discuss momentarily. Vero briefly takes her eyes off the road (see fig. 8.1) to search for a phone ringing in her purse on the passenger seat—our eyes are still fixed on her—when the car hits something. Though the sudden impact seems violent and shocking, the consequences initially appear manageable—for Vero at least. She merely loses her sunglasses and bangs her head slightly against the steering wheel. She stops the car and recovers her breath.

Vero reaches for the door handle to get out of the car, but then hesitates and changes her mind (see fig. 8.2). After a brief pause she slowly drives away from the scene only to stop again around the next bend in the road. There she does get out, unlike the camera, which slightly (therefore perhaps all the more awkwardly) tilts but remains inside the car. Vero paces up and down, literally headless from the spectator's point of view, as her body is truncated by the edges of the car's windshield. Rain—that allegorical eraser—starts falling in thick drops on the windshield (a diegetic screen of sorts) until the title frame cuts the scene (see fig. 8.3).

Figure 8.1. The scene leading up to the accident in *The Headless Woman*.¹⁰

Figures 8.2, 8.3. The immediate aftermath of the accident in *The Headless Woman*.

Ceylan's *Three Monkeys* starts with an objective windshield shot of a male, middle-aged driver fighting off sleep behind the wheel (see fig. 8.4). He is not yet known to the first-time viewer as Servet, a name that translates as "riches" or "fortune." Servet is a contractor-cum-politician and living embodiment of the new money that comes with the intersection of global capitalism and politics. Aside from this opening shot, Ceylan's three-minute-long prologue is composed of two mirroring scenes, each consisting of a single long take.

The first of these starts when we cut from the windshield shot to a view of the back of a car, which serves as an establishing shot of sorts: we now see that the man is driving at moderate speed on a desolate country road at night, surrounded by trees (fig. 8.5). Having been trailed by the camera for a while, the car gradu-

Figures 8.4, 8.5. The scene leading to the accident in *Three Monkeys*.

ally drives away into the distance. To the viewer, the circumference of the light cast by the car's headlights appears to shrink to a mere dot on a big black screen. Meanwhile, the noise of the car gradually gives way to the ambient sound of the surrounding forest, with its crickets and chirping birds. Break lights provide a last red glow before the car takes a turn and disappears altogether, leaving us literally in the dark about the events taking place just behind the road's bend in the distance. Within this total blackness we can hear a faint noise of screeching tires.

The second half of the prologue reverses the order of things. This time around the scene starts off with a black screen. The chirping of crickets and birds is now all but suppressed by the steady sound of pouring rain. We hear a car approaching before we get to see its headlights coming from behind a distant bend in the road. The light beam reveals a barely discernible man running from the middle ground of this shot to hide behind a car parked in the foreground; only the roof of this car is visible along the bottom edge of the frame. The approaching car stops when it arrives at an indistinct body lying in the middle of the road, in the middle ground of the shot (see fig. 8.6).

We hear car doors opening, but no one gets out. A man's voice asks a woman what she thinks she is doing, to which she replies: "To have a look, the guy looks alive." "Don't be ridiculous," the male voice urges her to stay inside the car, "we'll call the police." On that note they drive off. Servet now reappears from behind the car parked in the foreground. He walks around the vehicle, gets in, and wipes the wheel with a tissue. The scene cuts to the title frame as Servet drives off, accompanied by a roaring thunderbolt to punctuate the end of the prologue.

Wanting "to have a look" but not being allowed one: it is as though the man in the car were Ceylan himself, frustrating the viewer's desire as much as the woman's. Indeed, the viewing position is so awkwardly restrained that this, more than anything, seems to be point of the entire scene. Since it seems clear enough what has happened (and since Servet, unlike us and unlike Vero in *The Headless Woman*, *knows* what he has hit), we are to figure out why Ceylan robbed us of our view of such an *obvious* event. What is the function of *this* particular constraint? This question becomes all the more pressing once we realize that Ceylan, like

Figure 8.6. The immediate aftermath of the accident in *Three Monkeys*.

Martel, puts the *virtual point of view* to work. Let us first see what this concept entails and how it works in the scene from *The Headless Woman* and then return to Ceylan's prologue.

The Virtual Point of View in *The Headless Woman*

Let us examine the brief interruption of the long lateral take that constitutes almost the entire accident scene in *The Headless Woman*, which I had omitted from my description but promised to discuss later. It concerns a brief rear window shot onto the scene of the accident, and occurs when Vero drives away from it. It is so brief indeed that we are probably unable to discriminate what the shot shows upon first viewing. At best, we may be able to see that *something* is lying in "the middle of the road" (which so happens to be the name of the band whose song "Soley, Soley" is playing on Vero's car radio during the accident). With pause buttons and other digital tools at our disposal, however, we can readily determine this to be a dog (see fig. 8.7 and close up).

James Quandt makes an interesting point when he writes in his review of *The Headless Woman* that this particular shot "has been described as subjective, as being from Vero's point of view, but probably isn't" (Quandt 2009, 95). And indeed, we do not see the frame of the rearview mirror itself within the frame of the shot, as is customary in such cases—think of Marion anxiously spotting the police car behind her in *Psycho*, or *Taxi Driver*'s amazing final shot. Vero neither glances in the direction of the mirror when we cut back to her—the scene does not follow the editing conventions for an eyeline match—nor does she show any signs of having observed or of trying to discern anything significant in the mirror. I would doubt, then, what Amy Taubin asserts in her review of *The Headless Woman*: "In the rearview mirror we see, as she [Vero] also must, her victim lying in the road but whether it is a dog or a child or both is unclear" (Taubin 2009, 23). Given our pause button, it is clear enough what Taubin doubts: that we see a dog and not a child. What we ought to doubt is what Taubin states with confidence: that we are looking through a mirror, and that Vero is (or must be) doing the same. Given that Vero did not get out of the car, thus avoiding the knowledge of what she had hit, it would make sense for her to want to avoid *this* confrontational (if mediated) view as well.

Figure 8.7 and close up. Virtual point of view.

Much of the rest of the film revolves around the question of whether Vero (believes she) had hit a dog or a child, and Taubin indeed has reasons to doubt that the film provides any unequivocal answers in that direction. But when it comes to the particular shot under consideration, I would rather side with Quandt when he doubts the subjective nature of the rear window shot, however hesitantly ("it probably isn't"). Yet he too seems to miss an important point when he parenthetically adds: "(The film's central mystery rests on the ontological status of that one image)" (Quandt 2009, 95). Although Quandt does not elaborate on this suggestive comment, I would argue that the ontological status of this image is an interesting one indeed, even if the film's mystery in no way depends on it—a crucial point that requires elaboration.

By doubting that the rear window shot offers a subjective perspective, we need not assert that it provides an objective one instead: the point of view is too specifically restricted to a particular place for that, and what it shows from this position is too suspiciously unclear. That is: the point of view is *localized but not materialized* within the diegetic world. Ostensibly, someone must have turned around to see this, yet no one was actually there to make this turn: we lack an actual character to assign this view to. I would therefore suggest we call this point of view a virtual one. The virtuality of the point of view does not necessarily undermine the reality of the shot—we need not doubt that there was something (a dog) on the road—but by lacking a stable relation to a center of perception, the shot renders its actuality inoperable or impracticable.[11]

This virtual ontological status of the point of view is in fact already apparent in the long take which this rear-window shot interrupts. In it, the immobile camera persists in a profile view of Vero sitting behind the steering wheel. As such, this is a conventional camera position for scenes shot inside a car. But if it is awkward already to maintain this lateral framing for so long (especially because nothing very specific is happening or to be seen for the most part), it becomes really suspicious at the moment of the collision, as it effectively prevents us from seeing what is happening in front of the car. The camera now strikes one not only as a passive recording device that does *not show anything specific*, but also as a preventive actor that *specifically refuses to show something*, thus withholding or restricting our knowledge of the nature of the accident. As with the inserted shot, this is neither an objective point of view—the cinematic equivalent of an omniscient narrator, which would have shown us what had happened from the best possible position—nor is the point of view subjective, as we have no reason to assume that somebody is actually occupying the passenger seat. With this uncomfortably insistent yet dispassionate recording of the entire scene, Martel puts a cinematic convention to use by turning it into a very deliberate localization: the point of view is conspicuously situated within the car, but as with the inserted shot of the dog it lacks the materialization or incarnation that would justify such a position. The final pan that reframes the literally headless woman in front of the car at the end of the scene only serves to underscore this awkwardness.

Martel's own descriptions of her camera as "a character with whom I identify very closely" and as "someone who belongs to the world of the narrated" can seem misleading.[12] Such specifications do not quite apply to our instances of the virtual point of view—not, at least, if we take Martel's words literally. Had the camera been a character indeed, it could have picked up Vero's phone and prevented an accident to begin with. The sheer fact that it cannot do this *despite* being located in the car, or more generally the fact that Vero and the camera do not interact with and cannot acknowledge one another, underscores Cavell's insistence that the camera exists on a different plane than the protagonist and is thus marked by a fundamental, metaphysical distance or outsideness—a defining feature, we saw, of cinematic skepticism. On the other hand, despite its lack of interaction, the camera does suggest some localized presence within the diegetic world. The specification of this presence as a virtual one is therefore pertinent in a Deleuzian sense of something real but not actual.[13]

Martel offers a better characterization of her camera when she describes herself as "playing doctor" by using the technical aspects of cinema as though they were "medical instruments." The camera, she mentioned in an interview, "is like a microscope. Behind it, I feel as though I am examining my characters—though I [also] have a very strong feeling that the closer I get, the less I know" (Matheou 2010, 30). In another conversation she puts it as follows:

> There's a medical aspect in my filmmaking in that I try to get as close as possible to my subject in an almost microscopic way and from that draw more general reflections. The set of a film can be similar to an office where X-rays or CAT scans are made of the body. All these technical aspects allow us to come closer and closer to discovering and putting out into the world the mystery that is by nature secret and mysterious, and that's the mind itself. (Oumano 2011, 177)[14]

This citation suggests that the central mystery of the film does not primarily concern the question whether Vero hit a dog or actually killed a person on the road, but whether we can gather what goes on in her mind. All we have at our disposal to read Vero's mind is her body, and one of the central mysteries for Martel concerns the gap existing between the two ("the closer I get, the less I know"). By situating her camera between subjective and objective positions, Martel seems intent to "record" this gap between body and soul, between mind and world.

We can elaborate on the significance of this virtual point of view by understanding it as a particular instantiation or variation of what Deleuze dubbed "free indirect vision," which in turn is a specific rendering of Pier Paolo Pasolini's appropriation of *free indirect discourse* for the cinema.[15] Here, however, we should be careful not to take the term too narrowly, as Matt Losada does in his reading of *The Headless Woman*: if free indirect discourse were limited to a camera assuming a subjective presence *by simulating or mimicking a character's way of seeing* even when objective points of view are used (that is, ultimately, even when the protagonist him- or herself is in view), we run the risk of missing the point entirely.[16] Martel's camera, despite its insistent fixation on Vero, is anything but immersive or mimetic. Likewise, we would miss another, if related point of Martel's film were we to assume that the "information provided to the viewer is restricted to that known to the protagonist," as is the case in Losada's understanding of free indirect discourse (Losada 2010, 308). It is true that, by withholding our view onto the road, Martel seems to reduce our knowledge of the accident to Vero's. Yet I would counter that *The Headless Woman* is precisely premised on a discrepancy between two bodies of knowledge, both restricted but unequally so: the protagonist's and the film's, or what comes to the same thing, Vero's and ours.

The Virtual Point of View in *Three Monkeys*

Ceylan likewise puts the virtual point of view to use in the prologue to *Three Monkeys* discussed above. We can see it at work when the car drives away into the distance. As in the case of Martel, who gave new significance to the conventional positioning of the camera on the passenger seat, Ceylan turns the convention of a trailing camera into a meaningful gesture by having the car drive away from it. This does not happen because the car accelerates, but because the trailing camera slows down and in so doing ceases to offer what until then seemed to be an objective point of view. Indeed, as the sounds from the forest increase and gradually replace the noise of the car, our sense of physical presence grows accordingly. By all appearances, somebody or something through whose senses we now experience the world not only stopped tracking, but stopped moving altogether. Despite this, no character appears to grant us a subjective vision. The shot shows no signs of a driver or passenger perspective: it is not framed by a dashboard, rearview mirror, or hood, nor do we see headlights shining forth. We are not offered a reverse shot revealing the identity or nature of the perceiver either. As a result, we should not only, and rightly, feel constrained because of our situatedness (we are so ostensibly *here*—left in the dark among the crickets—whereas we really want to be *there*—on the other side of the bend), but also because we do not even know what body—let alone what mind—we are asked to impersonate.

The effect of this virtual point of view is further enhanced in the subsequent scene. Although it consists of a single long take, the scene switches between subjective and objective perspectives due to the virtuoso interaction between camera work and mise-en-scène, which radically destabilizes the point of view.

The initially immobile camera is positioned behind and slightly above Servet's parked car. When the other car—the one with the couple—enters the scene of the accident, Servet runs to hide behind his vehicle, hence behind the camera. He sides, or coincides, with us (viewers) as he comes to embody the objective point of view, thus invisibly turning it into a subjective one. This fluctuation between subjective and objective shots is made even more pertinent when Servet's face reappears. Initially he looks off-screen to the right to watch the couple drive away (see fig. 8.8). To wit: we witness him witnessing the witnesses. Servet then turns his head to look at the body on the road, offering us an *over the shoulder* (OTS) shot—a subjective shot allowing us to look with, or, so to speak, *through* the character (see fig. 8.9). When he turns his head to look off-screen again, we no longer look with him, but at him, and we are no longer hidden with him, but from him. Without moving, then, the viewer has been displaced from a position behind the car to a position behind the screen, which is given further significance when the camera, hitherto immobile, suddenly pans down to allow us to look through the window of the car—the same allegorical screen employed by Martel—and watch how Servet gets behind the wheel. As if to underscore our invisible presence, the politician anxiously looks around him and checks his mirrors to make sure he is acting unseen before erasing his fingerprints from the wheel. This introduces the premise of the main body of the film, which centers on Servet bribing his longtime chauffeur Eyüp (played by famous folk singer Yavuz Bingöl) to take the rap and sit his time in jail in exchange for a continued payroll to support his wife and son. The prologue ends with a final gesture mimicking Servet's earlier turn of the head, the camera pans right to witness Servet driving away (see fig. 8.10).

As a whole, the prologue of *Three Monkeys* thus comes full circle: from the opening shot, which offered an objective look through the windshield/screen at Servet fighting off his sleep behind the wheel, we came to occupy a disembodied

Figures 8.8–8.10. Virtual point of view in *Three Monkeys*.

position within the diegetic world. After the cut Servet came to embody our position, until we were finally put back behind the window/screen, only to start the sequence again as we are left behind with the car driving off into the distance. This cyclical structure in fact anticipates the structure of the film as a whole.

Conclusion: Ethics of Cinematic Skepticism, the Virtual POV, and the Global Turn

That Servet's car drives *away from us* at the end of Ceylan's prologue, leaving us behind, or out, as though it were crossing some metaphysical border we cannot now pass along with it, may well signify the radical outsideness that qualifies our relation to any film. Although we do not mistake a diegetic, fictive world for a real one, we do not doubt either that it is constructed out of shots involving real (prediegetic) people and settings that are, so to speak, *of* our world. The camera's recordings are taken automatically, and, once projected, they declare with equal automatism that their reality is one we can only engage with by taking views *of* it (rather than taking part *in* it).

Cavell's view on the relation between film and skepticism mostly privileges the connection between the skeptic's conclusion and film's automatism—each of which effectively foregrounds this radical isolation and outsideness of the viewing/doubting subject. I nevertheless insisted on Cavell's distinction between three positions in regard to skepticism. Beyond the radical positions of skeptic's conclusion and the desire to overcome skeptical doubt altogether, this includes the acknowledgment of the skeptical *impetus*, a fragile and instable position that affirms human forms of knowing as finite. Far from canceling out the extreme skeptical positions, it rather remains under the constant threat of falling back into either. Together these three positions make up the dynamic interplay I dub cinematic skepticism proper.

This is to say that the application of a particular technique—here: the virtual point of view—or the inclusion of a certain kind of shot—say: a car driving away from us—does not in itself suffice to tag any film as an instantiation of cinematic skepticism, let alone as a successful one. It is also to deny that cinematic skepticism is either a film genre or a medium-specific quality. Rather, I posit that cinematic skepticism pervades the history of cinema, occurring across genres and commonly accepted divisions (say, between classical and modern film, or between fiction and documentary film, or between first, second, and third cinemas), though it remains the task of the critic to examine whether and how any film advances its concept.[17]

I did propose the collision film as a genre. As such, it gained prominence with the global emergence of new cinema in the 1990s. I argued to read the accidents featured in collision films allegorically as the quite literal impact of contemporary experience in a networked world. The collision itself does not serve a spectacular purpose, nor do its physical effects drive the plot. Rather, the sudden, radically unforeseeable and usually unintentional confrontation leads to an interruption or disruption of the ways the involved characters have lived and understood their lives. Unable to go on without response, protagonists face a choice: they will need to break new moral grounds or cover the accident's traces that may implicate their involvement. Knowledge of the nature of the accident is certainly relevant, if insufficient to determine this choice.

The virtual point of view gives further significance to this break in a before and after. Approached negatively, this perspective strips cinematic conventions of their conviction by robbing objective shots of their objects. In the case study, the conventional camera placement on the passenger's seat (*The Headless Woman*), or its common activity of trailing a car (*Three Monkeys*), restricts more than it reveals. By explicitly withholding the narratively relevant object or event from view, the virtual point of view marks a presence within the diegetic world that nevertheless cannot be *meaningfully* attributed to a viewing subject (or to a sensory object, for that matter). Thus offering neither an objective nor a subjective perspective, the virtual point of view even goes beyond such literary devices as free indirect discourse or a restricted third-person perspective, since these still attribute the perspectives to a relevant character or narrator present at the occasion. I argued that the virtual point of view marks the very gap not only between subjective and objective shots, but between the worlds before and after the accident, or indeed between the world on screen and the world we inhabit. It marks a point of radical outsideness *within* the diegetic world, as though to offer a view of an invisible, metaphysical line.

Martel and Ceylan thus give specific significance to the virtual point of view. By relating this significance to its appearance within the collision film as an emerging genre of world cinema, I am not suggesting that the virtual point of view is restricted to or typical of this genre, only that is has a specific significance within it, and even then to different effects in the respective instances I discussed. In *The Headless Woman* the effect is that the questions of what has just happened and what is going to happen double in intensity: we are asked to compare what we (think we) know to what we think Vero (thinks she) knows. The gap opened up by this initial splitting of time is—by the discontinuity between the immediate past and future—and the parallel splitting of limited bodies of knowledge widens dramatically over the course of the film, as the viewer is not in a position to tell Vero's paranoia apart from a cover-up story in which virtually everyone appears complicit.

In *Three Monkeys*, the effect differs: here the question of what (we think) the protagonist (in the opening scene) knows is less pressing: we see Servet looking at a body that remains indistinct to us, but whose identification never becomes an issue in the film. We spy on aftermaths of events, and are yet kept at a distance, separated from the actual events by an abyss that forces us retrospectively to infer what must have taken place. And this is, in fact, the blueprint for the entire movie, which develops according to a *procedure of conjecture*. That is: the film does not in fact show any of its *nuclei*; it rather implies them. Anything that would normally perform a cardinal function in a narrative and thus allows the viewer to reconstruct the logical and chronological order of events into a story is in fact withheld from view in the film.[18] For the most part, all we get to see or hear are the reactions rather than the actions, the moments before and/or after, rather than the actual events themselves. But if the gap keeps widening in Martel's film, in Ceylan it keeps covering itself over. From the moments before and after events we can gather, infer, guess, and connect the dots to assume what must have happened: a web of slight, casual, indirect, and insinuating signs will do to confirm or seal our conjectures. Indeed, we would put ourselves in an awkward position were we to deny or even question what we think must be going on. As Ceylan has mentioned in an interview, his characters revel in their *pretentions not to know*, in their "hypocrisy of appearances" (Cardullo 2015, 106).

The virtual point of view is thus employed to different effects in the respective films. Yet in both cases it mobilizes the concept of cinematic skepticism by expressing that our forms of knowing have their limitations, and equally that our (recovery from our broken) relation to the world is not grounded in knowledge. Just as the virtual point of view is not restricted to or typical of the collision film, however, this new genre itself is not restricted to or typical of cinematic skepticism: not all collision films can be interpreted as meaningful instantiations of it. Rather, cinematic skepticism occurs across genres new and old, and may or may not be given new significance as the medium turns to sound, to color, or to the digital.

Notes

1. On film philosophy and the central place Cavell occupies in it, see, for example, Rodowick 2015, Robert Sinnerbrink 2015, and Steven Mulhall 2011, among many others.

2. On the difference between moral and epistemological arguments, see Gerrits 2010. For examples of film's and TV's relation to skepticism of other minds, see Gerrits 2012.

3. An expanded version of "The World Viewed" appeared in 1979; it includes the lengthy essay "More of the World Viewed." Quotations in this chapter refer to this expanded edition.

4. See Bazin's essay "The Ontology of the Photographic Image," in Bazin 2004.

5. Unlike some early realist film theorists, Cavell does not claim that photographic film in fact manages to overcome the limitations of human perception to effectively counter the skeptical conclusion. On this point, I disagree with Malcolm Turvey, who puts Cavell on par with what he calls "the revelationist tradition" (See Turvey 2008).

6. On this subgenre, see especially Elsaesser 2009.

7. This list is not meant to be exhaustive, nor is it meant to deny the existence of collision films prior to the 1990s. Notable predecessors range from *Lolita* (Stanley Kubrick 1962, remade in 1997 by Adrian Lyne) to Tati's last film *Trafic* (1971), and from Peter Weir's Ozploitation film *The Cars that Ate Paris* (Australia 1974) to Kazan's *The Arrangement* (USA 1969).

8. As with any specification of a genre or subgenre, a certain degree of arbitrariness cannot be avoided in determining its scope. It is not impossible to imagine a subgenre that includes other sudden events with high impact, such as airplane crashes or gun violence. Yet whereas the airplane crash indeed features frequently enough since the success of Marshall's 1993 film *Alive*, to say nothing of its hype in post-9/11 cinema, I would set it apart from the collision film as it does not meet the crucial criterion of a momentary loss of control and the subsequent question of responsibility. It would rather belong to the category of disaster movies. Gun violence, on the other hand, seems overdetermined in this respect: even when stray bullets or shooting accidents are considered, the sense of responsibility is assumed rather than put under pressure, and for that reason lacks allegorical significance. Other films do in fact consider questions of moral responsibility and push protagonists to reconsider their relation to the world, while they do not strictly involve cars. Hirukazo Koreeda's *Maborosi* (1995) would be an excellent example of this.

9. While the film is in Spanish, the Italian reference is unlikely to get lost on Argentine viewers. Not only is the Spanish *verdad/veras/verosimilitud* closely enough related to the Italian to gauge the significance of the protagonist's name; we should also note the fact, highly relevant in the context of this film, that Italian immigration forms one of the largest and central ethnic origins of modern Argentinians, with 62.5 percent of the total population having some degree of Italian descent.

It is further worth noting that Verónica—Vero's full name—is a term used for the basic pass in bullfighting, namely, the act of a matador letting his cloak trail over the bull's head as it runs past him. Here too the term resonates with the larger themes of the film, and indeed with Martel's basic story-telling technique, which I have elsewhere dubbed *Changüí*, namely, the trick of pulling the rug from under the viewer's feet. I thank Luiza Moreira for this insight.

10. All images in this essay are frame captures from the DVDs as indicated in the Works Cited page.

11. The term *virtual point of view* borrows from Deleuze's interpretation of the Bergsonian concept of the virtual. For Bergson's take on the "virtual image" as differentiated from both objective and subjective images, see Bergson 1988, 130–31. On Deleuze's interpretation, see especially Deleuze 1988, 40–43, and note 12.

12. Oubiña, quoted on page 87.

13. In this sense, Martel's film makes for an interesting comparison with Kim Ki-Duk's *3 Iron* (aka *Bin Jip*, 2004), a home-invasion film that Thomas Elsaesser interpreted in terms of the virtual and hence with the "new ontology characterized by 'ubiquity' . . . (and its corollary, invisible presence . . .)" (Elsaesser 2009, 12, 14).

14. This citation explains the significance of the X-ray office, visited by Vero during her brief hospitalization after the accident in a scene marked by a disturbing false sound bridge.

15. For Deleuze's use of the term *free indirect vision*, see Deleuze 1989, esp. 148–49; Pasolini developed the concept of free indirect discourse for the cinema in Pasolini 2005, see in particular the essays "Free Indirect Discourse" and "The 'Cinema of Poetry.'"

16. Losada uses this narrow definition in his reading of *The Headless Woman* to suggest that Martel's stylistic decisions are based on her "immersion in the mind of a character" (Losada 2010, 308). He does not, to be sure, specifically have the scene of the accident in mind when discussing the concept. Indeed, he claims that the film's opening is to be excluded from his analysis, claiming that in the "opening eight minutes or so the narration is fairly objective and omniscient . . . but then comes the trauma" (310). I am arguing rather that these minutes are precisely not objective and omniscient, any more than they are indicative of free indirect discourse in this narrow sense.

17. Cavell's own proposed genres within classical Hollywood cinema, the remarriage comedy and the melodrama of the unknown woman, involve films that would obviously engage cinematic skepticism, whereas films that seem to inspire skepticism about the reality *of the fictional world* of film by exposing the filmmaking process are not equally obvious candidates. This is not to say that Hollywood films generally engage philosophical skepticism cinematically, only that they are as deserving of consideration as any film, which film theorists have frequently denied. On Cavell's genres, and on the very concept of genre, see Cavell 1981 and Cavell 1996. On Cavell's impatience for film's self-reference, see Cavell 1979, esp. chapter 16, "Exhibition and Self-Reference."

18. Nucleï or cardinal functions are narratological pivot points that decisively push the action in one direction or another. See Barthes's "Structural Analysis of Narratives" (Barthes 1977).

Works Cited

Barthes, Roland. 1977. *Image, Music, Text*, translated by Stephen Heath. London: Fotana.

Bergson, Henri. 1988. *Matter and memory*, translated by by Nancy Margaret Paul and W. Scott Palmer. New York: Zone Books.

Landis, John, dir. 1998. *Blues Brothers 2000*. Universal Pictures Home Entertainment.

Cardullo, R. J. 2015. *Nuri Bilge Ceylan: Essays and Interviews*. Berlin, Germany: Logos Verlag.

Cavell, Stanley. 1979. *The World Viewed: Reflections on the Ontology of Film* Cambridge, MA: Harvard University Press.

———. 1981. *Pursuits of Happiness: The Hollywood Comedy of Remarriage*. Cambridge, MA: Harvard University Press.

———. 1982 *The Claim of Reason: Wittgenstein, Skepticism, Morality, and Tragedy*. Oxford; New York: Oxford University Press.

———. 1996 *Contesting Tears: The Hollywood Melodrama of the Unknown Woman*. Chicago, IL: University of Chicago Press.

Deleuze, Gilles. 1988. *Bergsonism*, translated by Hugh Tomlinson and Barbara Habberjam. New York: Zone Books.

———. 1989. *The Time-Image*, translated by Hugh Tomlinson and Robert Galeta. London: Athlone Press.

Elsaesser, Thomas. 2009. "World Cinema: Realism, Evidence, Presence." In *Realism and the Audiovisual Media*, edited by Lucia Nagib and Cicilia Mello, 3–19. New York: Palgrave Macmillan.

Gerrits, Jeroen. 2019. *Cinematic Skepticism: Across Digital and Global Turns*. Albany: SUNY Press.

———. 2010. "Disagreement as Duty: On the Importance of the Self and Friendship in Cavell's Moral Philosophy." *European Journal of Pragmatism and American Philosophy* 2, no. 1.

———. 2012. "When Horror Becomes Human: Living Conditions in *Buffy the Vampire Slayer*." *MLN* 127, no. 5: 1059–70.

———. 2019. *Cinematic Skepticism: Across Digital and Global Turns*. Albany: SUNY Press, 2019.

Kant, Immanuel. 1998. *Critique of Pure Reason*, translated by Paul Guyer and Allen W. Wood. Cambridge, UK; New York: Cambridge University Press.

Matheou, Demetrios. 2010. "Vanishing Point." *Sight & Sound* 20, no. 3: 28–32, 28.
Mulhall, Stephen. 2008. *On Film*. London; New York: Routledge.
Page, Johanna. 2009. *Crisis and Capitalism in Contemporary Argentine Cinema*. Durham NC: Duke University Press.
Pasolini, Pier Paolo. 1988. *Heretical Empiricism*, translated by Ben Lawton and Louise K. Barnett. Bloomington: Indiana University Press.
Quandt, James. 2009. "Art of Fugue." *Artforum International* 47, no. 10: 95.
Rodowick, D. N. 2015. *Philosophy's Artful Conversation*. Cambridge, MA: Harvard University Press.
Sinnerbrink, Robert. 2016. *Cinematic Ethics: Exploring Ethical Experience through Film*. New York: Routledge.
Taubin, Amy. 2009. "Identification of a Woman." *Film Comment* 45, no. 4: 20–23.
Martel, Lucrecia, dir. 2009. *The Headless Woman*. Culver City, CA: Strand Releasing Home Video.
Ceylan, Nuri Bilge, dir. 2008. *Three Monkeys*. Zeitgeist Films.
Turvey, Malcolm. 2008. *Doubting Vision: Film and the Revelationist Tradition*. Oxford. UK; New York: Oxford University Press.

Chapter 9

Polycentrism, Periphery, and the Place of Brazilian Cinema in World Cinema

Cecília Mello

The aim of this chapter is to reflect on how the category "world" as applied to cinema translates into the Brazilian academic and audiovisual environment in the twenty-first century. It starts by offering an overview of the main theories and concepts related to the idea of "world cinema" in the British and American academic debate. In general terms, there was a time when the category "world cinema" was partly rejected as being mostly a label of convenience, designating films not produced in the US and parts of Europe, while it was, at the same time, reclaimed so as to be used from a positive and polycentric perspective. "World cinema" may then be redefined through a democratic and inclusive approach that rejects the binary division between center and periphery (Nagib 2006). More recently, this debate has extended to the place of Brazil in the cartographies of world cinema, as seen, for instance, in the XVI Meeting of the Brazilian Society of Cinema and Audiovisual Studies (SOCINE) organized in São Paulo in 2012.[1] The argument for polycentrism, which has played an important role in European and North American debates, has come into contact, in Brazil, with a long and well-established tradition of literary criticism. Starting with the work of Antonio Candido, at the University of São Paulo, this tradition has been carried forward by the highly influential work of Roberto Schwarz, which is grounded on this binary scheme, in which Brazil is firmly placed "on the periphery of capitalism"

(Schwarz 2001). Is it possible, then, to embrace a polycentric approach and the idea of "world cinema" in Brazil today? And, more to the point, what are the political implications of shedding our peripheral status in order to free our understanding of the arts from the constant, obligatory reference to the constraints of the world economic system?

This question is set in a head-on collision course with two traditions of sociological thought that have informed the debate around the idea of "world cinema," from both a European and Latin American perspective. The first is dependency theory and the Latin American dependency model (see Cardoso & Faletto 1970), with implications in Brazil and beyond in the fields of literature (Schwarz 2001) and cinema, particularly in relation to what became known as Third Cinema in the 1960s and 1970s (see Martin 1997; Sales Gomes 2016; Rocha 2018). The second is world-systems theory (Wallerstein 2000), which shares its Marxist roots with dependency theory, but aims to refine it by adding a third element into the binary equation of core and periphery. This perspective has likewise been influential in literary (Moretti 1999 & 2000) and cinematic theory and criticism (Andrew 2006). Even if the two models and their relationship are more complex than this summary might suggest, they are nonetheless informed by the overarching Marxist principle of the impossibility to dissociate social-economic processes from artistic-cultural processes. Breaking with this principle means redefining the ways in which we think about cinema as a practice and an art whose specificities do not pertain exclusively to the social-economic system. This endeavor may well prove fruitless, and yet it is necessary to confront this challenge.

A Polycentric Approach

The term *world cinema* became increasingly debated in the first decade of the twenty-first century within cinema and audiovisual criticism and theory in the English language, and especially in the British academic environment. Volumes such as *Remapping World Cinema: Identity, Culture and Politics in Film* (2006), and the more recent collections *World Cinema, Transnational Perspectives* (2010) and *Theorizing World Cinema* (2012) are key works in this debate, whose centrality can also be felt in the increase of undergraduate and graduate courses in World Cinema(s) in the UK. Within this scenario, the most notable addition was the creation of the Centre for World Cinemas in 2006, a pioneering initiative of the

University of Leeds, first headed by Lúcia Nagib and more recently by Paul Cook, now under the name Centre for World Cinemas and Digital Cultures.

Broadly speaking, the debate around "world cinema" in our day is informed by a polycentric approach that, in tune with the digital revolution and globalization, rejects an understanding of the world system as based on the relationship between core and periphery. In "Situating World Cinema as a Theoretical Problem," Stephanie Dennison and Song Hwee Lim discuss two problematic ways in which "world cinema" tends to be categorized: (1) as the sum of all national cinemas in the world and (2) as everything that is not Hollywood cinema. "World cinema," they argue, would then be analogous to convenience labels such as "world music" and "world literature," "categories created in the Western world to refer to cultural products and practices that are mainly non-Western" (Dennison & Lim 2006, 1). The first categorization is flawed in that it presupposes the nation as a prevailing concept for organizing and understanding the world, and the second reinforces the hegemony of American cinema while also ignoring its diversity.[2] Both understandings would be at odds with our historical moment defined by globalization and by accentuated migratory fluxes, in which "dichotomies such as Western and non-Western, self and other, although entrenched in popular imagination, are beginning to dissolve" (Dennison & Lim 2006, 4). With this in mind, Dennison and Lim also highlight the need to separate the idea of "world cinema" from resistance discourse. They suggest that it is more productive to focus on the interconnection of cinematographic practices and cultures. Such an approach leads to the notions of hybridity, transculturalism, border-crossing, transnationalism, and translation, which have the potential of enriching the debate about the conceptualization of "world cinema."

But what is world cinema? Dennison and Lim do not believe this to be an appropriate question. Rejecting the impetus of theorization, the authors suggest that "world cinema" can be reconceived as a discipline, a methodology, and a perspective, rather than a concept. "World cinema" would be a theoretical question, destined to a "ceaseless problematisation, always a work-in-progress" (Dennison & Lim 2006, 9). A response to Dennison and Lim's foundational article, and to other reflections equally reticent in approximating the terms "world cinema" and "theory," was to appear six years later in the form of an edited collection that proposed—in its very title—to "theorise world cinema" (Nagib, Perriam, & Dudrah 2012). Editors Lúcia Nagib, Chris Perriam, and Rajinder Dudrah explain that their book is concerned with the place of "world cinema" in the cultural imaginary, thus presupposing its insertion in a wider discursive space. Their desire is to reposition some meanings and concepts that the theory and historiography of cinema have perpetuated for decades. In this light, "world cinema" could be seen as a renewed space for the theorization of cinema in the face of the recent discredit that haunts theory, beset by discourses about its end. To reposition meanings, according to the authors, means to challenge the diachronic and dichotomist obsession that informs film theory since André Bazin's division between classical and modern cinema (Bazin 2002). These distinctions are perpetuated by Gilles Deleuze in the categories "movement-image" and "time-image" (Deleuze 1985a; Deleuze 1985b), but also more recently, by Jacques Rancière in his theorization of a representational and aesthetic regime of art—respectively associated with Hollywood cinema and Bazinian realism (Rancière 2006). Such dichotomies also persist in David Bordwell, Janet Staiger, and Kristin Thompson's study of Hollywood classical cinema (Bordwell, Staiger, & Thompson 1988), and in Miriam Hansen's "vernacular modernism" (Hansen 2000). A similar pattern may be found in the opposition between Hollywood's narrative realism and Brechtian political antirealism as posited by Colin MacCabe and other contributors to *Screen* in the 1970s, as well as in Noël Burch's distinction between the institutional mode of representation and the primitive mode of representation. *Theorizing World Cinema* proposes a refusal of this dual mode. It calls instead for a polycentric approach to clear a path for original theorizing in cinema studies.

Yet the original theorizing that stems from world cinema does not resolve the elusiveness of the actual concept of "world cinema." The closest any recent reflection got to contributing to a positive definition of this category was perhaps Lúcia Nagib's "Towards a Positive Definition of World Cinema" (Nagib 2006). In tandem with Dennison and Lim, Nagib proposes the adoption of a democratic and inclusive approach to "world cinema," rejecting the binary division between center (Hollywood) and periphery (the rest of the world). She weaves an unflinching criticism of the use of the term in the British academic landscape and proposes that "world cinema" should be defined from a positive and polycentric perspective: it is not simply the cinema made in other parts of the world that are not Hollywood, or from other modes of production and address that are not those of Hollywood. This vision assumes the existence of a pattern and a diversion, thus obscuring local specificities, cultural influences, and different histories of cinema. But Nagib differs from Dennison and Lim when she suggests that "world cinema" is not a discipline, but a method of studying cinema that is capable of creating flexible geographies, moving through peaks of creation in different countries and different periods of time. "World cinema," she writes, "is simply the cinema of the world. It has no centre. It is not the other, but it is us. It has no beginning and no end, but is a global process. World cinema, as the world itself, is circulation" (Nagib 2006, 35).

Nagib's revolutionary proposition draws openly from the pioneering correction of Eurocentric criticism in cultural and media studies led by Ella Shohat and Robert Stam in *Unthinking Eurocentrism* (Shohat & Stam 1994). The authors' "polycentric multiculturalism" inspired Nagib's understanding of film history as a series of waves of films and movements that, through their correlations, create such flexible geographies. This leads to a complete rebuttal of the binary system.

> Can one really isolate foreign from local components of an art work? Could not the imported form itself be the result of multiple influences, often originating in the same regions that now import them back? On what basis is modernity considered an exclusively Western attribute, when Western modernist artists were constantly looking at Africa and Asia? A truly encompassing and democratic approach has to get rid of the binary system as a whole. (Nagib 2006, 33)

In Nagib's understanding of "world cinema," no single cinema mode occupies a center. She puts this idea to the test in her groundbreaking *World Cinema and the Ethics of Realism*, where she brings together peaks of creativity in film history that reveal a commitment to the truth through an ethics of realism (Nagib 2011). Rather than focusing on specific national cinemas, seen as isolated events, and rather than seeing individual manifestations as a form of resistance to the hegemony of Hollywood, Nagib asserts that "in multicultural, multi-ethnic societies like ours, cinematic expressions from various origins cannot be seen as 'the other' for the simple reason that they are us. More interesting than their difference is, in most cases, their interconnectedness" (Nagib 2011, 1).

"World cinema," taken as a polycentric phenomenon, thus hopes to reestablish equilibrium. It eschews dominance discourses—usually forged under the auspices of the so-called market forces—that tend to disregard the importance of cultural specificities in shaping cinematographic tendencies in different parts of the world. By the same token, arguing against the binary scheme also means revisiting the understanding of certain cinema movements as resistance to Hollywood's hegemony. One such example is, of course, the Latin American "Third Cinema" movement, which ensues from the Brazilian *cinema novo* in the 1960s, a cinema made in the periphery, in the Third World, and working as a form of resistance (Martin 1997). The polycentric approach is at odds with the claim that "Third Cinema" is an alternative in the face of a norm. It further challenges the enormous impact of postcolonialism on film theory, which was felt especially from the early 1990s onward, due to the rise of Cultural Studies and the ideas of, among others, Homi K. Bhabha and Arjun Appadurai. The work of Ackbar Abbas on culture in East Asia (Abbas 1997; Abbas 2010) and Hamid Naficy's "accented cinema" (Naficy 2001) are examples of this trend in film studies. The postcolonial approach occupies the vacuum left by the resistance movements of the 1960s, shifting the focus from the class struggle to the plight of oppressed minorities. It is not by chance that the rise of this perspective coincides with the decline of communism as a viable political and economic project. The approach to cinema through the lens of postcolonial theory is evidenced by the proliferation in film studies of adjectives such as "migrant," "diasporic," "hybrid," "multicultural," "transnational," "frontier," "intercultural," "interstitial," "underground," and "accented" as modifiers to "cinema," individual films, and directors. A volume such as *Cinema at the Periphery* from 2010, edited by Dina Iordanova, David Martin-Jones, and Belén Vidal, takes this position in defending the discovery of different facets of cinematographic creation, emerging from a global exchange that is far from symmetric, and thus working as a form of resistance. These and many other approaches are therefore concerned with highlighting a type of cinema, accentuating its difference, presenting it as the other of Hollywood. Thus, even if they appear as alternatives to the Marxist perspective that contrasts core and periphery, they perpetuate, despite themselves, a binary view. "World cinema" as a method hopes to eradicate such binary assumptions.

An Atlas of World Cinema

Prior to Nagib, as well as Dennison and Lim's aforementioned contributions in 2006, Dudley Andrew's "An Atlas of World Cinema," which appeared as the first chapter in the *Remapping World Cinema* collection, sees the immense territory of world cinema as the terrain for the emergence of different maps. According to Andrew, the composition of an atlas would be a more fecund approach, replacing both the binary (Hollywood vs. the rest of the world) and the isolationist (national cinemas) perspectives.

Such an approach examines overriding factors, then zeroes in on specific 'cinema sites'—provides coordinates for navigating this world of world cinema. No need to dock in every port as if on a *tour du monde* with some 'Michelin guide' textbook. Displacement, not coverage, matters most; let us travel where we will, so long as every local cinema is examined with an eye to its complex ecology. My approach might best be conceived as an atlas of types of maps, each providing a different orientation to unfamiliar terrain, bringing out different aspects, elements and dimensions. Each approach, or map, models a type of view: hence, the *Atlas*. (2005, 19)

Andrew's proposition for an Atlas, of course, follows Franco Moretti's *Atlas of the European Novel 1800–1900* (1999) and his provocative piece "Conjectures on World Literature," published in the first issue of the relaunched *New Left Review* (2000). Moretti's argument is well-known. He suggests replacing "close-reading," which would prevent one from looking beyond the canon, since it presupposes that only certain—very few—works are worth reading and studying, with "distant reading," which "allows you to focus on units that are much smaller or much larger than the text: devices, themes, tropes—or genres and systems" (Moretti 2000, 57). To this wider lens, Moretti applies a "law" of literary evolution that he takes from Fredric Jameson, and which goes as this: "In cultures that belong to the periphery of the literary system (which means: almost all cultures, inside and outside Europe), the modern novel first arises not as an autonomous development but as a compromise between a western formal influence (usually French or English) and local materials" (Moretti 2000, 58). This compromise, which takes different forms despite the pressure toward homogeneity from the Anglo-French core, makes up the system of world literature, a system of variations, single but not uniform (Moretti 2000, 64). Finally, Moretti explains how his notion of "compromise" differs from Jameson's: "For him, the relationship is fundamentally a binary one: 'the abstract formal patterns of Western novel construction' and 'the raw material of Japanese social experience': form and content, basically. For me, it's more of a triangle: foreign form, local material—and local form" (Moretti 2000, 64–65).

Andrew's proposition does not follow Moretti's part and parcel. He opposes, for instance, Moretti's defence of "distant reading," that is, the strict sociological approach, proposing instead to examine films as "cognitive maps" while at the same time placing them on the map (Andrew 2006, 24). But he follows Moretti by considering the hegemonic influence of classical Hollywood cinema through Miriam Hansen's notion of "vernacular modernism." This conceptualization corresponds to the cinematographic version of the argument that sees the novel as an imported form that has an impact around the whole world, creating modern literary forms everywhere. At the same time, in a similar move to Moretti's introduction of a third element to Jameson's rule, Andrew proposes a shift of focus, moving from Hollywood, whose weight would be too accentuated in Hansen's original model, to regional interactions with story-telling traditions.

Despite the originality of the idea of the Atlas, which provides a more complex understanding of the forces of literature and cinema in the world, I agree with Nagib who still identifies epistemological problems in the persistence of a binary vision in both Moretti and Andrew's propositions (Andrew 2006, 33). Whereas Moretti introduces a third element in the binary scheme proposed by Jameson, his view of world literature is still firmly erected on the dialectic between core and periphery derived from political economy. His thesis—"world literature: one and unequal"—borrows from the world-system school of historical social science, drawing on an understanding of the world as defined by capitalism. For Moretti, the system of world literature is likewise "profoundly unequal" (Moretti 2000, 55, 56). Similarly, Andrew's shift of focus away from Hollywood does little to brush off the binary scheme; his work often slips back into the "us" and "them, "center" and "periphery" dichotomies.[3]

Taking these observations into consideration, the originality of the polycentric approach arguably lies in providing a vindicating resolution for those commonly seen to occupy the periphery, by doing away with the peripheral positionality within the world of cinema. Although it is an attractive proposition, it still raises problems, especially when one writes from the periphery of capitalism. There are questions to be asked. First, if "world cinema" appears in the form of peaks of creation scattered around the world, how does that differ from the idea of world cinema as an ensemble of multiple national cinemas, framed by their most relevant moments as for example "the French *nouvelle vague*," "the Brazilian *cinema novo*," "Taiwan New Cinema," "Dogma 95," and so on? And what happens to waves of popular cinema and the American commercial cinema, suspiciously absent from so many polycentric world cinema books/studies/courses? Second, should "world cinema" remain an elusive theoretical category that must rely on other categories to be meaningful (realist, transnationalist, accented, or art cinema)? Or is it simply a method rather than a theoretical category? This last question emerges from the various ways in which "world cinema" is used in the titles of the most important studies in the subject today. The following list suffices to illustrate this variation: Elsaesser's *World Cinema: Realism, Evidence, Presence*, in which he claims that "world cinema has always defined itself against Hollywood on the basis of its greater realism" (Elsaesser 2009, 3); Nagib's *World Cinema and the Ethics of Realism* (2011) and her more recent chapter "'Realist Cinema as World Cinema" (Nagib 2017); or Tiago de Luca's "Realism of the senses: a tendency in contemporary world cinema" (2012), John Caughie's "Morvern Callar, Art Cinema and the 'Monstrous Archive'" (2012), Paul Julian Smith's "Transnational Cinemas: the Cases of Mexico, Argentina and Brazil" (2012), and Song Hwee Lim's "Speaking in Tongues: Ang Lee, Accented Cinema, Hollywood" (2012), in *Theorizing World Cinema*. If that is indeed the case, what is the importance of theorizing "world cinema"? What is the difference between saying, for instance, "a tendency in contemporary world cinema" and "a tendency in contemporary cinema"? Does the term "world cinema" risk being a hollow shell? Or is its use more political than theoretical?

Another question emerges from this line of inquiry: Why is it that "world cinema" appears so frequently—in both its "negative" (what it is not) and "positive" (what it is) definitions—in the British academic world, and almost exclusively in the hegemonic English language, yet not so frequently in other academic environments? This question requires a more detailed analysis that takes into consideration the process of affiliation of cinema degrees/courses with literature and language courses in British universities, issues related to postcolonialism and the subsequent emergence of cultural studies in the United Kingdom, as well as other academic, historical, political and social matters that prepared the terrain for this debate. These considerations lead to discussions beyond the scope of this chapter. However, they still raise a pertinent problem: if "world cinema" is so weighted with the scholarly debate in the UK, what happens to the term when the debate extends to the place of Brazilian cinema within "world cinema" maps, but also the place of "world cinema" in Brazil? It is worth pointing out that the place of cinema courses in Brazil differs widely from that in the UK. Cinema Studies emerged as an independent university degree in Brazil in the 1960s, following a trajectory more akin to the French tradition—the main model for the University of São Paulo since its inception in the 1930s. The study of cinema was not subordinated to language and literature departments and degrees, and both theory and practice have coexisted on equal terms in most of Brazil's bachelor's degrees in film. Within this landscape, what can we in Brazil do with the term "world cinema"? Is *cinema mundial* in fact the best translation of the English term *world cinema*?

Finally, and perhaps more importantly, what is the political importance of the defence of polycentrism in relation to the arts (cinema, literature) in a country that has remained for a long time and on many levels "on the periphery"? Are these categories (center-periphery/world/polycentrism) the adequate ones for addressing the place of Brazilian cinema in the world today?

Back to the Periphery

In the pages that follow, I propose further to investigate how the category "world cinema" has roots in the "world literature" debate, and is thus implicated in a discussion characteristic of Brazilian literary criticism, that of the cultural practices in the periphery of capitalism. As is well known, Franco Moretti drew some of his ideas from the highly influential work of Brazilian critic Roberto Schwarz, whose arguments are firmly placed within the dialectics of center and periphery. Moretti particularly gleaned two concepts from Schwarz, the first being that of "foreign debt," taken from the essay "The Importing of the Novel to Brazil and Its Contradictions in the Work of Alencar." Interestingly, John Gledson decided to include this article in *Misplaced Ideas*, a collection of Schwarz's essays he edited for Verso in 1992 against the author's will. To Schwarz, it seemed that no one would be interested in reading an essay about José de Alencar, author of the "second-class novel" *Senhora*. But Gledson insisted on translating it, because he saw in the idea of the traveling of forms an argument of importance (see Schwarcz and Botelho 2008, 154). Moretti, for one, drew heavily from it.

> "Foreign debt is as inevitable in Brazilian letters as in any other field," writes Roberto Schwarz in a splendid essay on "The Importing of the Novel to Brazil": "it's not simply an easily dispensable part of the work in which it appears, but a complex feature of it." (Moretti 2000, 56)

Foreign debt refers to how colonized countries import models from the colonizers, the novel being one such model, imported to Brazil—the periphery—from the center—Europe. This notion is complemented by the issue of literary form, thought of by Schwarz as being laden with foreign debt, a notion equally espoused by Moretti: "the foreign presence 'interferes' with the very utterance of the novel. The one-and-unequal literary system is not just an external network here, it doesn't remain outside the text: it's embedded well into its form" (Moretti 2000, 65–66).

Moretti's reading of Schwarz introduces the notion of "foreign debt" and its translation into literary form—concepts that are anchored in the arguments of dependency theory—into a framework of thought derived from the world-systems perspective. Moretti's *Atlas of the European Novel* and his understanding of "world literature" are important references for current constructions of "world cinema." Dudley Andrew carries the baton forward (from social theory into literary criticism and theory and finally into cinema studies) by proposing *An Atlas of World Cinema*.

The reconstruction of this intellectual trajectory finally leaves us nowhere to hide. It throws the question of "world cinema" in Brazil back into the tradition of thought of the University of São Paulo, from where I am writing these words. This dialectical tradition was generally seen as taking a clear form when the Marxism study group was formed in 1958. The group consisted of young professors and students from the University of São Paulo, such as José Arthur Giannotti, Fernando Henrique Cardoso, Ruth Cardoso, Octavio Ianni, Paul Singer, Fernando Novais, Bento Prado Junior, Roberto Schwarz, Michael Lowy, Juarez Brandão Lopes, Francisco Weffort, Gabriel Bolaffi, and others. The group aimed to undertake a careful reading of Marx's *Das Kapital*, trying to ascertain how his historical materialism could be put into dialogue with Brazilian sociological thought.[4]

The main name behind the University of São Paulo's intellectual formation and growth was, of course, Antonio Candido, whose understanding of the law of Brazilian spiritual life as being ruled by the dialectics of localism and cosmopolitanism, which is manifested in different modes, encapsulates a dialectical tradition of thought perpetuated for decades (Candido 2006, 117). Schwarz is a disciple of Candido, and his perspective is informed by the thought of Adorno, Lukács, Brecht, and Benjamin. His aim was to find the connection between literature and social process. According to Schwarz, this connection does not lie in the surface of thematic elements, but rather in the literary form, or its structure. The literary apparatus captures and dramatizes the structure of a country, which is transformed into a rule of writing. Schwarz's ideas are analogous to Fernando Henrique Cardoso's understanding of dependency theory, and translate into the world of the arts and culture concepts that were originally developed in sociology and, more specifically, within the Marxism study group at the University of São Paulo.

In his highly influential, contentious, and quite often misunderstood essay "Misplaced Ideas," Schwarz sees liberalism in Brazil as an idea out of place, unable to describe the reality of the country, marked by the central importance of slavery and the social practice of favor. In Europe, however, liberalism is faced with the reality of the class struggle that emerges in the mid-nineteenth century; this process reveals how liberalism and universalism are both hollow and ideological from the start. Schwarz describes the Brazilian experience as that of incongruity,

> of ill-assortedness—unmanageable contrasts, disproportions, nonsense, anachronisms, outrageous compromises and the like, [where] the social strata that benefited the most from a slave-system exclusively based on agricultural production attempted to create an illusion for their own use of an ambience with urban and European characteristics. (Schwarz 1992, 25, 26)

Moving from political economy to the aesthetic realm, Schwarz then suggests that the novel was a literary form equally out of place in this country, for its historical preconditions, such as bourgeois society, were inexistent in Brazil in the nineteenth century. "For the arts," he claims, "there was always a way to adore, quote, ape, sack, adapt or devour these manners and fashions, so that they would reflect, in their defectiveness, a cultural embarrassment in which we would recognize ourselves" (Schwarz 1992, 28).[5]

Schwarz's "defectiveness" echoes Paulo Emílio Sales Gomes's famous observation on the Brazilian "creative lack of competence in copying" (Sales Gomes 2016, 190).[6] Paulo Emílio's voice has been the most influential one concerned with Brazilian cinema's own "misplaced ideas." In 1960 he wrote his famous essay "A Colonial Situation," where he decreed that Brazilian cinema was and had always been stuck in a state of colonialism, a view that, according to Schwarz, accurately summed up "the situation that developmental nationalism hoped to overcome in the cultural sphere" (Sales Gomes 2016, 47–54; Schwarz 1999, 156). Schwarz aligns Paulo Emílio's early phase with developmental nationalism, historically locating his resistance discourse as a continuation of the "divorce between cultural aspirations and local conditions that is typical of colonies or ex-colonies" (Schwarz 1999, 156). Along the same lines, Ismail Xavier speaks of a "secular asymmetry" stretching behind Brazilian cinema's colonial situation.

In 1960, Paulo Emílio's talk during the First National Convention of Cinematographic Criticism began by analysing the critics' dissatisfaction with Brazilian cinema and the generalized frustration of the filmmakers in face of the precarious conditions in which they worked. This dissatisfaction did not unfold in an effective analysis of the neo-colonial economic-political conditions of the cinema, dominated by Hollywood conglomerates. . . . The "colonial situation," in short, was an expression of an already secular asymmetry since in the realm of cinema the division between central and peripheral countries became clear. The subaltern experience of this asymmetry was the dominant experience of Brazilians, who nevertheless insisted on making viable cinematographic production with scarce resources for an internal market that already had an owner. (Xavier 2016, 17)

In 1973, Paulo Emílio would treat a similar issue from the point of view of underdevelopment in his groundbreaking "Cinema: Trajectory in Underdevelopment" (Sales Gomes 2016), where he attempts to draw a panorama of the history of Brazilian cinema, having, as Xavier points out, the movement put forward by Antonio Candido in the field of literature as his main reference (Xavier 2016, 186–205, 19). But what he finds out is that this trajectory was hopelessly flawed: in keeping with the triangular notion of "authors, works and public," the desired overcoming of underdevelopment was constantly postponed. In this sense, it could be said that Paulo Emílio inevitably played down the importance of *cinema novo* in the Brazilian cinematographic panorama. *Cinema novo* had been unable to find a public, and so was unable to overcome underdevelopment.

The last point raises a few important questions. First, would this not be a dilemma akin to the very nature of artistic creation, rather than a mark of underdevelopment? Is "developed" art and artistic production that which reaches a large audience? Was it not the very merit of *cinema novo* and Third Cinema to prove that you do not need money to make great art, that is, to overcome underdevelopment? If our cinema cannot but be submitted to our historical condition of colonization and exploitation, then when will we ever see the light at the end of the tunnel? Would it be far-fetched to suggest that cinema, and political cinema at that, need not be thought of as being in harness to political and economic history?

Paulo Emílio's understanding of Brazilian cinema through the colonial lens is combined with an unwavering defence of the need and obligation on the part of Brazilian scholars and critics to see and study Brazilian cinema, thus embracing its mediocre condition. This leads to partisan claims that sound outlandish today: he argues, for instance, that any Brazilian film, even a bad one, will give a joy of understanding to the Brazilian spectator that no Bergman could, or that it is understandable that we see some foreign films, but to study them in depth is an action of no consequence. . . . The bad film, just for the simple fact that it emanates from our society, has to do with us all, and it often acquires a revelatory function. (Sales Gomes 2016, 389, 341)

These are indeed utterly anachronistic views, but Paulo Emílio is far from being a naive believer in a return to or conquest of some purely national cinematic expression, or of an original Brazil. His aforementioned polemic/political statements should not be taken in isolation and at face value. The recent work of Carlos Augusto Calil in editing the collections *Uma situação colonial* (2016) and *O cinema no século* (2015) is essential for reevaluating the depth and consistency of his work. Moreover, Paulo Emílio did not often practice what he preached, for he wrote extensively—as a critic—on foreign cinema. In an earlier phase of his career, while in exile, he extensively researched French filmmaker genius Jean Vigo. His book *Jean Vigo* was originally published in French in 1957 by Éditions du Seuil. It garnered praise from none other than André Bazin, and remains one of the most important books on Vigo (Fagundes Telles 1984, iii).

But in Brazilian academic circles old habits die hard. Despite Paulo Emílio's arguably broad cosmopolitan outlook, his work is still often understood through the lens of a commitment to an inward-looking search for identity. Given Brazil's condition as a relatively "new" country, this is understandable. It can, however, lead to a certain isolation in relation to the rest of the world, especially in relation to Africa and Asia—Japan being the notable exception for reasons of immigration. In Brazil we are much behind the United Kingdom and the United States, for instance, where researchers from all over the world write about cinema from all over the world. Language barriers, above all, need to be overcome. So, in order to nurture a truly polycentric view on different levels, should we not intensify Brazil's interconnections and transnational collaborations? That would also be a way of putting our cinema on the map of world cinema.

Before moving forward to the next section, I would also like to highlight how Schwarz's ideas, despite their impact and longevity in Brazilian academic circles, have been the subject of debate and criticism from their inception. They are frequently counterpointed with Silviano Santiago's influential "The In-Between Place in Latin American Discourse," from 1970. In this essay, Santiago mobilizes a plethora of then-recent French critical theories (reception theory, deconstructionism, poststructuralism, etc.) in order to suggest that the particular condition of Latin

American discourse "finds its specific ambit in the 'in-between' place, which is that of the deviation from the norm, the mark of the difference inscribed in the very original text that destroys its purity and unity" (Palti 2006, 162–63). Santiago's poststructuralist focus on "difference," which also defines to a certain extent the work of Edward Said, shifts Schwarz's dialectical emphasis on political economy and class inequality to the realm of culture and its silenced minorities (see Telles 2004, 79). This is, as explained by his disciple and film scholar Denilson Lopes, "the difference between the Marxist root of Schwarz's criticism and the Nietzschean root of the focus on difference that characterises Santiago's view" (Lopes 2012, 25). This focus on difference also diverges from the old resistance discourses typical of Third Cinema, dropping the Marxist lens and bringing in dislocation, diasporic, and accented experiences more akin to postmodern approaches.

The focus on minorities, as proposed by Santiago and his followers in Brazil, leads to a new vitality in studies of black, women, and queer cinema, for instance. However, under the renewed desire to defend oppressed groups by attacking inequality, the film form often runs the risk of being dissociated from the subject matter, which inevitably acquires primacy. As a consequence, as Nagib warns us, there is a risk that a film will be valued more by whatever high moral values (as judged by the critic) it puts forth than by its level of aesthetic invention, leading to "naive analyses that end up discussing the film's story as if it were true, as if one was dealing with real characters" (Nagib quoted in Sobrinho and Mello 2009, 223–24). Moreover, Santiago's "in-between place" is reminiscent of Moretti's and Andrew's "third element" in the binary structure of core and periphery, that is, the triangular notion that does not solve the issue of truly abolishing hierarchies, and that becomes even frailer by purporting to do so.

The World of Cinema

For the purposes of this chapter, the review of Schwarz's, Paulo Emílio's and Santiago's arguments suffices to call attention to the binary scheme that is persistent in their account of the world system, opposing core and periphery or including a third item in the equation. This approach stands in contrast to the democratic and polycentric view of world cinema articulated by Shohat and Stam, as well as Nagib. The polycentric approach does not amount to a negation of the world's geopolitical walls, neither does it attempt to find the "in-between spaces," the "semiperipheries," and the "accented art" of the triangular view. Rather, it springs from the belief that the world of cinema and the world of the arts can be understood under different schemes and systems than those of political economy. In the context of literary criticism, a step in this direction was taken by Efraín Kristal's " 'Considering Coldly . . .': A Response to Franco Moretti," published in the *New Left Review* in 2002. This engaging piece puts forward an poignant criticism of Moretti's "Conjectures on World Literature."

> I am arguing, however, in favour of a view of world literature in which the novel is not necessarily the privileged genre for understanding literary developments of social importance in the periphery; in which the West does not have a monopoly over the creation of forms that count; in which themes and forms can move in several directions—from the centre to the periphery, from the periphery to the centre, from one periphery to another, while some original forms of consequence may not move much at all; and in which strategies of transfer in any direction may involve rejections, swerves, as well as transformations of various kinds, even from one genre to another. (Kristal 2002, 73–74)

Moving further in his article, Kristal dares to place the word "periphery" in quotation marks, asserting the restrictiveness of limiting the study of "peripheral" literature to "local compromises with metropolitan norms."

> Writers in Asia, Africa, Eastern Europe and elsewhere can do exactly what Moretti would readily allow writers in the centre: create forms—'self-generating' as Gerald Martin has described them in the case of Latin American literature—that have decisively transformed the course of literary history at large. (Kristal 74)

Moretti's reply to Kristal in "More Conjectures," published in *New Left Review* in 2003, claims that the movement from center to periphery is much more frequent and therefore consequential to the world literary system, eclipsing all discreet if at all real movements from periphery to center and from periphery to periphery (Moretti 2003, 75–76). Ironically, Moretti's own "Conjectures" showed how perhaps academic flows are less trapped within the world system than artistic ones—for ideas can indeed move from the periphery (Schwarz) to the center (Moretti). More to the point, though, Kristal's ideas resonate with Nagib's polycentric notion of world cinema, expressed, for instance, in her argument against Bordwell and Thompson's reference to Ozu's strategies as violating Hollywood continuity rules (Kristal 2006, 32). And it also resonates with her claim that indeed self-generating forms can also lead to original theories such as Xavier's "historical allegories," an important branch in postcolonial theory that can be and has been applied to other cinemas across the globe (see, for instance, Pieldner 2006, where Xavier's theory is employed in the study of a Romanian film from 2015).

As for movements from periphery to periphery and periphery to the center, perhaps they are much more frequent within the world of cinema than they are in the world of literature. Cinema is, after all, a traveling medium in essence, able to breach long distances both through distribution/exhibition and through editing. No wonder New German Cinema dialogued profusely with the earlier Brazilian *cinema novo*, and that echoes of 1960s Latin American Third Cinema can be felt in Southeast Asian cinema from the 1970s onward. New forms appear in different places and, moreover, they do not remain contained within national borders. Today, for instance, some of contemporary cinema's most creative directors, such as Carlos Reygadas, Jia Zhangke, Tsai Ming-liang, Gus Van Sant, Apichatpong Weerasethakul, Béla Tarr, and Pedro Costa, emerging from Mexico, China, Taiwan, United States, Thailand, Hungary, and Portugal, are connected in their adherence to realism through the use of the long take, be it on digital, super 16 mm, or 35 mm, combined with real locations and characters. This phenomenon can and should be understood in its transnational connections and, at the same time, through its regional peculiarities (see Nagib & Mello 2009; De Luca 2014).

Today, the center-periphery scheme also seems to be increasingly at odds with Hollywood's own role as a transnational, globalized industry (Cook 2013), as well as with the national and international market and distribution flows. An overview of the recent history of South Korean cinema, for instance, reveals how a combination of government incentive in the form of quotas and financing, the funding of the Korean Film Council, and the role of the Chaebols (large industrial conglomerates) in film production, marketing, and distribution, secured the growth of the national market share not against but alongside that of the international market share, which means that in fact the cinematographic market itself grew.[6] By the same token, Reed Hastings, the creator of Netflix, said recently in an interview to a Brazilian magazine that the company grew from 0 subscribers eleven years ago to 50 million in 2018, which represents half of the American households. And, more importantly, contrary to expectations, their main competitor HBO, did not suffer from the growth of Netflix. On the contrary, the audience of HBO grew from

30 to 35 million. "There is room for everyone in this ever-expanding industry," Hastings finally declared (quoted in Vilicic 2018, 16).

But could Korean cinema and Netflix be notable exceptions? In "Fin de Siécle," Schwarz evokes Robert Kurz's powerful reminder that "the market is not open to all," an important caveat to the faith in the productive forces of globalization (Schwarz 1999, 161). In the past, Schwarz had also displayed a certain resistance against the importing and reproducing of "metropolitan tendencies" and trendy terms, of American and European models that are quick to become so appealing to academic tastes in Brazil (Schwarz 1992b). This does not mean, of course, that one should engage in the most fruitless of endeavors, that of searching for the authentic and the national, for genuine culture. It means, rather, that it is perhaps wiser to dialogue with "world cinema" rather than to embrace it as a method, a term, or a concept.

I have sided with Nagib's polycentric approach throughout this chapter because it sees cinema as not necessarily in harness with the market forces of the world system. In fact, some of the most inventive and reinvigorating forces in cinema have been those that advocate a space for art, and poor art at that, within the landscape of production: Chinese cinema's Sixth Generation and contemporary digital documentary practices, made in the fringes of the system, are excellent illustrations of this claim. And so is the Mumblecore movement in the United States, Pedro Costa's cinema in Portugal, the Iranian cinema of Jafar Panahi, as well as the Brazilian *cinema novo*, the British Free Cinema, and Derek Jarman's Super 8 experiments. I would also like to point out that the polycentric approach should not be seen as a product of globalization and the digital revolution, for to assume so would characterize an epistemological and ontological flaw. Rather, cinema was a polycentric phenomenon from its inception, emerging in different parts of the world and not entirely conditioned by market forces, production settings, and codified practices. It is thus desirable to insert our Brazilian cinema into new cartographies rather than keep it at the periphery, where it does not need to be. Overcoming underdevelopment in the arts does not require money and market.

Brazil's Rarefied Dialectic

My final proposition in this chapter is to qualify the view of world cinema delineated above. I will do so by suggesting that Brazilian cinema is a fruitful ground on which to trace these discussions, precisely because it solves the issue of difference and dependency without completely doing away with historical materialism. Perhaps the key to this conundrum is to be found in a well-known passage from Paulo Emílio. Beyond calling attention to complexities of his thought, this passage may also provide a clue to the place of world cinema in Brazil, and of Brazilian cinema in world cinema. He writes,

> We are neither European nor North American. Lacking an original culture, nothing is foreign to us because everything is. The painful construction of ourselves develops within the rarefied dialectic of not being and being the other. (Sales Gomes 2016, 190)

In Paulo Emílio's rarefied dialectic, we are at once absent and another, defined by indefinability, moving between everything and nothing. Within this realm, binarisms, in-between places and triangles collapse, and a multitude of interconnections appear. Does this not resonate slightly with Nagib's proposition that world cinema is not the other, for it is us (Nagib 2006)? Could the Brazilian rarefied dialectic serve as a prism through which to see the cinema of the world, for it shares characteristics that are intrinsic to the traveling medium of cinema? But, more importantly, does not the rarefied dialectic of Brazilian cinema suggest that it is possible to be at the periphery without being the other?

This line of argument could, at first glance, prompt a contentious return to a revised form of dependency theory as developed by Fernando Henrique Cardoso (1996), emerging from the technological/digital revolution and globalization and purporting that economic growth is not anathema to the peripheral condition. For Cardoso, globalization does not lead to a symmetrical world, but the current asymmetries should be revaluated under a new light. This should reveal that the condition of dependency is not a mechanical one. Rather, dependency does not hinder transformation, for it is possible to grow in the periphery. The project of translating this into cinematic criticism and bringing Paulo Emílio's rarefied dialectic into the twenty-first century would mean that our cinema in Brazil could be at the center and still be dependent; it could exist in an asymmetrical cinematographic world and represent a norm. There is no in-between space, only our space, developed and peripheral, interconnected and a force in its own right. Could this mean that "world cinema" can finally return to being just "cinema," anytime, anywhere? I believe it can, for it is in its own nature to travel and to interconnect. The seas are now filled with pirates, and the forces at play have never been more complex.

Acknowledgments

This chapter is in many ways the result of conversations I have had in the past years with Luiza Franco Moreira, Roberto Franco Moreira, Lúcia Nagib, and João Lemos. I am grateful to all of them for their invaluable suggestions.

Notes

1. The introductory parts of this chapter were first written for a paper delivered at the XVI Encontro Socine "Brazilian Cinema and the New Cartographies of World Cinema" (São Paulo, 2012). The book *World Cinema: As Cartografias do Cinema Mundial* is a collection of papers from the conference, edited by Stephanie Dennison in 2013.

2. See examples of "world cinema" as a collection of national cinemas in, for instance, Chapman 2003; Dissanayake 1998; Nowell-Smith 1997. The same editorial trend was followed in Brazil when the term first appeared in Portuguese as *cinema mundial* (see Baptista and Mascarello 2008; Mascarello 2006; Meleiro 2007).

3. Similar epistemological problems can be identified in Andrew's "Time Zones and Jetlag: The Flows and Phases of World Cinema" (2007), where he proposes five phases in the periodization of "world cinema history." These, he claims, alongside the identification of patterns that can raise a film to the category of "world cinema" in the eyes of distributors, critics, scholars, and cinephiles, can help to categorize the full phenomenon of world cinema toward a historical understanding (60). The five phases proposed by Andrew correspond to historical benchmarks in the twentieth century, and they are called the "cosmopolitan" phase (1918), the "national" phase (1945), the "federative" phase (1968), the "world" phase (1989), and the "global" phase (today). The "world" phase, according to Andrew's categorization, begins in 1968, and it is associated to the cinemas coming from places "never before thought of as cinematically interesting or viable" (77), such as the Taiwanese cinema of Hou Hsiao-hsien, the Chinese cinema of Zhang Yimou, and the Iranian cinema of Abbas Kiarostami. These emerge in the 1970s and fill the "vacuum caused by the retreat of the modernist art cinema" (77), functioning as authentic, picturesque visions to the eyes of festivals and cinephiles around the world. So Andrew's "world cinema" phase falls into the category of that which is not European or American, that is, the rest of the world, revealing the persistence of the bipolar notion of world cinema (to which Andrew opposes "global cinema," more characterised by polycentrism).

4. For more on the Marxism study group see Schwarz, Roberto (1999), "Um seminário de Marx," in *Sequências Brasileiras*, 86–105.

5. The most consistent criticism to Schwarz's formula came almost immediately from Maria Sylvia de Carvalho Franco, whose PhD thesis was decisive in influencing his essay in

the first place (Schwarcz & Botelho 2008, 149). In an interview published not long after "Misplaced Ideas" and titled "As ideias estão no lugar" ("The ideas are in place" 1976), Carvalho Franco contends that liberal ideas in Brazil were neither more nor less out of place than the pro-slavery ones, for they all constituted an integral part of the country's complex reality. Her argument is openly Marxist in that the periphery and the center are part of one capitalist system. As such, it would make sense that Brazil would receive the liberal ideas from Europe while profiting from slavery.

6. In the body of the text, the name Paulo Emílio Sales Gomes will be abbreviated as "Paulo Emílio," in accordance with Brazilian usage.

7. I would like to thank my colleague, filmmaker Roberto Franco Moreira for pointing this out to me.

Works Cited

Abbas, Ackbar. 1997. *Culture and the Politics of Disappearance*. Minneapolis: University of Minnesota Press.

———. 2010. "Affective Spaces in Hong Kong/Chinese Cinemas." In *Cinema at the City's Edge: Film and Urban Networks in East Asia*, edited by Yomi Braester and James Tweedie, 25–36. Hong Kong: Hong Kong University Press.

Andrew, Dudley. 2006. "An Atlas of World Cinema." In *Remapping World Cinema: Identity, Culture and Politics in Film*, edited by Stephanie Dennison and Song Hwee Lim, 19–29. London and New York: Wallflower Press.

———. 2007. "Time Zones and Jetlag: The Flows and Phases of World Cinema." In *World Cinemas: Transnational Perspectives*, edited by Natasa Durovicova and Kathleen Newman, 59–89. London and New York: Routledge.

———. 2016. "Fatih Akin's Moral Geometry." In *The Global Auteur: The Politics of Authorship in 21st Century Cinema*, edited by Seung-hoon Jeong and Jeremi Szaniawski, 179–98. London and New York: Bloomsbury Academic.

Baptista, Mauro, and Mascarello, Fernando, eds. 2008. *Cinema Mundial Contemporâneo*. Campinas, Brazil: Papirus.

Bazin, André, 2002. *Qu'est-ce que le cinéma?* Paris: Les Éditions du Cerf.

Berry, Chris. 2010. "What Is Transnational Cinema? Thinking from the Chinese Situation." In *Transnational Cinemas* 1, no. 2: 111–27.

Bordwell, David, Staiger, Janet and Thompson, Kristin. 1988. *The Classical Hollywood Cinema: Film Style and Mode of Production to 1960*. London: Routledge.

Botelho, André. 2013. "Teoria e História na Sociologia Brasileira: A Crítica de Maria Sylvia de Carvalho Franco." *Lua Nova* 90: 331–66.

Burch, Noel. 1981. *Theory of Film Practice*. Princeton, NJ: Princeton University Press.

Candido, Antonio. 2004. "Dialética da malandragem." In *O Discurso e a Cidade*, 17–46. São Paulo e Rio de Janeiro, Brazil: Duas Cidades/Ouro sobre Azul.
———. 1975. *Formação da literatura brasileira*. 2 volumes. São Paulo, Brazil: Edusp/Itatiaia.
———. 2006. *Literatura e Sociedade*. Rio de Janeiro, Brazil: Ouro sobre Azul.
Cardoso, Fernando Henrique. 1996. "Relações Norte-Sul no Contexto Atual: Uma Nova Dependência?" In *O Brasil e a Economia Global*, edited by Renato Baumann, 5–15. Rio de Janeiro, Brazil: Campus.
Cardoso, Fernando Henrique and Faletto, Enzo. 1970. *Dependência e Desenvolvimento na América Latina: Ensaio de Interpretação Sociológica*. Rio de Janeiro, Brazil: Editora LTC.
Caughie, John. 2012. "*Morvern Callar*, Art Cinema and 'Monstrous Archive.'" In *Theorizing World Cinema*, ed. Lúcia Nagib, Chris Perriam, and Rajinder Dudrah, 3–20. London: I. B. Tauris.
Chapman, James. 2003. *Cinemas of the World: Film and Society from 1895 to Present*. London: Reaktion.
Cook, Paul. 2013. "A Importância de um 'S': O Leeds Centre for World Cinemas, Transnacionalismo, Policentrismo e o Desafio de Hollywood." In *World Cinema: As Novas Cartografias do Cinema Mundial*, edited by Stephanie Dennison, 13–34. Campinas, Brazil: Papirus.
De Luca, Tiago. 2012. "Realism of the Senses: A Tendency in Contemporary World Cinema." In *Theorizing World Cinema*, edited by Lúcia Nagib, Chris Perriam, and Rajinder Dudrah, 183–206. London: I. B. Tauris.
———. 2014. *Realism of the Senses in World Cinema: The Experience of Physical Reality*. London: I. B. Tauris.
Deleuze, Gilles. 1985a. *Cinéma 1: L'Image-Mouvement*. Paris: Les Editions de Minuit.
———. 1985b. *Cinéma 2: L'Image-Temps*. Paris: Les Editions de Minuit.
Dennison, Stephanie. 2013. "Introdução." In *World Cinema: As Novas Cartografias do Cinema Mundial*, edited by Stephanie Dennison, 11–20. Campinas, Brazil: Papirus.
Dennison, Stephanie, Song Hwee and Lim. 2006. "Situating World Cinema as a Theoretical." In *Remapping World Cinema: Identity, Culture and Politics in Film*, edited by Stephanie Dennison and Song Hwee Lim, 1–15. London and New York: Wallflower Press.
Dennison, Stephanie, and Song Hwee Lim, eds. 2006. *Remapping World Cinema: Identity, Culture and Politics in Film*. London and New York: Wallflower Press.
Dissanayake, Wimal. 1998. "Issues in World Cinema." In *The Oxford Guide to Film Studies*, edited by John Hill and Pamela Church Gibson, 527–34. Oxford, UK: Oxford University Press.
Durovicova, Natasa, and Newman, Kathleen, eds. 2007. *World Cinemas: Transnational Perspectives*. London and New York: Routledge.
Elsaesser, Thomas. 2009. "World Cinema: Realism, Evidence, Presence." In *Realism and the Audiovisual Media*, edited by Lúcia Nagib and Cecília Mello, 3–19. Basingstoke, UK: Palgrave Macmillan.

Fagundes Telles, Lygia. 1984. "Permanência de Paulo Emílio." In *Jean Vigo* by Paulo Emílio Sales Gomes; translated by Elisabeth Almeida, 1–3. Rio de Janeiro, Brazil: Paz e Terra.

Franco, Maria Sylvia de Carvalho. 1970. *O moderno e suas diferenças*. Tese (Livre Docência)—Faculdade de Filosofia, Letras e Ciências Humanas, Universidade de São Paulo.

———. 1976. "As ideias estão no lugar." *Cadernos de Debates* 1: 61–64.

Furtado, Celso. 2010. *Formação Econômica do Brasil*. São Paulo, Brazil: Companhia das Letras.

Hansen, Miriam B. 2000. "The Mass Production of the Senses: Classical Cinema as Vernacular Modernism." In *Reinventing Film Studies*, edited by Christine Gledhill and Linda Williams, 332–50. London: Arnold.

Higbee, Will, and Lim, Song Hwee. 2010. "Concepts of Transnational Cinema: Towards a Critical Transnationalism in Film Studies." *Transnational Cinemas* 1, no. 1: 7–21.

Holanda, Sérgio Buarque. 2006. *Raízes do Brasil*. São Paulo, Brazil: Companhia das Letras.

Iordanova, Dina, David Martin-Jones, and Belén Vidal, eds. 2010. *Cinema at the Periphery*. Detroit: Wayne State University Press.

Kristal, Efraín. 2002. "'Considering Coldly . . .': A Response to Franco Moretti." *New Left Review* 15 (May–June): 61–74.

Lim, Song Hwee. 2012. "Speaking in Tongues: Ang Lee, Accented Cinema, Hollywood." In *Theorizing World Cinema*, edited by Lúcia Nagib, Chris Perriam, and Rajinder Dudrah, 129–44. London: I. B. Tauris.

Lopes, Denilson. 2012. *No coração do mundo: paisagens transculturais*. Rio de Janeiro, Brazil: Rocco.

Lukács, Georg. 2003. *História e consciência de classe*. São Paulo, Brazil: Editora Martins Fontes.

Martin, Michael T., ed. 1997. *New Latin American Cinema Volume 1: Theory, Practice and Transcontinental Articulations*. Detroit, MI: Wayne State University Press.

Mascarello, Fernando, ed. 2006. *História do Cinema Mundial*. Campinas: Papirus.

Meleiro, Alessandra, ed. 2007. *Cinema no Mundo: Indústria, Política, Mercado*. São Paulo, Brazil: Escrituras.

Moretti, Franco. 1999. *Atlas of the European Novel 1800–1900*. London and New York: Verso.

———. 2000. "Conjectures on World Literature." *New Left Review* 1: 54–68.

———. 2003. "More Conjunctures." *New Left Review*, 20: 73–81.

Naficy, Hamid. 2001. *An Accented Cinema: Exilic and Diasporic Filmmaking*. Princeton, NJ: Princeton University Press.

Nagib, Lúcia. 2011. *World Cinema and the Ethics of Realism*. New York: Continuum.

———. 2006. "Towards a Positive Definition of World Cinema." In *Remapping World Cinema: Identity, Culture and Politics in Film*, edited by Stephanie Dennison and Song Hwee Lim, 30–37. London and New York: Wallflower.

———. 2017. "Realist Cinema as World Cinema." In *The Routledge Companion to World Cinema*, edited by R. Stone and P. Cooke, 310–22. Abingdon-on-Thames, UK: Routledge.

Nagib, Lúcia, Chris Perriam, and Rajinder Dudrah, eds. 2012. *Theorizing World Cinema*. London: I. B. Tauris.
Nagib, Lúcia and Cecília Mello, eds. 2009. *Realism and the Audiovisual Media*. Basingstoke, UK: Palgrave Macmillan.
Nowell-Smith, Geoffrey, ed. 1997. *The Oxford History of World Cinema*. Oxford, UK: Oxford University Press.
Palti, Elías José. 2006. "The Problem of 'Misplaced Ideas' Revisited: Beyond the 'History of Ideas' in Latin America." *Journal of the History of Ideas* 67, no. 1: 149–79.
Pieldner, Judit. 2016. "History, Cultural Memory and Intermediality in Radu Jude's Aferim!" *Acta Universitatis. Sapientiae, Film and Media Studies* 13: 89–105.
Rancière, Jacques. 2006. *Film Fables*, translated by Emiliano Battista. Oxford, UK: Berg.
Rocha, Glauber. 2018. *On Cinema*, edited by Ismail Xavier. London: I. B. Tauris.
Said, Edward W. 2003. *Orientalism*. London: Penguin.
Sales Gomes, Paulo Emílio. 2015. *O cinema no século*, edited by Carlos Augusto Calil. São Paulo, Brazil: Companhia das Letras.
Sales Gomes, Paulo Emílio. 2016. "Uma situação colonial?," "Cinema: Trajetória no subdesenvolvimento," "A alegria do mau filme brasileiro," and "Explicapresentação." In *Uma situação colonial?*, edited by Carlos Augusto Calil, 47–54, 186–205, 388–89, and 340–42. São Paulo, Brazil: Companhia das Letras.
———. 1984. *Jean Vigo*. Rio de Janeiro, Brazil: Paz e Terra.
Schwarcz, Lília, and Botelho, André. 2008. "*Ao vencedor as batatas* 30 anos: crítica da cultura e processo social: entrevista com Roberto Schwarz." *Revista Brasileira de Ciências Sociais* 23, no. 67: 147–60.
Schwarz, Roberto. 1992a. *Misplaced Ideas: Essays on Brazilian Culture*, edited by John Gledson. London and New York: Verso.
———. 1992b. "Brazilian Culture: Nationalism by Elimination." In *Misplaced Ideas: Essays on Brazilian Culture*, edited by John Gledson, 1–18. London and New York: Verso.
———. 1997. *Duas meninas*. São Paulo, Brazil: Companhia das Letras.
———. 1999. *Sequências brasileiras*. São Paulo, Brazil: Companhia das Letras.
———. 2001. *A Master on the Periphery of Capitalism*, translated and with an introduction by John Gledson. London and Durham, NC: Duke University Press.
———. 2008. *O pai de família e outros estudos*. São Paulo, Brazil: Companhia das Letras.
———. 2012a. *Ao vencedor as batatas*. São Paulo, Brazil: Editora 34/Duas Cidades.
———. 2012b. *Que horas são?* São Paulo, Brazil: Companhia das Letras.
Sobrinho, Gilberto, and Mello, Cecília. 2009. "Entrevista com Lúcia Nagib." in *Conexão: Comunicação e Cultura* 8: 213–25.
Shohat, Ella, and Robert Stam. 1994. *Unthinking Eurocentrism: Multiculturalism and the Media*. London: Routledge.

Smith, Paul Julian. 2012. "Transnational Cinemas: The Cases of Mexico, Argentina and Brazil." In *Theorizing World Cinema*, edited by Lúcia Nagib, Chris Perriam, and Rajinder Dudrah, 63–76. London: I. B. Tauris.

Telles, Renata. 2004. "Latino-Americanismo e Orientalismo: Roberto Schwarz, Silviano Santiago e Edward Said." *Terra roxa e outras terras: Revista de Estudos Literários* 4: 71–87.

Vilicic, Filipe. 2018. "A Qualidade Subiu: Entrevista com Reed Hastings." *Veja* 51, no. 7: 13–17.

Wallerstein, Immanuel. 2000. *The Essential Wallerstein*. New York: New Press.

Xavier, Ismail. 2016. "Prefácio: A crítica não indiferente." In *Uma situação colonial?* Paulo Emílio Sales Gomes, 12–30. São Paulo, Brazil: Companhia das Letras.

CONTRIBUTORS

Patrick Dove is professor of Hispanic literature and culture at Indiana University. His research explores intersections between literature, philosophy, and politics. He is author of two books; the most recent, *Literature and "Interregnum": Globalization, War, and the Crisis of Sovereignty in Latin America* (SUNY 2016), explores literary responses to the crisis of aesthetic and political modernity in recent Southern Cone narrative. He is currently working on a book project that looks at war and the production of social space in Central America.

Jeroen Gerrits is associate professor of comparative literature and codirector of the program in Philosophy, Literature and the History of Criticism at Binghamton University (SUNY). His monograph *Cinematic Skepticism: Across Digital and Global Turns* (SUNY 2019) connects the film philosophies of Stanley Cavell and Gilles Deleuze to argue that skepticism is an ethical problem that pervades contemporary world cinema. Other publications on the intersection of cinema, media, and philosophy include "Raúl Ruiz's Adaptation *The Blind Owl* (1987): A Chilean Exilic Film between Iranian Surrealism and the European Alpha City," "When Horror Becomes Human: Living Conditions in *Buffy the Vampire Slayer*," and "Cavell, Film, Feminisme: *Stella Dallas and* the Controversy Concerning the Unknown Woman."

Hannan Hever is the Jacob and Hilda Blaustein Professor of Hebrew Language and Literature and Comparative Literature at Yale University, with an affiliation in the program of Judaic Studies. He has published extensively in Modern Hebrew literature and culture, the theory of literature, and culture critique from political theology from political theology, postnational, and postcolonial perspectives. Hever received his PhD in 1984 from the Hebrew University-Jerusalem, where he taught from 1979 to 1989. Between 1989 and 2000 he taught at Tel Aviv University, and then returned to the Hebrew University, until he joined Yale in 2013. He also taught at Northwestern University, Michigan University-Ann Arbor, Jewish Theological Seminary, and at

235

Columbia University. Hever is an Israeli literary critic and editor. Among his books are *Producing the Modern Hebrew Canon: Nation Building and Minority Discourse* (NYU Press, 2002); *Nativism, Zionism and Beyond: Three Essays on Nativist Hebrew Poetry* (B. G. Rudolph Lectures in Judaic Studies, Syracuse University Press, 2014); *Beautiful Motherland of Death: Aesthetics and Politics in U. Z. Greenberg's Poetry* (Am Oved, 2004, Heb.); *They Shall Dwell at the Haven of the Sea: The Sea in Modern Hebrew Culture* (Van Leer Institution and Hakbutz Ha-Meuchad, 2007, Heb.); *With the Power of God: Political Theology in Modern Hebrew Literature* (2014, Heb.); *To Inherent the Land, To Conquer the Space: The Birth of Hebrew Poetry in Eretz Yisrael* (Mosad Bialik, 2015, Heb.); *Suddenly the Sight of War: Nationalism and Violence in the Hebrew Poetry of the 1940s* (Stanford University Press, 2016); *We are Broken Rhymes: The Politics of Trauma in Israeli Literature* (2017, Heb.), and *Hebrew Literature and the 1948, Essays on Philology and Responsibility* (Brill, 2019). He has recently completed a book titled *Political Theology of the Hassidic Tale*.

Richard E. Lee is Bartle Professor of Sociology at Binghamton University, where he concentrates on the study of long-term, large-scale social change from the world-systems perspective, and director of the Fernand Braudel Center and editor of *Review*. He is the author of *Life and Times of Cultural Studies: The Politics and Transformation of the Structures of Knowledge* (Duke University Press, 2003), *Knowledge Matters: The Structures of Knowledge and the Crisis of the Modern World-System* (University of Queensland Press, 2011), and numerous edited collections. His research focuses on the long-term intellectual and disciplinary structures of knowledge formation, in writings that range across the sciences, social sciences, and humanities, and most lately, the role of music in the reproduction of the capitalist world-economy.

Benjamin Liu is associate professor in the Department of Hispanic Studies at the University of California, Riverside. Liu studies the literatures and cultures of the medieval Iberian peninsula. He is the author of *Medieval Joke Poetry: The Cantigas d'Escarnho e de Mal Dizer* (Harvard Studies in Comparative Literature, 2004), articles in *Yearbook of Comparative and General Literature*, *Medieval Encounters*, *Bulletin of Hispanic Studies*, *La Corónica*, and *Nueva Revista de Filología Hispánica*, as well as several book chapters, the most recent of which is "Ricote, Mariana y el patrón oro" in *Cervantes y la economía*, edited by Miguel-Ángel Galindo Martín

(Cuenca: Universidad de Castilla-La Mancha, 2007). His current research project considers various economic modes of interfaith relations in early Spanish literature, examining how the circulation of money and goods among Christians, Muslims, and Jews configures complex interpersonal networks among these groups. He is also developing new research on travel literature and trade in the Middle Ages.

Karim Mattar is an associate professor of English at the University of Colorado at Boulder. He completed his DPhil in English at the University of Oxford in 2013. He works on world literature in the context of global capitalist modernity, and his research and teaching interests include the history of the novel, comparative Middle Eastern literatures and cultures, and critical theory. He has recently completed two books, a monograph titled *Specters of World Literature: Orientalism, Modernity, and the Novel in the Middle East* (Edinburgh University Press, 2020) and a coedited volume titled *The Edinburgh Companion to the Postcolonial Middle East* (Edinburgh University Press, 2019; edited with Anna Ball). Current and future research projects include books on "The Ethics of Affiliation: Literature and the Trauma of History in Israel/Palestine" and "Literatures of Global Crisis." He is fluent in Arabic, and has a working competency in French, German, Turkish, and Persian.

Cecília Mello is associate professor of Film and Audiovisual Media at the Department of Film, Radio and Television, University of São Paulo, Brazil. Her research focuses on world cinema—with an emphasis on British and Chinese cinemas—and on issues of audiovisual realism, cinema and urban spaces, and intermediality. She is the author of several articles and book chapters in Brazil and abroad, editor and coeditor of four books and the author of *The Cinema of Jia Zhangke: Realism and Memory in Chinese Film* (London: Bloomsbury, 2019).

Luiza Franco Moreira is professor of comparative literature at Binghamton University. Her scholarship focuses on the comparative literary history of the Americas. She is the author of *Meninos, Poetas e Heróis: Cassiano Ricardo do Modernismo ao Estado Novo* (EDUSP, 2001) and editor of the anthology *Os Melhores Poemas de Cassiano Ricardo* (Global, 2003). She has published articles in *Comparative Literature Studies*, *Revista de Indias*, *Terceira Margem*, *Cultural Critique*, *Revista Iberoamericana*, and *Revista de Crítica Literaria Latinoamericana*, as well as several chapters in edited collections.

Tarek Shamma is an associate professor at the Comparative Literature Department and the Translation Research and Instruction Program, Binghamton University. He has taught at universities in Syria, United Arab Emirates, Qatar, and the United States. His works include *Translation and the Manipulation of Difference: Arabic Literature in Nineteenth Century England* (St. Jerome, 2014). He is currently working at an anthology of Arabic discourse on translation, to be published by Routledge.

INDEX

2666, 156–164

adab, 5, 83–89, 91–93
Africa, 6, 154, 213, 222, 224
'ajamiyya, 29–30, 33, 42
Al-Andalus (Andalucía), 3, 21, 41, 84, 102
aljamiado, 4, 30–34, 38–40
Andrade, Carlos Drummond de (Drummond), 5, 111–122, 132, 138–139
apostasy, 53–54, 56, 63, 65, 74
Apter, Emily, 29, 62, 76, 91, 138
Arabic: (language), 3–4, 10–14, 16–19, 21–22, 25, 31–35, 42, 69–71, 84–93; literature (*see under* literature); poetry (*see under* poetry)
Aristotle, 3, 9–15, 18, 20–25, 163
Ataç, Nurullah, 92–94
Auerbach, Erich, 5, 59–60
Averroes, 3–4, 10–11, 16, 21–26, 29. *See also* Ibn Rushd, Abu al-Walid

Bazin, André, 185, 212, 222
Beecroft, Alexander, 1, 113, 137, 140
Benjamin, Walter, 31, 77, 219
Bialik, H.N., 60, 66–68, 70
Bishop, Elizabeth, 5, 111–139
Black Book, The, 5, 83, 86, 92, 95–99, 103–106
Bolaño, Roberto, 5–6, 155–164
Borges, Jorge Luis, 5–6, 29, 147–158, 162–163

Braudel, Fernand, 30, 168
Brazil, 111, 114–115, 119, 123–126, 132, 138–140, 209–210, 217–219, 222–223, 226–228
Brazilian: literature, 114–117, 119; poetry, 114–120, 124, 136
Britto, Paulo Henriques, 116, 119, 139–140
Brown, Ashley, 114–115, 118, 124

Cairo, 41–42, 84, 87, 153
Candido, Antonio, 116–117, 126, 209, 219, 221
capitalism, 114, 157, 159, 167–170
Casanova, Pascale, 1, 84–85, 89, 113, 136, 145
Cavell, Stanley, 6, 183–186, 197, 201, 204
Cervantes, Miguel de, 30–31
Ceylan, Nuri Bilge, 6, 183, 187–194, 198–203
cinema: criticism, 210, 213, 220, 227; new, 186–187, 202, 216, 225; Third (see Third Cinema); world, 6–7, 184, 187, 202, 209–219, 222, 226–228
cinema novo, 213, 216, 221, 225–226
classification system, 6, 90, 168, 177–178
Cohen, Walter, 1, 113, 137
collision film, 188, 202–203
comedy, 9–10, 14–15, 128
Communism, 132–135, 139, 214
Coplas del hijante de Puey Moçón, 4, 29, 33–34

core (center), 3, 167, 177, 215
core/periphery model (center-periphery model), 3, 6, 58, 85, 90, 136, 209–212, 214–216, 218, 223, 225
criticism: cinema, 210, 213, 220, 227; literary, 16, 22, 74, 88, 147, 152, 163, 209, 218–219, 222–224
"Crusoe in England," 111–114, 119, 124–131, 135–136

Damrosch, David, 88, 91–92, 113, 136, 137–138
Dante, 119, 152–153
Defoe, Daniel, 112, 124–135, 140
Deleuze, Gilles, 197, 205, 212
Derrida, Jaques, 6, 64, 151, 161
"*Divagações sobre a Ilha,*" 132–133
division of labor, 6, 167–170
Drummond. *See* Andrade, Carlos Drummond de (Drummond)

edebiyat, 93–94
"El Aleph," 147–148, 152–153, 155, 163
English. *See* language, English
Enlightenment, 49, 84–85, 87. See also *Nahda*
European: languages, 2–3, 72, 137 (*see also* individual languages); literature, 45, 72, 85, 137

fitra, 13, 16–17, 20
French, 1, 29, 137, 222

German, 62, 75, 97
Germany, 36, 60, 187–188
Gnosis, 54, 56–57, 66
Goethe, 46, 72, 88
Gomes, Paulo Emílio Sales, 220–223, 227–229

Granada, 31, 34, 37–38
Greek: literature, 10, 12, 22–25; poetry, 12, 21–24

Haj, 35, 40–42
Harvey, L. P., 34–36, 39–50
ha'atakah, 68–71. *See also* translation
Headless Woman, The, 6, 183, 187–198, 202, 205
Hebrew: literature, 4–5, 45–79; poetry, 60, 66–67, 72
Hegel, 57–59, 153
hegemony, 1–4, 156, 170–172, 176, 211, 213
Heidegger, Martin, 6, 151, 153, 162–164
historical materialism, 47–48, 58–59, 219, 227
Hollywood, 188, 211–217, 221, 225
Holy Land, 46, 50, 64, 67, 73
Hopkins, Terence, 113, 168
Hurufism, 86, 96, 100, 102–103

Ibn Rushd, Abu al-Walid, 3, 10, 21, 29. *See also* Averroes
India, 34, 88, 138
"Infância," 112, 119–126, 131
interstate system, 6, 167, 169–170, 175–176
Islam, 4–5, 9, 13, 16, 20, 31
Israel, 5, 46, 48, 50–53, 55–58, 64–68, 73–74
Istanbul, 84, 95–96, 99

Jewish: literature (*see under* literature); nationality, 4–5, 74–77; "Question," 49–50, 54, 60–61, 64–67; religion (*see under* religion)
Juárez, Ciudad, 157–161

240

Kant, Immanuel, 160, 183–185
Kilito, Abdalfattah, 14, 29–33
Krochmal, R. Nachman, 5, 48, 54–57, 61, 64–65, 69, 71, 76

language: English, 5, 62, 72, 97, 136–138, 210, 215, 217–218; French, 1, 29, 137, 222; German, 62, 75, 97; Latin, 31, 62, 97, 137; Portuguese, 115–118, 123–124, 131, 136–139; Spanish, 4, 30–33, 38, 156. *See also* Arabic (language); Persian; Turkish; Yiddish
languages: European, 2–3, 72, 137; literary, 1–3, 113, 136–137
Latin, 31, 62, 97, 137
Latin America, 5, 139, 146–147, 156–157, 164, 210, 213, 224
Library of Congress, 6, 172, 175–179
literary criticism. *See* criticism, literary
literature: Arabic, 9, 12, 14, 24, 85, 88–89, 94; Brazilian, 114–117, 119; European, 45, 72, 85, 137; Greek, 10, 12, 22–25; Hebrew, 4–5, 45–79; Jewish, 45–48, 51–52, 55–56, 65; Turkish, 91–95; world, 1–8, 29, 45–48, 51–53, 59–63, 68–73, 76–79, 84–92, 96–98, 103, 111–114, 124–125, 131–132, 135–140, 145–148, 155–156, 215–219, 224–225. See also *adab; edebiyat*

Mancebo de Arévalo, 34–35, 40
Martel, Lucrecia, 6, 183, 187–190, 194–199, 202–205
Marx, Karl, 57–59, 219
Matta bin Yunus, Abu Bishr (Matta), 3, 9–21
Mecca, 4, 32–35, 39–41, 84, 100
Mexico, 157–161
Middle East, 34, 84–92

mimesis, 14, 21–23, 157
Mimesis, 5, 59
Miron, Dan, 45, 52–53, 57–58
modernism, 112–119, 124–125, 131, 136, 212, 216
modernity, 5–6, 51, 54, 84–98, 102–103, 145–146, 157–158, 161–162
Moretti, Franco, 1–3, 88, 145, 215–219, 223–224
Moriscos, 30–38
Mufti, Aamir, 85, 88–90
Muslims, 4, 20, 32–33, 41–42, 89

Nagib, Lúcia, 211–217, 223–227
Nahda, 84, 87, 94. *See also* Enlightenment
new cinema, 186–187, 202, 216, 225
novels, 3, 34–35, 38, 89–90, 94–99, 215–220

Ottoman Empire, 36, 39, 92–96

Palestine, 45, 49–50, 61–63
Pamuk, Orhan, 4–5, 83, 86, 92, 95–103
Paulo Emílio Sales Gomes, 220–223, 227–229
periphery, 60, 136, 216, 224–229
Persian, 29, 72, 84, 87, 93–94, 97, 100
philosophers, 9–16, 21–23, 69, 184
philosophy, 4, 11–13, 16–25, 54, 70, 171, 184
Plato, 24, 133, 155–157
Poetics, 3–4, 9–16, 21–26
poetry: 40, 86–87, 111–112, 123–127, 131–139; Arabic, 9, 12–15, 21–24, 31–32, 86–87; Brazilian, 114–120, 124, 136; Greek, 12, 21–24; Hebrew, 60, 66–67, 72
point of view, virtual. *See* virtual point of view

political theology, 50–53, 56, 61, 64–67, 70, 73–77
Portuguese. *See* language, Portuguese
Puey Monçón, 4, 29, 33–35, 39–42

Quran, 13, 20, 23–24, 30–32, 84, 101–102

realism, 94–95, 186, 212–213, 217
religion: 20, 86, 91–92, 95–96, 103, 137; Jewish, 4–5, 46–47, 51–56, 65, 71, 76–77. *See also* Hurufism; Islam
Republic of Turkey, 92–94, 99–102
revelation, 61, 77–78, 148–149, 152–155, 162
Robinson Crusoe, 111–112, 120–127, 132
Rosenzweig, Franz, 61, 75–78

Sacks, Jeffery, 85–90
Sadan, Dov, 4–5, 45–70, 73–79
Scholem, Gershom, 61–64, 75
Schwarz, Roberto, 2, 209, 218–226
script, 4, 30–33, 46, 70, 92, 100
Second World War, 60, 132, 137, 176–177
secularism, 5, 53, 86, 91–92, 95–96, 103
skepticism, 6, 183–189, 197, 201–205
Soviet Union, 60, 118, 132–134
Spanish, 4, 30–33, 38, 156. See also 'ajamiyya

targum, 68–70. *See also* translation
Three Monkeys, 6, 183, 187–193, 198–203
Third Cinema, 202, 210, 213–226
Torah, 54–56, 61, 65, 71, 77

tragedy, 10, 14–15
translation, 3–22, 25, 29–34, 52, 59–64, 68–72, 75–78, 96–98, 117–124, 135–139. See also *fitra*
transliteration, 4, 29–34, 42. See also *aljamiado*
travel writing, 4, 29–30, 34–35, 86
Turkey, 37, 86, 91–96, 99–103, 183, 187–188
Turkish: (language), 38, 84, 92, 97; literature, 91–95

United Kingdom (UK), 181, 210, 217, 222
United States (USA), 1, 111–12, 117, 123, 138–139, 156, 171–179, 187–188, 209, 222, 225–226
university, 6, 172–175, 179, 217

virtual point of view, 6, 184, 189, 194, 197–205

Wallerstein, Immanuel, 2–3, 113, 168
world: cinema (*see* cinema, world); -economy, 167, 176–177, 181; literature (*see* literature, world); literary system, 1, 84, 86, 90, 136–137, 224; -system, 3, 6, 113, 145, 167–173, 181, 211, 216, 223–224; War II (*see* Second World War)

Yiddish, 47–48, 67
Yishuv, 45, 49, 64

Zionism, 50–51, 55–57, 64, 70

www.ingramcontent.com/pod-product-compliance
Lightning Source LLC
Chambersburg PA
CBHW030539230426
43665CB00010B/952